NEON NOIR

Contemporary American Crime Fiction

WOODY HAUT

Library of Congress Catalog Card Number: 98-86410

A catalogue record for this book is available from the British Library on request

The right of Woody Haut to be identified as the author of this work has been asserted by him in accordance with the Copyright, Designs and Patents Act 1988

First published in 1999 by
Serpent's Tail, 4 Blackstock Mews, London N4

Website: www.serpentstail.com

Set in 10pt Baskerville by Avon Dataset Ltd, Bidford on Avon, Warwickshire

Printed in Great Britain by Mackays of Chatham plc, Chatham, Kent

10 9 8 7 6 5 4 3 2 1

Contents

Acknowledgements

This one is dedicated to the memory of Albert Haut, 1903–1976, whose photographs and stories of pre-war urban America proved the perfect introduction to the world of neon noir. Thanks also to Mavis for reading the manuscript at various stages, and to Laurence O'Toole at Serpent's Tail for his insight and editorial expertise.

I

INTRODUCTION: SKIP-TRACING THE CULTURE

Criminal incongruities; locating the evidence; selling the genre

- *Item*: December 7, 1996. Crime writer Eugene Izzi is found dangling from the window of a fourteenth storey office block in Chicago. He is wearing a bullet-proof vest; in his pockets are a set of brass knuckles, a tear gas canister, notes referring to telephone threats from a militia group, and three computer disks containing, according to police, "writing consistent with the prose of a crime writer".[1] The doors are locked from the inside and an unfired gun is on the floor near his desk. Witnesses say it looks like a scene from one of Izzi's novels. While the media speculates on whether it was suicide or murder, rumours that the disks contain the story of a crime writer found dead after being pursued by members of a secret Indiana militia go unconfirmed.

- *Item*: January, 1997. Believing his wife, Margo, is involved in a lesbian relationship with crime writer Patricia Cornwell, former FBI counter-espionage agent, Eugene Bennett, enters Margo's Methodist church in Manasas, Virginia, and takes the pastor hostage. Margo arrives and, though an expert in interrogation and hostage crisis situations, comes close to shooting her husband. At the trial, Eugene insists it was Ed, the other half of his personality – split through decades of state deceit – who committed the crime. He maintains that, after confronting Margo with evidence of her relationship, she mocked him and asked why it had taken so long to find out. Meanwhile, in Cornwell's *Hornet's Nest*, the police chief, Judy Hammer, has also tired of her dull husband: "[He] was so much like a spineless, spiteful woman that his wife wondered how it was possible she

should have ended up in a lesbian relationship with a man."
Hornet's Nest is part of a three book deal for which Cornwell was
paid $24 million.[2]

- *Item*: Having, by his own admission, used the murder of his
mother to achieve notoriety as a crime writer, James Ellroy writes
a non-fiction book which he hopes will atone for his past
exploitation. *My Dark Places* concerns Ellroy's past life, his
mother's death and his unsuccessful attempt to track down her
murderer. Having in the past created fictional characters –
including several based on his mother – who interact with the
famous and infamous, Ellroy must now create a real character
and piece together a plot which can stand alongside his past
fictionalisations.

Contemporary crime writers, seeking to replicate life at street-
level, have created a genre whose predominant artifice is
its apparent lack of artifice; consequently, the line separating
fiction and reality has become increasingly blurred. The
origins of this anomaly might well be located in the political
lethargy, cover-ups and crimes that followed the Vietnam
war. Prior to the 1970s, crime fiction seldom sought such
simulation. Raymond Chandler's amorphous depictions of
LA are, however evocative, parodies of the culture. While
Chester Himes admitted that the Harlem he portrayed was, in
the end, a product of his imagination.[3] Even Jim Thompson,
whose work accurately depicts the internal thoughts of twisted
psychopaths, would never have suggested his work replicated
reality.

So common has such simulation become that few crime
writers can expect to exert the same impact as Newton
Thornberg, James Crumley, George V. Higgins and James Ellroy,
who, in the mid to late 1970s, emerged with novels seemingly so
authentic as to reinterpret the national narrative. This obsession
with verisimilitude, from George V. Higgins's off-centred
dialogue to Andrew Vachss's descent into the world of child
exploitation, requires one to reappraise the genre's relationship
to the culture. Consequently, contemporary noir fiction, often

vicarious and voyeuristic, can be read as quasi-anthropological texts, or as narratives evoking prurient interests; descriptions of what America has become, or chapters in a survivalist's handbook. Despite a handful of writers preoccupied with the poetry of violence or the grand gestures of everyday life, the genre continues its drift towards simulation, extremism and confession. As a character in James Crumley's *One to Count Cadence* puts it, "Art deceives as well as history; Life imitates Art as often as Art does Life; History seems to have little connection to either one."[4]

Locating the Evidence

To examine a culture, one need only investigate its crimes.[5] Thus the fictionalisation of crime has become a favourite pastime and a means of analysing society. A popular and often lucrative genre,[6] contemporary crime fiction addresses the social contradictions and conditions of a decaying society. In personalising the political and politicising the personal, crime fiction takes the temperature of a culture obsessed by paranoia, hooked, as it were, on packageable insights, instant replays, soundbites and various post-mortem proddings.

Neon Noir concerns crime fiction from the mid-1960s to the 1990s. Following on from *Pulp Culture*,[7] it places the genre in a political perspective, reading the era alongside particular authors and texts. Yet *Neon Noir* makes no attempt to be a definitive history of contemporary crime fiction. As in *Pulp Culture*, the writers included in this study reflect the author's personal tastes. Positioning themselves on the furthest reaches of the literary establishment, the writers, many of whom are part of the tradition of the *literary worker* – that is, those who must work to contract – include some not normally associated with crime fiction. Consequently the likes of Robert Stone (*Dog Soldiers*) and Michael Herr (*Dispatches*) – whose work has influenced contemporary crime fiction – will be discussed alongside James Ellroy, Richard Stark, Sara Paretsky, and Elmore Leonard.

Meanwhile, conspicuous by their absence, are best-selling authors like Scott Turow, Tom Clancy and John Grisham, who, in search of the lowest cultural denominator, are neither hard-boiled, nor inheritors of the pulp culture tradition.

The book is entitled *Neon Noir* for two reasons. One, because the term implies a predominantly urban genre; and, two, because it suggests an electronic culture consisting of half-lit signs adorning cheap hotels, the sound of crackling synapses induced by hallucinogenics and the war in Vietnam, the power of the media, and the flash of self- promotion as crime writers hammer out stories on the frontage of the information super-highway.

Neon noir writers are descendants of such hardboiled pulp culture writers as Jim Thompson, David Goodis, Charles Williams, and Dorothy B. Hughes. Emerging from the maelstrom of the 1960s, neon noirists would be deeply affected by the Vietnam war and the political atmosphere surrounding it. Dividing the nation, the war instilled an atmosphere of paranoia, a condition exacerbated by government secrecy, inflexible policies, and the effect of drugs on the political consciousness of numerous dissidents. In the following years, the Watergate investigation and congressional hearings regarding the role of the CIA would confirm public suspicion about government duplicity and corruption, and contribute further to the forging of noir narratives as paranoid as the era from which they derive. Accordingly, writers like Elmore Leonard, James Lee Burke and Lawrence Block, having worked in other genres – westerns, lowlife fiction, science-fiction, softcore porn – produced narratives which investigate the relationship between public and private crime. Striving for realism and accessibility, their work is typified by a straightforward prose style, tinged, in many cases, with vernacularisms and a dark and irreverent humour. Battling the bottle, drug-addled, or beaten down by society, neon noir protagonists are no longer wise-cracking know-it-alls, but psychologically scarred inhabitants of a morally ambiguous world in which people are capable of perpetrating any and every outrage.

Neon noir fiction would also be affected by the Reagan–Bush era's obsession with deregulation and privatisation. Such policies would contribute to a corresponding deregulation and privatisation of the genre, as well as its investigative process. Beginning in the early 1980s, noir texts were suddenly content to distort and even disregard past rules concerning narrative voice, plot and subject matter. In following a path of privatisation, crime fiction also became more personalised, as concerned with the protagonist's journey and battle against the forces-that-be as with solving crime. Portraying the effects of deregulation and privatisation – social inequality, corruption, violent crime and a culture driven to extremes by the era's cut-throat economics – noir fiction's narrative grew more dispersed, while its investigation of crime remained unconnected to any specific political perspective. This populist approach appealed to readers feeling increasingly powerless in a society saturated by street and state crime, whether muggings, drive-by killings, insider dealing, or foreign invasions. With the continuation of such crimes, post-Vietnam war crime writers like Ellroy, Higgins and Jerome Charyn, would, in turn, influence another generation of noirists. The likes of Jack O'Donnell, and George Pelecanos, schooled on noir fiction, film and TV, would regard violence as part and parcel of urban life. Interpreting the culture along formalistic lines, their writing, though referring to past noir styles, continues to push the boundaries of crime fiction to greater extremes.

The two generations – one having witnessed the war and the culture surrounding it and the other having, in some instances, noted the era in retrospect – rely on a common reality: a culture of violence stimulated by the push and pull of the free market.[8] Accordingly, both would prove popular with readers seeking narratives capable of recreating a recognisable world. This despite the fact that few readers are likely to be victims of the kind of crime they encounter in their fiction.[9] Yet their paranoia

– induced by cultural disparities and media sensationalism – is such that they seek out narratives that replicate that part of the culture they most fear. Depicting the culture at its most excessive, crime fiction walks a thin line between criticising the culture and numbing its readers with rollercoaster narratives whose politics have yet to be articulated.

With advertisements distorting him into a lone survivor inhabiting a dangerous urban landscape, the noir protagonist has become a marketable commodity. More *Die Hard* than *Thin Man*, one notes this new breed of noirist – young, white and stylishly dressed – swaggering past rappers and winos, or dancing with svelte black women in ghetto nightclubs. Possessing perfect instincts, he is, despite the chaos surrounding him, in control of his life, the territory and the narrative. The consummate consumer, he is a means of self-empowerment in an age of neon powerlessness. Not content to stay in the present, this mock-noirist has even been chased into the future, inhabiting sci-fi films – whether *Blade Runner*, *Total Recall* or *Strange Days* – and speculative fiction simulating films and novels that only exist in the minds of those who passively consume such products.

Meanwhile, their more legitimate counterparts, unlike pulp culture protagonists, are as likely to appear in hardback as in cheap paperback originals or mass market editions. After all, paperback publishing, which, during the late 1940s, heralded the possibility of a literate nation, has, since the early 1960s, ceased to be politically contentious. To most readers, paperbacks merely represent an economically accessible form of literary product, the politics of which is rarely questioned. Though paperback publishing as a commonplace phenomenon is not without significance, its effect has been lessened by the excesses of mass culture. Meanwhile, some noirists, realising the contradiction entailed in profiting from novels that depict crime and violence, have suggested that their writing might, in itself, be a confidence trick, if not an illicit activity. Veteran

crime writer Ed McBain has half-jokingly said, "Writing a com-
mercially successful novel comes high on the list of white-collar
crime",[10] while K. C. Constantine, putting the role of the crime
writer in another perspective, has written, "[Is] there any doubt
that a storyteller is society's stoolie?"[11]

So commodified and populist has the genre become that, when
asked about his reading habits, Bill Clinton named Walter
Mosley as his favourite author. In doing so, the President went
some way towards single-handedly reducing the power of crime
fiction to function in a subversive manner. Given the Great
Comforter's propensity for poll-mongering, one suspects that
Clinton's choice had more to do with cultural correctness than
literary acumen. Yet, if Clinton, given his politics, reads Mosley,
one could be forgiven for questioning whether the latter can be
said to occupy a position on the cutting edge of noir fiction.
Certainly Mosley's novel, *A Red Death*, which depicts the
McCarthy era, remains, on the surface, oddly non-political.
Though Clinton and Mosley are products of the same generation, one wonders how someone rarely outside the corridors of
power could understand the nuances of an oppositional genre,
or appreciate the subtlety of Mosley's fiction. After all, the
political thrust of post-Vietnam war noirists has been, at the
very least, to critique the dominant narrative and reclaim the
genre from the pseudo-Chandlerites; not to join the literary or
political mainstream. However, Clinton's pronouncement, if
nothing else, indicates the extent to which crime fiction can
appeal to a cross-section of the population, from ordinary
punters to credibility-seeking Presidents.

Selling the Genre

While writers such as Charles Willeford and Chester Himes
were able to make the transition from pulp culture to neon noir
fiction, the likes of Jim Thompson, Charles Williams and David
Goodis were less successful.[12] One reason for their failure was

that they came from a period in which ambiguity offered a degree of protection against McCarthyism. In general, pulp culture fiction, with its contractual and cultural constraints, could not contend with the confrontational politics of the 1960s. A class-based literature – primarily oriented towards working-class readers – it had literally lost its class. Readers either expected more or were subsumed by the promise of prosperity and slicker forms of escapism. Nevertheless, the era ended with some excellent critiques, the most notable of which might be Willeford's *The Woman Chaser*. Summing up the hesitancies of the pulp culture era, its protagonist senses the nation's changing narrative, saying, "Some of my story is too personal to write in the first person, and some of it is too personal to write in the third person. Most of it is too personal to write at all."[13] Thus Willeford's character speculates not only on whether to simulate reality, and, if he chooses to do so, the voice in which he will speak, but, in a more general way, on the relationship between author and protagonist. Significantly, two years after the publication of *Woman Chaser*, Willeford's *Cockfighter* would appear. In this novel written from the perspective of someone who has chosen not to speak, Willeford formally acknowledges the genre's shift in perspective and, parodying unfriendly witnesses, silent majorities and strong silent types, bridges the narrative chasm separating the two eras.

If it wanted to survive, noir fiction had little choice but to meet the demands of the era, readdress itself to state crime while continuing to investigate human foible, fear, and a world in which, to paraphrase Ross Macdonald, the hunter and the hunted are often indistinguishable. These days readers have come to expect uncertainty, deviancy, moral ambiguity, iconoclasm, and a narrative suggesting cultural and psychological fragmentation. Nor are readers, after Watergate, Irangate, the Savings and Loan scandal and the Gulf War, easily shocked when it comes to state crime. Aware of the trajectory of contemporary life, and the fact that the guilty often escape punishment, few expect fictional crime narratives to neatly resolve themselves in the traditional manner. Writers as diverse as Andrew Coburn, who writes with subtlety about East Coast suburban crime, and Jerome Charyn, whose Jewish grand gesture fiction centres on New York, constantly subvert expectations with plot twists and outrageous resolutions as open-ended as their investigations. Referring to subjects and signs with which earlier crime writers would have been unfamiliar, neon noir writers continue to represent life in an increasingly fragmented and corrupt society.

Given the era's policies and the pursuit of excess at any cost, a proliferation of crime novels appeared in the 1980s. The commodification of the genre, along with chronic inflation,[14] meant that crime fiction would invariably over-price itself, while crime writers, not wanting to alienate potential readers, would refrain from political reductionism. This resistance to political categorisation suggests that writers no longer believed the language and ideologies of their predecessors capable of addressing contemporary issues. Preferring to leave himself open to interpretation, James Ellroy, for example, would refer to himself as an extreme right-winger, yet write about the Hollywood witch hunts from what could be called a left-wing perspective. This resistance to categorisation also points to the influence of economic considerations on the contents and packaging of noir fiction. After all, the business of crime fiction, like any such enterprise, is based on hype, which, in turn, functions as the conceptual engine of a consumer culture. Appealing to all ideologies simultaneously, corporate publishing absorbs contradictions, while encouraging – though never at the expense of profit – the depoliticalisation of that which it produces. Regardless of volume, format and price, neon noir fiction threatens to become as expendable as its pulp culture predecessors. Yet this has a positive aspect; for noir fiction, existing within a historical and cultural context, rarely pretends to be anything other than what it is: expendable product whose appeal extends no further than replication and critique. With crime fiction so easily commodified, corporate publishers and the media adjust their response to the genre, creating demand through supply, a circular process that begins and ends with the market and its manipulation.[15] These days, every crime novel is a possible movie, and every author is a would-be celebrity. Consequently, some authors, to protect themselves, choose to take the most extreme position possible.

Neon noir fiction, which could be said to begin with Richard Stark's *Point Blank*, reaches its apogee with James Ellroy's *White Jazz*. After Ellroy's fragmented assault, the crime novel would have to reassess its place in the culture. For Ellroy's work suggests that crime fiction is at its most subversive not when it retreats into the confines of the genre, but when it stretches its narrative boundaries and rules regarding subject, style and plot. With its historical resonances, *White Jazz* mirrors the last days of the Reagan–Bush era, and, in doing so, becomes the quintessential noir product. "The last word in atrocity, cynicism and horror", wrote André Gide in reference to Dashiell Hammett's 1929 *Red Harvest*. He might just as well have been referring to *White Jazz*. But times change. These days, Hammett is the epitome of good taste, while Ellroy has become the most recent example of extremism in pursuit of vice.

The chapters that follow cover a variety of subjects and a number of writers. The first four chapters place neon noir fiction in a historical context, while the last two investigate specific themes. "From Pulp to Neon: Searching for the war in the wreckage of pulp culture fiction" addresses itself to writers seeking to make the transition from pulp culture to neon noir fiction. Starting with the Vietnam war – conspicuous by its absence in noir fiction during the 1960s – the chapter explores how the genre would reflect a divided nation. "Total Crime: Negotiating the memory of Vietnam" considers the aftermath of the Vietnam war, the Nixon era, Watergate, and the Congressional hearings on the CIA. In doing so, it discusses the genre's changing subject matter and readership, as well as the war-as-crime narrative. "Figures in the Mirror: Private-eye fiction from Watergate to Whitewater" deals specifically with detective fiction and its role in investigating the culture. It follows the rise and fall of post-Watergate fiction and its relationship to history in a post-pulp culture era. "Extremists in Pursuit of Vice: The origins and practice of deregulated crime fiction" looks at the genre against the backdrop of the Reagan–Bush era, and obsessions with serial killers, racial division, class warfare, and the apparent breakdown of society.

"From Mean Streets to Dream Streets: The portrayal of cities in contemporary noir fiction" discusses crime fiction in relationship to the cities in which it takes place. Considering how urban space has changed over the years, it focuses on three cities: Los Angeles seen through the fiction of Ellroy, Arthur Lyons, Walter Mosley, and Joseph Wambaugh; Miami via the fiction of Elmore Leonard, Charles Willeford and Carl Hiassen; New York through the fiction of Jerome Charyn and Nick Tosches; and the imaginary contemporary city through the work of Jack O'Connell. Here one notes that utopias have become dystopias, the stalker has replaced the *flâneur,* and public spaces have become zones of paranoia and repression. The final chapter, "Turning Out the Lights: Post-mortem aesthetics; the politics of murder in the work of Thomas B. Harris and Bradley Denton; pastiche noir; and the future of crime fiction" widens the discussion and draws the main body of the study to a close. Given that crime fiction and film are so closely linked, *Neon Noir* ends with "Screening Neon", which lists and comments upon examples of modern film noir as they relate to the fiction discussed in the preceding chapters.

Though neon noir fiction reflects the warp and woof of society, it rarely does so to the point of negating the inner workings of the genre or of exposing itself to political categorisation. While most contemporary noirists maintain a firm grip on the moral centre of their fictional world, others demonstrate a more flexible relationship. Responding to a crime-ridden, economically extreme, and morally uncertain culture, the latter carve out narratives that manoeuvre between fiction and replication, self-reference and artifice. It's these critiques to which *Neon Noir* pays particular attention.

2

FROM PULP TO NEON

Searching for the war in the wreckage of pulp culture fiction: Ross Macdonald, John D. MacDonald, Chester Himes, Jim Thompson, Charles Willeford, Joe Gores and Richard Stark

The Vietnam War, from 1964 to 1973,[1] was the cold war in neon. Not only was it the first war to be regularly featured on television,[2] but it marked the beginning of an era of financial, political and narrative deregulation in which the US "faced the problem of the war-bloated deficit and the gap in the balance of payments caused by US direct foreign investment and expenditure overseas".[3] Warfare had also become deregulated, as strafe bombing, counter-insurgency terror, and discontent amongst ordinary soldiers undermined traditional notions of battlefield conduct. The same could be said of public order, as civil insurrections swept through a series of American cities. Forced to pass liberal domestic legislation at home, President Lyndon Johnson and his Great Society would continue to treat foreign enemies – exemplified by the "mere gook rule"[4] – with contempt. In the end, the war had become a deadly testing ground, irrevocably altering America's already twisted narrative.[5]

With its My Lai-type massacres, PHOENIX program,[6] and gunboat diplomacy, America's involvement in Vietnam made its past crimes appear insignificant. Out of this morass, a new type of crime fiction would emerge. For the war would influence an entire generation of crime writers. Some like James Crumley would find themselves in Southeast Asia. Others like

James Ellroy would sit the war out, high on drugs or preoccupied by small-time thievery. Experiencing the war – or numbing oneself against it – would, however, take its toll. For the war represented America's most expensive (approximately $140 billion), prolonged and deadly intervention into Third World territory. It's not surprising that, despite gathering opposition, crime writers were slow to respond to the crisis, much less show signs of dissent. Fearing controversy, silence, for many, would be the best policy. The war would signal an economic and cultural shift, causing subsequent crime fiction, not to mention future military policy and political discourse, to seek new markets and marketing strategies. Just as Vietnam veterans would return to haunt the nation, reminding it of its criminal past, so crime writers, in recalling the ghosts of past critiques, would come to haunt America's literary narrative. Locating a new readership and a market based on expendability and dissonance, crime fiction, dependent on the permutations of society, would articulate public concern, and the excesses caused by the war and assorted free market policies.

However, the war presented crime fiction with a dilemma. To engage with the culture, the genre had to find a way to investigate state crime without sacrificing its status as popular literature. Either it could ignore state crime and face extinction as a critical genre; address itself to the problem and face censure; or make oblique references within a more general cultural critique. Veering between the first and third options, crime fiction would alter its orientation only when writers with a more urgent relationship to the war began to emerge from their literary bunkers.

Though crime fiction occupies a special place in American literary culture, it remains a popular but marginal pursuit.[7] Ironical that, while mainstream literature has been used to illustrate the superiority of US culture, hardboiled fiction, as American as jazz, has offered writers in other countries (for example, Jean-Patrick Manchette, Jean-Claude Izzo, Hélène Couturier, and Didier Daeninckx in France; Leonardo Sciascia in Italy; Manuel Velazquez Montalbán in Spain; Derek Raymond and Ted Lewis in Britain; Rolo Diez and Paco Ignacio Taibo in Mexico; Enrique Medina in Argentina) an oppositional perspective, and an investigatory style that is as political as it is engaging.

That being the case, why, during the years of the Vietnam war, did most crime writers, working in a genre whose roots are in proletariat fiction, refrain from criticising the war? Despite the fact that, had they wanted to write about the war, many, working to contract, could well have been silenced by their, or their publishers', desire to sell books.[8] Others might have felt that, as storytellers, it was not their place to criticise the war. After all, crime novelists were still literary workers, not yet celebrities, nor possessing the luxury of being able to court controversy. Moreover, some writers, detached from the roots of the genre, or, siding with the state, doubtlessly supported the war. Yet, taking into account the seemingly apolitical stance of many hardboiled narratives, there is, within the crevices of most texts, an implicit critique, if only regarding the hypocrisy of the culture, and the values that sustain a system that seeks to penetrate foreign countries. At the same time, the genre's decline as an oppositional literature would lead to its rejuvenation, as future noir writers and readers sought narratives more in line with the neon reality of the era.

Ross Macdonald

With the war draining money from a more-than-affluent economy, the contradiction between wealth and repression had become so apparent that an oppositional culture could not help but emerge. This *underground* culture would issue critiques regarding the war, as well as the politics, history and ideology behind it. The underground culture took many forms, from alternative newspapers and radio stations to advice groups for draft resisters, free medical clinics and legal advice centres. It also produced communiques – manifestos, poetry, comic books

– of *samizdat* proportions, and, at least for the duration of the war, exerted a profound effect on American society. Moreover, the term *underground* resonated with meaning, bringing to mind resistance movements, the underground railway and, from a later perspective, tunnels dug by the Vietnamese during the war.[9] It also formed the title of one of Ross Macdonald's most popular novels. Written and published during the war, Macdonald's 1971 *The Underground Man* became a metaphor that linked the oppositional culture and readers, writers and protagonists of crime fiction. Moreover, thanks to Eudora Welty's 1971 essay on *The Underground Man* in the *New York Times Book Review*, Macdonald's book would be the first modern crime novel to be regarded as serious literature.

If one considers it alongside Macdonald's other work, *The Underground Man*'s significance relates more to its title than to its text, which is neither better nor worse than any of his other finely honed humanitarian crime novels. With a publishing career that began in the 1940s, Macdonald, in this novel, was able to attach a tag so pertinent that it helped crime fiction reassume its role as a literature capable of articulating and criticising the era. At the same time, *The Underground Man* represents an investigation of the author's well-trodden theme, more relevant than ever, regarding the sins of the fathers. For Macdonald's emphasis on familial relationships – usually con-sisting of plots about fathers searching for sons, sons searching for fathers, or families in search of themselves[10] – typified a period which, despite feminist murmurings, focused primarily on male protagonists and the psychological intricacies of their behaviour.

Not the first crime writer to be influenced by psychoanalysis (Thompson, McCoy, Highsmith, and Woolrich were amongst those noirists who had already fallen under its spell), Macdonald's protagonist, Lew Archer, could be regarded as a kind of *Laingian* detective, relentlessly attacking the totalitarian-ism of family life. In a variation on Macdonald's often-used theme, Archer, at the conclusion of *The Underground Man*, protects young Fritz from his mother, who urges her son to keep quiet and not incriminate himself lest he wind up in jail or a mental hospital. In an era of domineering mothers and hen-pecked fathers, Archer says, "Don't let her scare you, Fritz ... You won't be put in jail for anything you did because she made you." When Fritz's mother claims Archer is trying to turn her son against her, Archer says, "Maybe it's time, Mrs Snow. You've been using your son as a scapegoat, telling yourself that you've been looking after him ... He could get better help from a stranger."[11]

Not only does Archer manage to keep his wits, but he voices serious social concerns. While reading the classified ads of the *LA Times* – "they sometimes tell you more about Los Angeles than the news"[12] – Archer, in the opening pages of *The Underground Man*, is visited by a neighbour who informs him of a forest fire in Santa Teresa, one similar to a fire that had threatened Macdonald's Santa Barbara a few years prior to the publication of the novel. The fire reminds readers of environmental matters, particularly America's defoliation of Vietnam. However, that will be as close to the war as Macdonald ventures. Having opened the genre to a middle-class readership, Macdonald, whose politics are, from the 1960s onwards, consistently liberal, is careful where he treads. After all, he was writing at a time when the war was only beginning to find dissenters amongst the middle class.[13]

Accordingly, it is from a middle-class perspective that Macdonald writes about the counter-culture – an unavoidable subject if one is addressing 1960s family life. Crandall, the father of the missing girl, Susan, says of his daughter's boyfriend:

> "I tried to straighten the boy out on his philosophy of life. I asked him in a friendly way what he planned to do with himself, and he said all he wanted was just to get by. I didn't think that was a satisfactory answer, and I asked him what would happen to the country if everybody took that attitude. He said it had already happened to the country. I don't know

what he meant by that, but I didn't like his tone."[14]

Later, crime writers would investigate the counter-culture from a different perspective, that of ex-participant rather than observer. However, no crime writer would investigate the state of family life as deeply and with as much compassion as Macdonald. So egalitarian is Archer that, in the early 1970s, Macdonald can include feminism in his fiction, if not in his perspective: "He gave me a tentative look to see if we could get together on an anti-feminist platform."[15] Looking after the interests of his clients and all innocent parties, and despite his preoccupation with psychotherapy, Macdonald's perspective changed very little over the years. Though he refers to the culture that creates, and is created by, the Vietnam war, he does so from the viewpoint of an eco-ambassador, rather than a left-wing critic. Dealing with effects rather than causes, Archer, with his finger on the pulse, ignores a war that has yet to personally affect him.

John D. MacDonald

With a more direct, if less subtle, relationship to the era, John D. MacDonald, author of some seventy novels, sets his work amongst the putrefied middle class. *Dress Her in Indigo*, published in 1969, features his customary protagonist, Travis McGee. Renowned for his thundering moralisms and corrosive observations regarding the shortcomings of others, McGee, in this novel, treks to Mexico to locate the teenage daughter of a well-to-do Florida businessman. The girl's father believes his only child has been killed in a road accident. Once over the border, McGee, who refers to himself as a "salvage consultant", finds she is very much alive, and part of a community that includes hippies, drug addicts, homosexuals, lesbians, and a wealthy countess. Though John D. MacDonald is less realistic and more simplistic than Ross Macdonald, he is more intolerant when it comes to middle-class pretensions. Preferring to tell it like it was, *Dress Her in Indigo*, with its tabloid sensationalism, reads as though it might have been commissioned by an over-worked editor at *Argosy*. A throwback to pulp culture writers like Howard Browne and Thomas B. Dewey, Macdonald pushes the right cultural buttons, but to no lasting effect. When a character mentions the newly discovered "communications gap",[16] McGee, exercising his wit, responds, saying, "Anybody who gives it any thought knows that there has always been a communications gap between everybody. If any two people could ever really get inside each other's head, it would scare the pee out of both of them."[17]

Ironically, MacDonald is not afraid to mention Vietnam, even if it comes from the mouth of a simpatico father of a drop-out:

> "They've taken a good long look at our world, and they don't like it. They don't like the corruption, and the way the power structure takes care of its own, and the way we're all being hammered down into being a bunch of numbers in a whole country full of computers. So what they want to do is get away from all the machinery that makes Vietnams and makes slums and discrimination and legalized theft and murder."[18]

Though he hardly dwells on the subject, one wonders why John D. MacDonald could mention the *V-word* when his more politically correct namesake avoided it. Could it be that Ross Macdonald does not want to offend his middle-class readership? Or that John D. MacDonald has such a well-defined following that he can be confident, even cynical, regarding his subject matter? Enough, that is, to allow his characters some well-chosen words:

> "[There] are people – young and old – that I like, and people that I do not like. The former are always in short supply. I am turned off by humourless fanaticism, whether it's revolu-tionary mumbo-jumbo by a young one, or loud lessons from the scripture by an old one. We are all comical, touching, slapstick animals, walking on our hind legs, trying to make it a

noble journey from womb to tomb and the people who can't
see it all that way bore the hell out of me."[19]

Aware of the cultural narrative, MacDonald mocks it with
impunity. Rejecting the advances of the aging countess, McGee
tells her, "[I] wrote you down in one of the pages of my life, and
now the pages have been turned and we cannot go back and
reread them." But the woman, having survived World War Two,
says, "Because the book is very long and life is very short. Nice
try ducks. But I did the writing, and all I wrote was a preface."[20]
Yet one wonders how a war that killed over 50,000 Americans
and countless Vietnamese[21] might fit into her unwritten text,
and if its absence – like the absence of the war in crime fiction
– is merely a way to justify her apathy.

Though he mentions Vietnam, MacDonald refrains from
criticising the war or the male mind-set that allows it to continue. Not surprising, since he's part of that tradition of male
protagonists portrayed, for different reasons, by writers from
Hemingway to Willeford. Naturally, McGee takes exception to
the lesbian relationship involving Eva, a wealthy French woman,
and Bix, the girl he has been sent to locate. In a scene meant to
arouse prurient interests, McGee ties up the French woman,
while Bix, recovering from her drugged stupor, turns on her
lover. Her venomous remarks humble McGee enough to acknowledge that Eva, however perverse, has at least enabled Bix to
overcome her drug addiction. When he returns her to her
crippled father, Bix looks at this pathetic crumple of humanity,
turns to McGee and says, "Have you brought me back to this
silly old fart. I'd rather be back with Eva."[22]

Last Shots: From Charles Williams to Chester Himes

In his 1966 *Don't Just Stand There*, Charles Williams, at the end
of his career, and less than a decade before his 1975 suicide,
says of a fictional former pulpist,

Sanborn . . . used to turn out three to four million words a
year under contract to several strings of magazines and under
half a dozen names . . . He'd hardly written anything since the
pulp magazines folded, but when he sat down at a typewriter
it sounded like a machine-gunner repelling an attack. He
erupted characters and plots like a broken fire main . . . It
wasn't lack of talent, but simply a matter of early conditioning
and the fact he was a little too old to adapt.[23]

During the mid-1960s, many pulp culture writers found themselves similarly placed. With the disappearance of the pulps,
and, with paperbacks no longer heralding the promise of a
literate nation, even the best pulp cultists, unable or unwilling
to continue their critique, would find the going difficult.

This was not the case with Chester Himes. Thanks to the
quality of his writing, his perspective, and the impact of the
Black Power movement, Himes was able to move to the cusp
separating pulp culture and neon noir writing. That Himes's
career, by the end of the 1960s, would grind to a halt has less to
do with the absence of Vietnam in his fiction than with the
author's inability to reconcile his cynicism regarding the present
with his false optimism about the future. Involved, if at a
distance, with the ongoing political struggle, Himes, in novels
like *Cotton Comes to Harlem* (published in France in 1964) and
Blind Man With a Pistol (his final Harlem detective novel, published in 1969) had, despite the war's disproportionate number
of African-American casualties, no need to dwell on Vietnam,
not at the expense of narratives regarding battles taking place
in the black community.

In keeping with an era of deregulation – whose policies,
from the *Great Society* to Reaganomics, would have a detrimental
effect on inner-city African-Americans[24] – crime and disorder
become, in Himes's final detective novel, the overriding reality.
Blind Man With a Pistol – Himes's only finished work to appear
after the spate of inner-city rebellions – centres on the struggle
for political power within the black community, and concerns

the first rumblings of an incipient and apocalyptic revolution. Published four years after Himes's meeting Malcolm X (though appreciating his politics, Himes had reservations about Malcolm's religious views), and a year after the assassination of Martin Luther King, Himes's Harlem has become a dystopia devoid of hope, where "unorganized violence is like a blind man with a pistol."

As Coffin Ed and Grave Digger traipse through Harlem in search of the person responsible for slitting the throat of a white male who frequents Harlem for homosexual sex, they realise the futility of working for the state. Left to drift through their community, they end up shooting rats that emerge from an about-to-be-demolished building. A bitter metaphor, made more so by the fact that, as they take their pot-shots, a blind black man, having emerged from the subway, fires into the crowd, killing a white policeman. Watching what might be mistaken for the shots that spark a revolution, Coffin Ed and Grave Digger are mere spectators in a struggle which they cannot hope to influence or control.

Himes's protagonists explain the identity of the shooter to Anderson, their white superior:

"Some call him lack of respect for law and order, some lack of opportunity, some the teachings of the Bible, some the sins of their fathers," Grave Digger expounded. "Some call him ignorance, some poverty, some rebellion. Me and Ed look at him with compassion. We're victims."[25]

At the end of the novel, when Grave Digger tells Anderson that the riot was started by a blind man with a pistol, the latter says, "That don't make any sense." To which Grave Digger can only say, "Sure don't."

Though hardly ineffective, the blind man's actions are as understandable as they are self-destructive. Warning against spontaneous violence, Himes finally confronts the contradictory role his two detectives – black cops working for the state –

have been forced to play. Unfortunately, Himes could take his fiction no further. In *Plan B*, Grave Digger, for the sake of the revolution, must kill Coffin Ed. It's as though Himes's final bombshell must explode in the author's hands. With Himes more adept at analysing the present, *Plan B* would reach the public in a form as incomplete as it is uncertain.

Jim Thompson

Riddled by illness and alcohol, Jim Thompson, during the final decade of his life, made a last-ditch effort to adjust to the post-pulp culture era. Initiating and abandoning some fourteen novels during this period, Thompson, who died in 1977, still managed to churn out a handful of truncated texts: the auto-biographical *South of Heaven*; novelisations of *Ironsides*, *The Undefeated* and *Nothing But a Man* (the latter, based on Michael Roemer's 1964 film about race and class amongst African-Americans in the South, earned Thompson, presumably on the assumption that he was black, an entry in an encyclopaedia of African-American literature[26]), and two neglected and eccentric novels, *King Blood*[27] and *Child of Rage*.

Though dismissed by Thompsonites,[28] *King Blood* and *Child of Rage* – neither, even by Thompson's standards, can be considered well-structured works of fiction – contain a social critique and trajectory that make them relevant to this study. What's more, both novels consciously court extremism. A hybrid of *King Lear*, *High Chaparral* and Lautremont's *Maldoror*, *King Blood* depicts a world as dark as anything Thompson produced. Restating Thompson's belief that America is doomed by its history, *King Blood*'s publication in 1973 – and even then, only in Britain – would coincide with America's unseemly and ignominious withdrawal from Vietnam.[29]

Taking place in the Oklahoma Territory at the turn of the century, *King Blood* centres on Critchfield King, third and youngest son of Ike King, the largest landholder in the region. The novel begins as Critch, now an adult, returns to his father's home, having been whisked away at an early age by his mother and her boyfriend, an itinerant con-man. On the journey, Critch steals $72,000 from a pair of sisters who, in turn, have taken the money from men who mistook them for prostitutes. In the midst of this novel, a mixture of myth, history, and warped melodrama, Thompson interjects autobiographical tidbits and poetic asides concerning a landscape created by Manifest Destiny – which is to say, the belief that America has the god-given right to colonise the continent,[30] – that, in turn, would create the conditions that would facilitate such foreign interventions as the war in Vietnam.

In describing the inhabitants of El Paso, Thompson paints a vivid picture of the West, and a society not yet overly regulated through government intervention:

> A few, out of hateful necessity, would manage to make the transformation from cowboy to clodhopper. Some would turn outlaw. Some would become peace officers, hunting down the very men they had once worked with and called friend. As for the remainder . . . well, who knew? What does happen to men who can find no other path for themselves than the one occupied by the juggernaut of an onrushing civilization?[31]

Here there is as little regard for the land as there is for life. As for the father of the psycho-sisters, the narrator maintains that he had "incestuously begun their education in sex", which "accounted for their cold-blooded treatment of men . . . Except for sex he had taught them nothing – unless it was that greed and ignorance are poor tools for a farmer." Another case of the sins of the fathers, though, in Thompson's world, sins can pass on to daughters as well as sons. Here the father exercises the same cruelty and neglect on his land as he does on his daughters:

> Year after year he had planted the same soil-robbing crops. Ignoring the warnings in the gradually decreasing yields. Fertilizing scantily, if at all; giving the depleted land no chance for restful fallowing. And then, when the once-good earth

would no longer bear, he had cursed it for the worthlessness which he himself had brought to it – and begun to cast about for still more land to ruin.[32]

Rejected by Popular Library and Gold Medal, *Child of Rage* was contracted by Lancer in 1971 and published a year later. Originally written for the French cinema,[33] it would be Thompson's last book to be published in America during his lifetime. More savage and deliberately controversial than *King Blood*, this novel also concerns history's dark legacy. A provocative and scatological attack on racism – not to mention God and motherhood – *Child of Rage* tackles such subjects as incest, miscegenation and black militancy. Partly inspired by Norman Mailer's wordplay in *Why Are We in Vietnam*, the novel is narrated by Allen Smith, an intelligent African-American teenager whose mother is white.[34] Like many other Thompson protagonists, Allen is split – one side "drew people to him and the other [who] drove them away"[35] – this time racially as well as psychologically.

Believing his mother loathes him because of his skin-colour, Allen, trapped by his Oedipal complex as well as his colour, is consumed with self-hatred. In fact, his self-loathing manifests itself in a special kind of Tourette's Syndrome, causing Allen to utter truths so cruel they alienate anyone close to him. Meanwhile, Allen's mother, an entrepreneurial prostitute, uses sex to control her son just as she has used it to control every male who has crossed her path.

In opting for the outrageous, Thompson assumes, as he does in *Nothing But a Man*, the perspective of an African-American. This at a time when street-wise white males were co-opting, often to a comic degree, African-American vocabulary, inflection and culture. But Thompson assumes his guise less for fashion than to investigate the psychosis of racism.[36] While *Nothing But a Man* is a flat novelisation of an earlier film, *Child of Rage* reads as though it has been filtered through various African-American texts of the period, as well as Thompson's past politics.[37] In crossing cultures, Thompson is doing what he has always done: namely, getting inside his protagonist. It's from this claustrophobic and paranoid perspective that Thompson investigates the culture. "The intelligent man can only function behind a mask of stupidity, or conformity",[38] says Allen, reiterating the viewpoint of past Thompson protagonists, as well as reflecting a protective armour adopted by many African-Americans from slavery to the present. Like Thompson's prime protagonist, Lou Ford, Allen is out to wreak havoc on history. Atoning for past sins, he exonerates no one: "We're all guilty. We come into life filled with sinful shit, and we have to get it kicked out of us before we can be raised to glory."[39]

Exiting on a note of controversy, Thompson hopes his transgressions are enough to have created the ultimate deregulated narrative. Utilising wordplay and scatological invective, he plunders the culture, notwithstanding his favourite bugaboo, popular psychology:

> All psychoses and neuroses, the motivations of son-of-a-bitchery, are rooted in sex, if we are to believe Freud. And Freud's all reik, even for jung man like me. Thus, the white son-of-a-bitch (or pseudo son-of-a-bitch) has as many motivations as the total number of people in all the other races combined, because he's screwed them all. Everywhere we look we can see the results of his jazzing: the forests and fields flattened by his indiscriminate flopping about, the stinking pollution of his heaving and panting, the rivers and lakes clogged and poisonous with his pissed-off semen.[40]

Though this novel was written under the influence of Vietnam, Thompson mentions the war only once. After a stinging onslaught which makes use of every imaginable racial epithet, Allen addresses himself to the Chinese, deploying once again a series of racial and sexual terms of abuse:

> Small wonder that the seed spawned by Asiatic copulation is

soured from the start. Small wonder that the yellow infant's
first words are, "Oy, vey!" which, roughly translated, means,
"Oh, shit!" And this is why we are in Vietnam.[41]

Consequently, Thompson acknowledges, if briefly, the primary
narrative of the period – the war in Southeast Asia. But that is
as far as he goes. For this former Wobbly and Communist
remains locked into a previous tradition in which environmental
determinism and eternal truths such as, "We never know when
we're going to get kissed or kissed-off",[42] take precedence over
more topical matters.

Though he realises the warp in his moral perspective, Allen
believes his thinking must be relative to his condition: "The
world had been reduced to my world, the periphery which I
moved within, and its single anus awaited my entry."[43] As for
God, He is "not dead, no. Madmen never die; they simply laugh
themselves into a catatonic state, from which they emerge still
laughing. And screaming and shrieking and shouting."[44] Finally,
Allen realises that, however moral, he is dependent on a culture
that pushes him from one extreme to another:

> [Whichever] way one ran, he had only to run far enough to
> wind up at this starting point, winded and exhausted by going
> nowhere at all. Perhaps directions had no existence beyond
> that pin-head planet called Earth; perhaps they had another
> dimension, as with the space-time quotient. And because we
> are too stupid to discover it and equated success with move-
> ment, we would all end up in an explosion of colliding bodies,
> clogging the cosmos with flying shit.[45]

So extreme is *Child of Rage* that Thompson, at the time of its
writing, must have realised his literary life was drawing to an
end. This final assault on the genre constitutes an attempt to
create a new crime novel, one that moves to the political and
linguistic edge. Though Thompson would never extricate himself from the pulp culture era, *Child of Rage* and *King Blood*,
with their uncompromising tone and style, are essential for

understanding America's twisted narrative, and the future of noir fiction. However distorted, they are the logical extremes of an already extreme literary career. Despite its deficiencies, *King Blood* reads like the final product of Manifest Destiny, a policy Thompson viewed as the metaphorical source of the American tragedy;[46] while the provocative *Child of Rage* can be considered Thompson's final attempt to move from the era of pulp culture into a neon world where nothing is repressed and no critique is too extreme.

Charles Willeford

With his pulp excursions into the world of used-car salesmen, art forgers, alcoholics, Hollywood hacks, and Miami cops, Charles Willeford, in a career spanning four decades, would articulate a series of dispassionate critiques regarding a culture so obsessed with violence, competition and macho posturing that, given the state of things, war appears unavoidable. One of Willeford's most devastating cultural critiques, *Cockfighter*, published in 1972 – the same year as Thompson's *Child of Rage* – earned the praise of such writers as Erskine Caldwell, Harry Crews and Elmore Leonard. Appearing a year after his *The Burnt Orange Heresy* – a more mainstream crime novel concerning art forgery, that bears comparison to Patricia High-smith's *Ripley Quartet* – *Cockfighter*, later faithfully filmed by Monte Hellman, centres on Frank Mansfield, a man so dedicated that he has vowed not to speak until he wins the southern championship. A personal matter, Frank's silence derives from an incident in which his bravado caused him to lose a prized cock and the coveted Cockfighter of the Year award.

Less a crime novel than a novel in which various crimes are depicted, *Cockfighter* is in the tradition of low-life fiction, such as Leonard Gardner's 1969 classic small-town boxing novel *Fat City*. As in Gardner's novel, *Cockfighter* describes a dubious sport. Written in the midst of a war more disgusting than cockfighting could ever be, the novel's excessive detail mirrors the discomforting images from Vietnam which, at the time, were appearing nightly on TV. Likewise, Frank Mansfield's self-enforced silence, as well as reminding the reader that crime writers were still reluctant to include the war in their novels, can be tentatively linked to the creation of the *silent majority*[47] and the current state of noir fiction.

Set in a series of small Southern towns, *Cockfighter* investigates the relationship between sport, chauvinism and war. Yet Willeford refrains from mentioning Vietnam. In fact, *Cockfighter* takes place in a place and time in which the war has evidently been erased from the public record. Nevertheless, the war, or at least the sensibility that created and sustained it, is written between every line, and is evident in the way Frank relates to others, particularly women. Obsessed, competitive and ego-centric, Frank is similar to Willeford's other protagonists: Hudson in *Woman Chaser*, Jake Blake in *Wild Wives*, and Russell Haxby in *High Priest of California*. Though not without sensitivity – he plays the guitar with great skill – cockfighting takes precedence over all other activities. As does his prickly ego. Receiving what he considers too much money for playing the guitar, and thinking Bernice, a wealthy older woman, is only interested in his body, Frank is so offended that he smashes his instrument and storms out of her house.

In prefacing *Cockfighter* with a quote from Ezra Pound – "What matters is not the idea a man holds, but the depth at which he holds it" – Willeford sums up a novel in which no apologies are made for Frank's sport or his moral imperative. But one should take the quote with a grain of salt. For Willeford would probably not have said the same about Pound's support for Mussolini, nor the media's support for American troops in Vietnam.[48] Obviously, some ideas are not excusable, no matter how deeply they are held. If nothing else, Frank is the consummate cocksman, who exploits *chicks* as well as cocks, including Dody, a sixteen-year-old daughter of itinerant farm workers. Twice her age, Frank punches her in the stomach and, as though she were a prize steer, gives her to a man old enough to be her grandfather.

Believing he possesses a moral sense second to none, Frank, like Allen in *Child of Rage*, deploys religious terminology to describe his situation. Regarding the unpleasant experience of having to listen to others, he says,

> Since my vow of silence I had become, unwillingly, a man who listened to confessions . . . [People] often told me things they would hesitate to tell to a priest, or even to their wives. At first, it bothered me, learning things about people I didn't want or need to know, but now I just listened – not liking it . . . but accepting the confessions as an unwelcome part of the deal I had made with myself.[49]

What Frank hates most about his muteness is the passivity that accompanies it. For this cockfighter cannot tolerate being anyone's object. After all, a mute cannot interrupt a conversation or remain the centre of attention. Listening to others is something that few of Willeford's protagonists can bear doing. As Frank's friend and one-time cocksman, who, having become henpecked, has retired from the sport, says to him, "You're a hard man to talk to since you lost your voice!"[50]

So self-centred is Frank that, in an era when 19 per cent of all US households live in poverty, he cannot understand why anyone would want to join a trade union: "The idea of any free American male paying gangsters money for the right to work has always struck me as one of the most preposterous customs we have."[51] As well as taking place at a time when trade union membership had dropped to just over a quarter of the workforce, Frank's use of the term "right to work" indicates that, though a self-acclaimed free thinker, he too has succumbed to an early example of linguistic manipulation.

From a Georgia farming family, Willeford's protagonist is engaged to Mary Elizabeth, a schoolteacher who hopes Frank will give up cockfighting. However, Frank is less bothered by her objections than by the thought of becoming a member of the bourgeoisie. So much does he despise the trappings of middle-class life that he gleefully evicts his brother from the family property. Fortunately, Frank equates bourgeois life with racism, and, to spite his brother, who has become a member of the White Citizen's Council, makes sure the black tenant farmer stays on after the family property has been sold.

What Frank says about cockfighters might also be said about those who read crime fiction, or look at the stars and stripes while dreaming of enlisting in the war in Vietnam:

> Unlike most American sportsmen, the cockfighting fan has an overwhelming tendency to become an active participant . . . He either likes [the action of two game-cocks battling to the death] or he doesn't. If he doesn't like it, he doesn't return to watch another fight. If he does like it, he accepts, sooner or later, everything about the sport – the good with the bad.[52]

This marriage of advocate and participant is reinforced when Frank's partner, a former New York advertising executive, says, "[There's] a lot of things I don't like about cockfighting, but a cocker's got to take the good with the bad."[53] Similar sentiments would be expressed by the silent majority regarding America's policy in Southeast Asia.

To Frank, cockfighting is as American as apple pie and foreign invasions. Citing a letter from Washington to Lafayette that refers to the "spirit of anarchy and confusion" displayed at a "cocking main",[54] Frank asserts that "cockfighters are still the most democratic group of men in the United States".[55] However, if "anarchy and confusion" are tempered only by forceful personalities, it hardly bodes well for democracy.

Eventually Frank makes it to the Southern Championship. In the final match, though both cocks die in combat, Frank's bird leaves the pit last, giving him the honours and the prize money. Having regained his voice, Frank finds it "rusty, strangled, different, not at all like I remembered".[56] Meanwhile, Mary

Elizabeth has run from the arena in horror, not because of the cockfight, which she abhors, but Frank's sporting demeanour: "I watched your face. It was awful. No pity, no love, no understanding, nothing! Hate! You hate everything, yourself, me, the world, everybody!"[57] Rather than stun Frank, her words reaffirm his worst qualities: "I didn't know this woman . . . This was a Mary Elizabeth I had hidden from myself all these years."[58] Driving home the sexual metaphor, he steps on the neck of his dead cock, tears off its head, and hands it to Mary Elizabeth, saying to himself, "After thirty-three years, I was a mature individual. I had never needed Mary Elizabeth, and she had never needed me . . . From now on I could look toward the future, and it had never been brighter."[59] With a dubious sense of victory and what constitutes the moral high ground, Frank decides to take Bernice to Puerto Rico. Unlike Mary Elizabeth, she apparently knows how to have fun.

With its blatant double-entendre, cockfighting constitutes the ultimate macho sport. But then Willeford's protagonists are rarely politically correct. Yet they are human, and susceptible to human foibles and misunderstandings. In *Cockfighter*, as in his other novels, Willeford refuses to give the reader an easy way out. Likewise, his wicked satires avoid happy endings and easily-arrived-at resolutions. Having communicated this same bleak vision throughout his career, Willeford, in depicting protagonists too obsessed to reflect on their situation, offers a critique of male behaviour which implies the eventual demise of the cocksman.

Like *Child of Rage*, *Cockfighter* prefigures the next phase of noir fiction, one in which any type of crime is fair game. Nevertheless, articulating crime on a fictional level necessitates a degree of personalisation. This would prove problematical when trying to articulate the relative anonymity of state and corporate crime. Significantly, as Willeford's *Cockfighter* and Thompson's *Child of Rage* were being hammered out, the era of flight-capital and debt had already begun. Involved in an increasingly unpopular war, the American government refused to take the political risks associated with financing the war with high taxes. While the cost of military procurement at home helped drive the American government's budget into deficit, military spending abroad had a similar effect on the American balance of payments. However, since the US dollar was the currency on which the international payment system was based, it was the preferred instrument in which countries held foreign-exchange reserves. Finding themselves flooded with dollars by the US balance-of-payments deficit, other countries responded by investing the excess in treasury bills sold by the US government to help finance its budget deficit. In effect, the US Marines had replaced Meyer Lansky's couriers, and the European central banks arranged the loan-back.[60] It was a situation that prompted government consultant Herman Khan, when told of this plan, to exclaim, "We've pulled off the biggest rip-off in history!"[61] Needless to say, that debt has yet to be paid. Though their fiction is populated by gamblers, con-men and criminals, neither Willeford nor Thompson could have dreamt up, much less contended with, such a narrative.

Richard Stark

Beginning in 1963 with the publication of *Point Blank* (original title: *The Hunter*), Richard Stark – a pseudonym for crime novelist Donald Westlake – produced a number of brutal, existential, and anti-corporate noir narratives featuring a former Mob employee named Parker. Cold-blooded, and as alienated as he is primeval, Parker has been forced by circumstances to become a freelancer who seeks retribution on his former partners-in-crime. Like the best crime fiction, Stark's narratives are subtly political, to the degree that French film-maker Jean-Luc Godard, in his Maoist phase, turned Stark's *The Jugger* into his film, *Made in USA*. In *Point Blank* – adapted for the screen in 1967 by John Boorman – Stark portrays the Mafia as the quint-essential corporation, and Parker, in pursuit of corporate criminals, as a havoc-causing urban terrorist. Written in a sparse cinematic style, Stark's work recalls Paul Cain's *Fast One* and the *Black Mask* school of writing.

At the same time, Stark's work prefigures fiction by the likes of Elmore Leonard, James Ellroy, and Eugene Izzi. Yet, in comparison, even their work can sometimes appear placid, if not cumbersome. This is all the more remarkable when one considers that Stark wrote most of his fiction during the Vietnam war when the genre was at a low point. Published in 1962, as the US was about to invade Laos, and JFK was maintaining that "the US, for more than a decade has been assisting the government of Vietnam to maintain their independence,"[62] *Point Blank* concerns a society on the verge of tearing itself apart. Moreover, Stark's depiction of the business world, with its cold steel, glass and modern decor, reflects the era's corporate self-confidence. Meanwhile, the morally ambiguous Parker, whose existence noticeably precedes his essence, is as violent as Mickey Spillane, but without any trace of the latter's retrograde politics. Double-crossed, shot and left for dead in a burning house, Parker escapes, from which point his penchant for violence assumes a dynamic of its own:

> "I'm going to drink his blood . . . I'm going to chew up his heart and spit it into the gutter for the dogs to raise a leg at. I'm going to peel the skin off him and rip out his veins and hang him with them."[63]

Fortunately, Stark's objective third-person narrative allows readers to distance themselves from the protagonist's outbursts. This, in turn, gives the novel a dreamlike quality, and turns the protagonist into a somnambulant whose desires must be fulfilled. Noting his appetites, the reader views him as though through the lens of a camera, one which, in separating the viewer and the viewed, prefigures TV images of the war and future surveillance systems. Of course, Stark's fiction stops short of full-scale realism. For, in a society saturated with noir imagery,

Stark's readers are all too familiar with criminal stylisations and modes of behaviour.

Here the ultimate signifier is the organisation-as-object. Noting that, however it is linguistically altered, the essence of the organisation remains the same, Parker says,

> "The funnies call it the syndicate. The goons and hustlers call it the Outfit. You call it the organization. I hope you people have fun with your words. But I don't care if you call yourselves the Red Cross, you owe me forty-five thousand dollars and you'll pay me back whether you like it or not."[64]

Apparently it's a class thing. For Carter, regional head of the Outfit, reminds Parker what he's up against:

> "Do you have any idea just how many employees are on our organization payroll, coast to coast? Just how many affiliate organizations in how many towns? How many officials we control at local and state level all across the country?"[65]

The ultimate corporation, the Outfit is no different to any other company. It's as American as Tammany Hall. And just as honest. Says Carter,

> "The organization is not unreasonable. It pays its debts, works within acceptable business ethics, and does its best to run at a profit. Except for the fact that it works outside the law, it conforms as closely as possible to the corporate concept . . . [If] you had come to me with a legitimate corporate debt, you would have no trouble. But you are asking us to reimburse you for a personal debt contracted by a former employee. No corporation in the world would agree to that."[66]

Making it clear just how much he dislikes corporate capitalism, Parker draws the line between freelancers like himself and the corporate criminals operating within the Outfit:

"There's you people with your organization, and there's us. We don't have any organization, but we're professionals. We know each other . . . We don't hit the syndicate. You're sitting there wide open – you can't squeal to the law, but we don't hit you."[67]

Told by Carter's boss, Fairfax, he will be killed if he does anything foolish, Parker, whose networking belies his status as an alienated loner, knows the truth: throughout the country there exists a vast underground comprised of freelance criminals: "You'd never find us. We aren't organized, we're just a guy here and a guy there that know each other. You're organized, so you're easy to find."[68]

Parker warns Fairfax, and explains how disorganised crime works:

"I just keep chopping off heads. But I also write letters . . . I tell them the syndicate hit me for forty-five Gs; do me a favor and hit them back when you've got the chance. Maybe half of them will say the hell with it. The other half are like me; they've got the job all cased . . . We walk into a syndicate place and we look around . . . – we think about it like a job. We don't do anything about it because you people are on the same side as us, but we think about it . . . So all of a sudden they've got the green light, they've got an excuse. They'll grab for it."[69]

Though *Point Blank* was written in the early 1960s, Parker reflects the decade's romanticism surrounding political violence and criminality. That Parker kills, hardly matters. An entryist in the world of organised crime, and a constant source of disruption, Parker's interventions bear a similarity to hit-and-run protests against the war, and such intrusions as the Weather Movement's intervention at the Students for Democratic Society's 1969 Chicago Conference. Not quite a natural born killer, Parker is kept going by his desire for disorder and revenge:

He wasn't sure himself any more how much was a tough front to impress the organization and how much was himself. He knew he was hard, he knew that he worried less about emotion than other people. But he'd never enjoyed the idea of a killing.[70]

With its anarchistic violence, Stark's fiction reflects the period when, between August 1969 and March 1970, seven major companies were bombed in New York, causing forty-three deaths and $21.8 million of damage. If nothing else, Parker reminds us that stealing money from corporate America, and damaging its property, can sometimes be politically expedient.

Regardless of whether the Outfit represents corporate capital- ism, government institutions, or left-wing vanguard parties, Parker is hell-bent on destruction. This brand of criminal libertarianism is similar not only to that which would become popular amongst contemporary crime writers, but it can also be gleaned from 1960s films like *Bonnie and Clyde* and Sergio Leone's *A Fistful of Dollars*, and in the ethics of lawlessness embodied in the songs that comprise Bob Dylan's *John Wesley Harding*. This is an altogether different libertarianism from its 1980s counterpart which, in many cases, camouflaged a neo- conservative ideology. Although the former is often trivialised, it has long played an important part in America's history, and, during the 1960s, exacerbated by the war and increased state power, contributed to street-level political movements, mass mobilisations against the war, student protests, political groupings, and, on the downside, to the election victories of Richard Nixon and Ronald Reagan. Pre-empting the mood of the era, Stark suggests that change will come from below, depending on the power of the unorganised. While Al Capone once said, "Organised crime is a contradiction in terms", disorganised crime, for Parker, remains an attractive proposition.

In depicting the era's chaos, Stark conveys the paranoia of the disorganised and powerless regarding the powerful. While paranoia has always been an essential ingredient in crime fiction, Stark would be one of the few crime writers to capture the psychological condition of the era, the result of overlaying the drug culture on the war machine. With the streets becoming the site of the urban nightmare – consisting of police excess, criminal activity and class conflict – Parker's paranoia is understandable. Conversely, suggesting to his disorganised cohorts that they oppose organised crime, Parker easily instils paranoia in others. Yet Stark's narratives are too embedded in the disjunctures of street-level politics to survive the dictates of state power. Appropriately, Stark's final novel, *Butcher's Moon*, would appear in 1974, just after the war's conclusion.

A sign of the times, Parker's paranoia ultimately gets the better of him – "Everybody had a pattern . . . He had a pattern, a messy complicated pattern, but it would change. Soon, now."[71] – and, as he waits for his forty-five thousand dollars, he finds he has become the object of the Outfit's attention. Realising his paranoia is justified, Parker, knowing that his days are numbered, takes the first tentative steps into a new criminal era.

To be effective, crime fiction would need a new audience. Ironically, it was retro-pulp writer Joe Gores who helped accomplish this. His 1975 *Hammett*, a well-researched but otherwise ordinary San Francisco-set narrative featuring Dashiell Hammett,[72] would renew interest in the latter writer, help legitimise the genre's past, and indicate a possible direction for future noir fiction. Conveying a sense of Hammett's life and perspective, Gores's novel contains a half-hearted political critique: "Every illegal activity in the book is going on right now in San Francisco . . . And without mob control. Why? . . . Because your local government got here first."[73] However, Gores's sporadic criticisms seem mild compared to Hammett's assessment of company capitalism in *Red Harvest*, or subsequent critiques by post-Vietnam noirists. Tracking Hammett as a detective and as a writer, Gores's novel attracted attention by riding a wave of nostalgia for a world of recognisable indicators[74] and, with the recent Watergate break-in, concern about government corruption. This even though *Hammett* was published at a time when novels by George V. Higgins and Elmore Leonard, whose work presented a much grittier representation of America, were widely available. Though the concept behind Gores's novel might be better than the final product, it remains an accessible and exemplary achievement, one which successfully connects the past and the present. Ironically, *Hammett* is neither as hardcore nor as accomplished as Gores's detective procedurals – *Final Notice*, *Interface* and *Dead Skip* – whose portrayal of a detective agency and unromantic view of the investigator would have less impact on readers.

Also briefly popular during the early 1970s were such softboilers as Roger Simon's *The Big Fix* and Andrew Bergman's *The Big Kiss-Off of 1944* and *Hollywood and LeVine*.[75] While Bergman's narratives are Chandler-influenced exercises in nostalgia, Simon's novel attempts to find a niche for disillusioned 1960s radicals and ex-Vietnam protesters. Seeking an identifiable and oppositional narrative, *The Big Fix* fails because, unlike future noir fiction, Simon cannot forge a believable style. More intellectual than tough-guy empiricist, Simon's protagonist, Moses Wine, is a middle-class ex-political activist who, during the Vietnam war, attended university rather than go to Southeast Asia or survive on the streets of urban America. As a Los Angeles-based private eye, he must locate a former sixties radical. In doing so, he discovers the extent to which times and people have changed. Bemoaning the end of the 1960s, *The Big Fix* can only parody hardboiled fiction. With their investigations rooted in the past, Simon and Bergman fail to realise that readers require substance and originality in their fiction, and that noir protagonists need to investigate themselves as much as the culture and the crime. Aiming their work at a specific audience, both authors ignore the fact that the genre abhors any sign of elitism.

* * *

With their critiques of the culture, Ross Macdonald, John D. MacDonald, Jim Thompson, Charles Willeford, Joe Gores and Richard Stark represent particular aspects of what would become a new era of crime fiction. Though Ross Macdonald refrains from mentioning the war in Vietnam, his narratives are about the schisms in family life and in a culture that allows the war to take place. As intelligent as he is tolerant, Archer is the product of a previous era when, with McCarthyism biting at the heels of anyone expressing an alternative narrative, it was best to keep a low profile. Nevertheless, Archer's obsession with the sins of the fathers enables Macdonald to catch the mood of a nation on the verge of upheaval. Meanwhile, John D. MacDonald's cynicism and his adherence to pulp aesthetics allow him to incorporate the war into his limited literary vocabulary. After all, such indiscretion was hardly going to offend his readers, nor halt the publication of his numerous novels. Portraying cultural discontinuities, MacDonald's fiction offers a tepid critique, for his position is that, though people are good and bad, the investigator remains the antennae of the culture, and so at its moral centre. In the end, Travis McGee is too self-centred and patronising to be an effective critic. Likewise, Gores's retro-pulp procedurals which, when placed against Watergate and the historical circumstances of the era, are political only in their line of enquiry.

Having ingested the era, Thompson's discomfort enabled him to spew out a narrative too extreme for its own good. Following the trajectory of his earlier work, he believed that to truly investigate the crimes of the era he would have to expand the boundaries of the genre. However, Thompson's narrative anarchism was ahead of its time and too inventive to sit alongside other examples of early 1970s crime fiction. Though *Child of Rage* constitutes a significant failure, Willeford's *Cockfighter* is an unmitigated success, bridging, as it does, two eras. Willeford would go on to write a number of low-life crime novels describing, as Thompson had done, the effect of America's past on the present. As for Richard Stark, his non-

judgemental cinematic approach to violence was emblematic of
the era's political reality. Though Vietnam is rarely mentioned
in the work of these writers, the war exists as an omnipresent
subtext. At the very least, their novels are tacit critiques of the
culture and the narrative that created and sustained the war.
Yet these writers were, for the most part, too much part of the
previous generation to allow Vietnam to dominate their work,
their lives, or their perception of the world.

3

TOTAL CRIME

Negotiating the memory of Vietnam: Robert Stone, Newton Thornberg, James Crumley and George V. Higgins

"It was not warfare. It was murder." (Philip Caputo, *A Rumor of War*)

Begun in a web of secrecy and lies, the Vietnam war would be conducted in the glare of public attention. Given the role of the media, new battlefield technology, and a narrative decentred by Vietnamese resistance, it has been called the first post-modern war.[1] But, with American forces frustrated by Vietnam's guerrilla tactics, it was also the most primitive of wars. Over 50,000[2] American soldiers were to die, while others returned home burnt-out, suffering from mental as well as physical injuries.[3]

Having been dealt its first military defeat, America began its hectic withdrawal in 1973. The war had been an immense waste and, as an attempt to control the political future of a small nation, an unqualified failure. Its lack of comprehensibility would result in a historical revisionism whose primary post-war theme concerned *peace with honour* and aborted attempts by presidents from Carter to Clinton to heal a divided nation. Thus public attention shifted from the event to its aftermath, from the war to a series of jumbled memories and a campaign, reaching its apogee during the Reagan–Bush years, to locate soldiers said to be still imprisoned in Vietnam. Like something out of a pulp novel by M. E. Chaber or Nixon-spook Howard Hunt, the MIA-POW issue, though largely unsubstantiated, was used as a pretext to withhold war reparations and to continue the Vietnam conflict by economic means. Meanwhile, the post-war electorate continued to grow increasingly disillusioned with the political process.[4]

In an era of neon politics – flash without substance – the reality of the war would soon be all but expunged from the nation's memory. Sanitised for public consumption, it would become an event in which servicemen, whatever their misgivings, courageously fought for their country. From another perspective, the war indicated the lengths to which the nation's political and military establishment were willing to go to establish, via the *domino theory* (a commonly used term during the 1960s to justify US involvement in Vietnam, based on the belief that once Vietnam fell to the communists, other countries in the region and the world would follow), a dubious cold war narrative.[5]

Yet out of the war's wreckage, another narrative emerged. Using the war and its memory as a background to their work, crime writers would eventually articulate and arbitrate that narrative. Through ground-level observation and experience, they were able to note America's duplicity and the effect it would have on the body politic. Of course, these writers might have reached the same conclusion earlier had they read *The Pentagon Papers*,[6] which, as the conflict's secret narrative, provided the public with the evidence that the war had been the result of a foreign policy programme followed by US political leaders since the 1940s.

The manipulation of truth by those in charge of the war,[7] coupled with the inability of soldiers to comprehend their place within the conflict, resulted in a series of dark and paranoid texts by Vietnam war chroniclers like Michael Herr and Gustav Hasford. Conveying their wartime experiences in a vividly contemporary manner, Vietnam war writers were the first to extrapolate the era's primary crime, and, in doing so, suggest an uneasy, if personal, resolution for a narrative which, since the early 1960s, had been comprised of rhetoric, blood and brinkmanship. None of these chroniclers, with the exception of James Crumley – whose 1969 *One to Count Cadence* takes place when America was merely sending "advisors" rather than soldiers to Vietnam – could be considered crime writers. Nevertheless, they wrote about criminal activities. Not wanting to wallow in a pastiche of a genre that appeared to be on its last legs, they gravitated towards a form – be it memoir or its fictional variant – on which they could overlay their disordered experiences.

Also after the war, the likes of James Crumley, Robert Stone, Newton Thornberg, and George V. Higgins began publishing novels dealing with the effect of a war compromised by political ignorance, deception and national discontent – the latter spreading to military bases, where it took the form of strikes, disobeying orders, and the *fragging*[8] of officers by disgruntled troops. Noting how the war had changed the nation, their texts contain memories of combat and journeys into unchartered territory, whether real or metaphorical. Addled by the war, drugs, drink and oppositional politics, the protagonists of these novels do their best to survive in a world that has altered beyond recognition. With the line separating perpetrator and investigator having become blurred,[9] they are inevitably drawn into a noir existence. With a live-and-let-live attitude and scant regard for the law, these anti-heroes retreat into a primeval existentialism in which survival and quelling one's demons are what matter, while the heroic quest becomes a matter of getting through the day.

Ironically, it was the war's lack of meaning that would make it conducive to writers. For, other than the flimsy notion that the US was protecting Vietnam from communism, the war's rationale was never adequately explained.[10] Moreover, fighting so long for so little meant the war had no single narrative, no plot, nor logical sequence. This can be gleaned in the following interpretation of a Vietnamese analysis of the war:

Son's assessment of the American strategy is that "it did not

specially center on anything" and that "the Americans and
their puppets had no definite way of utilizing their mobile
and occupational forces . . ." For this reason even when
conflict was "head on," that conflict would be articulated in
terms of passivity, since action did not necessarily lead to
anything more than action itself. Moreover, the communists
saw to it that the "corps" would be disarticulated along various
mobile "fronts" all at the same time. In doing so they insured
that "action" would be reduced to random or marginalized
events which even if successfully won by the Americans would
not mean victory. As so many soldiers said to themselves over
and over again, "what a waste."[11]

This sense of infringement would later turn into the paranoia
generating crime fiction and a society besieged by criminals.

Son's assessment would be corroborated by Tim O'Brien:
"[Ordinary soldiers] did not have targets. They did not have a
cause. They did not know if it was a war of ideology or
economics or hegemony or spite."[12] Like an overly long crime
novel that no one could read, yet no one could ignore, the
fighting continued. And the real criminals remained hidden.
Meanwhile, the *other*, in the form of National Liberation Front
and the North Vietnamese army, made repeated incursions into
an already dispersed narrative, dissecting and deconstructing it
at will. To understand the war, one analysed its text, piecing
together the historical and cultural narrative that produced it.
This investigation would be the predominant feature of many
future crime novels. As John Douglas, head of the FBI
Investigative Support Unit, and model for Jack Crawford in
Silence of the Lambs, says,

Detectives and crime-scene analysts have to take a bunch of
disparate and seemingly unrelated clues and make them into a
coherent narrative, so story-telling ability is an important
talent, particularly in homicide investigations, where the
victim can't relate his or her own story.[13]

While Herr's description of military action in Vietnam reminds one of how serial killers or obsessive investigators home in on their prey:

> We took space back quickly, expensively, with total panic and close to maximum brutality. Our machine was devastating. And versatile. It could do everything but stop. As one American Major said, in a successful attempt at attaining history, "We had to destroy Ben Tre in order to save it."[14]

As the war machine quickened, and the crimes continued, the subject moved towards incomprehensibility. Once back in the US, many *ex-grunts* would, like their noir counterparts, reject authority, while others would turn into dissenters, schizoids, survivalists or criminals.

Accepting the Vietnam war as "a compromise with the conservative forces in the States, as a trade-off for his program of liberal domestic reforms",[15] Lyndon Johnson, in 1965, reiterated the gun ethic of the West, one which informs westerns as well as crime fiction. Having, in his presidential campaign, maintained that Americans would not die in Vietnam, Johnson, in response to a Viet Cong mortar attack, changed his tune:

> We have kept our gun over the mantel and our shells in the cupboard for a long time now. And what was the result? They are killing our men while they sleep in the night. I can't ask American soldiers out there to continue to fight with one hand tied behind their backs.[16]

The ethic of the west, *shoot first and ask questions later*, turned into a licence to kill, whether for soldiers, cops, or psychos. Meanwhile, for cultural investigators, it was a matter of writing it down, and leaving the post-mortem for others to decipher.

Though, prior to the early 1970s, the Vietnam war was, in crime fiction, conspicuous by its absence, new political and social pressures at home resulted in the subject eventually finding its way on to the page. By the 1980s, an intimate knowledge of the war and the era surrounding it would be integral to any credible noir text. Furthermore, many protagonists would be portrayed as having served in Vietnam, a place where, under fire, gung-ho perspectives regarding the war, authority, and country, had to be reconsidered. Once stateside and uneasily ensconced in a fractured domestic narrative, these protagonists would naturally regard government, anonymous corporations and rightwing fanatics with suspicion. Though threatening to create a new cliché, crime fiction, for the first time since the pulp culture era, had, thanks to the war, an oppositional edge, and a reason to exist.

Witnessing the war and subsequent events was something that street-level crime writers – whether Andrew Coburn, Lawrence Block, Jerome Charyn, Elmore Leonard or James Ellroy – had in common. Whether or not they had fought or merely watched the war on TV, their writing is a *de facto* memory of those events. Likewise, readers, many of them politicised by the war, sought a crime fiction which reflected their memory of events.

To maintain credibility, crime fiction needed to be as immediate and truthful to urban life as Vietnam war chroniclers had been to the conflict in Southeast Asia. Because it contradicted the official line, the hard-edged perspective of Vietnam war chroniclers allowed future noir writers, from James Crumley to James Lee Burke, to discuss the war's effect on domestic life. In depicting the excesses of the war, the likes of Herr, Caputo, and Hasford reflected the culture's often uncritical celebration of violence, a condition that would resurface in the crime fiction of the following decade. And, in combining reportage with incisive personal perceptions, Vietnam war writing, with its concern for accurate reporting, would move between objective realism and a hard-edged descriptive prose that would become a stylistic template for future noir fiction.

Amongst the reports from the front, Michael Herr's 1977 *Dispatches*, with its razor-sharp, hallucinogenic view of the war, is the book that most accurately prefigures future noir fiction. A journal written from the perspective of a reporter lost in an unfamiliar and terrifying landscape, *Dispatches*, regarding style and voice, bears certain similarities to the work of James Ellroy and James Crumley.

> Going out at night the medics gave you pills. Dexedrine breath like dead snakes kept too long in a jar. I never saw the need for them myself, a little contact or anything that even sounded like contact would give me more speed than I could bear.[17]

As Herr indicates, the drug culture was alive and thriving in Vietnam. Yet no drug would be powerful enough to eliminate fears regarding one's possible demise.

Published in the year Jimmy Carter assumed office, *Dispatches*'s perspective would be comprehensible only to cultural dissidents. As gripping and horrific as any crime novel, Herr's narrative – angry, scared and confused – soon became an outsider's primary recollection of the war, co-opted by Francis Ford Coppola in *Apocalypse Now*, and by future noirists. Thousands of miles from home, Herr captures the era: "Vietnam, Vietnam, Vietnam, we've all been there."[18] For the war had permeated all aspects of the culture, a fact that Herr notes when he returns to the States:

> Out on the streets I couldn't tell the Vietnam veterans from the rock and roll veterans. The Sixties had made so many casualties, its war and its music had run power off the same circuit for so long they didn't even have to fuse . . . What I'd thought of as two obsessions were really only one, I don't know how to tell you how complicated that made my life. Freezing and burning and going down again into the sucking mud of the culture, hold on tight and move real slow.[19]

Similarly, future noirists would base their fiction on an equally skewed revisionism. As everyone's war and everyone's crime, Vietnam would become the subtext of numerous crime novels.

It would also be the theatre on whose stage straight-laced kids from middle-America hoped to reach maturity. At least that is what Tim O'Brien's fiction maintains. Lacking Herr's warped perspective and urgency, O'Brien produced two wartime coming-of-age books: a personal account, written from the viewpoint of an ordinary soldier, entitled *If I Die in a Combat Zone*, and a novel, *Going After Cacciato*. More wholesome than Herr, O'Brien refuses to succumb to the war's excesses; for that reason, his work, at first glance, appears more refined if less interesting. Yet, embedded in his faultless prose are a series of penetrating insights. Flying home from the war, the narrator in the former book peers out the window and realises he's compromised one principle but fulfilled another:

> You learned . . . that war is not all bad; it may not make a man of you, but it teaches you that manhood is not something to scoff . . . dead bodies are heavy, and it's better not to touch them; fear is paralysis, but it is better to be afraid than to move out to die . . . [You] have to pick the times not to be afraid, but when you are afraid you must hide it to save respect and reputation. You learned that . . . anyone can die in a war if he tries.[20]

It's a perspective that James Lee Burke's fictional private eye and Vietnam vet Dave Robicheaux would adopt as he wages a personal war against stateside criminals and profiteers.

No less moral, O'Brien's 1975 *Going After Cacciato* sums up what must have been the unstated fantasy of countless combatants: on a rainy day, a naive soldier decides he'd rather be in Paris. So Cacciato begins a journey on foot of some 8,600 miles, pursued by his fellow soldiers in the Third Squad, First Platoon, Alpha Company. But O'Brien's book is less about Cacciato than the response of others regarding his decision to walk away from the war. Part dream and part reality, the soldiers move through war-zones and enclaves of peace, speculating, at every step, on their fellow soldier:

Where did he go, and why? What were his motives, or did he have motives, and did motive matter? What tricks had he used to keep going? How had he eluded them? How did he slip away into deep jungle, and how, through jungle, had they continued the chase?[21]

In seeking answers, the soldiers question their own motives for taking part in a war they don't quite understand. Consequently, they are denied "simple things: a sense of victory or satisfaction, or necessary sacrifice". Handling their situation as best they can, the soldiers perform their duties in a state of perpetual confusion:

> They did not know the feeling of taking a place and keeping it . . . They did not have targets. They did not have a cause . . . They did not know strategies. They did not know the terms of the war . . . When they took a prisoner . . . they did not know the questions to ask . . . They did not know how to feel. Whether, when seeing a dead Vietnamese, to be happy or sad or relieved; . . . whether to engage the enemy or elude him. They did not know how to feel when they saw villages burning . . . They did not know good from evil.[22]

Too young to realise they are implicated in a criminal narrative, these soldiers are guilty of being in the wrong place at the wrong time. O'Brien's narrator realises the war is wrong morally, if not politically. Nevertheless, he remains committed to seeing it through: "My obligation is to people, not to principle or politics or justice."[23] It's a theme that appears in crime fiction, as cops or investigators, knowing they are doing someone else's dirty work, cannot stop themselves from staying on the case. Just as narratives gather speed until the inevitable explosion occurs, so noir protagonists find themselves racing towards their own destruction – or deconstruction – unable to do anything about it.

Gustav Hasford's 1979 *The Short-Timers*, on which Kubrick

based the film *Full Metal Jacket*, addresses the war through a dark and subversive humour. However, the implication is that it will take more than humour – derived from a parody of Chandler-influenced fiction – to survive the war and convey its horrors, or, once stateside, to negotiate one's way back into the culture. Though Hasford's over-the-top LA crime novel, *A Gypsy Good Time*, appeared in 1992, shortly after the author's death, *The Short-Timers* is the more crime-ridden of the two books. Depicting the gruelling journey taken by Marines from basic training to the killing-zones of Southeast Asia, it views Vietnam as an absurd and calamitous playground, its dark narrative reminding the reader that the crimes later portrayed in noir fiction – serial murder, rape and violence against women and child abuse – did not become obsessive concerns until the war's conclusion. Not that the war created these misdeeds, but the conditions which produced the war also produced the atmosphere in which such crimes thrive.[24]

It's only when he comes under fire that Hasford's protagonist, the college-educated combat correspondent Leonard Pratt, begins to count the cost of his situation. While his superiors cannot tell if Pratt, aka Joker, is serious or merely deranged, the latter's humour keeps the horrors of the war at bay. Eventually the war wrecks his humour and hopes for the future. Yet Pratt's observations are as acute as those of most noir protagonists. So anonymous letters sent by concerned civilians are "like shoes for the dead, who do not walk".[25] And, after his first kill, Pratt admits that "blood had blemished my Yankee Doodle dream that everything would have a happy ending, and that I, when the war was over, would return to hometown America in a white silk uniform, a rainbow of campaign ribbons across my chest, brave beyond belief, the military Jesus".[26] There's a bitterness in Hasford's novel that's missing in O'Brien's fiction, and blotted out by drugs in Herr's *Dispatches*, but which becomes a basic ingredient in later crime fiction. Says Pratt, "The ugly that civilians choose to see in war focuses on spilled guts. To see human beings clearly, that is ugly. To carry death in your smile, that is ugly."[27] While Herr sees the cultural effect of the war, Hasford, who served as a correspondent for the First Division, notes its effect on the lives of its participants: "Upon each of our brains the war has lodged itself, a blackcrab feeding."[28] Related to America's policy of expansionism,[29] each of these authors describes how the US has negotiated its special relationship with crime and casual violence.

What these Vietnam war texts have in common is a nostalgia for a self-enclosed narrative, and a realisation that, in all likelihood, none will be forthcoming. Like the best examples of noir fiction, each contains a personal struggle with history and the culture.[30] Such texts counter the belief that war, much less history, proceeds, even at the best of times, along logical and linear lines. After all, this was a time when Barry Goldwater, in his 1964 presidential campaign, was advocating that America use atomic weapons in Vietnam and end the conflict once and for all. An unrealistic view, but one which, if accomplished, would have turned the conflict into a recognisable war with a clear-cut, if genocidal, resolution. That the war would not take on the appearance of a recognisable conflict, can be discerned in Philip Caputo's *A Rumor of War*, which concerns the murder of two Vietnamese civilians. As has been pointed out, it was America's inability to turn the war into a linear event, as much as the immorality of the conflict, that led to its defeat.[31] For Generals and media commentators were unable to cope with a war that lacked logistical development or specific targets. Not surprisingly, future noir fiction would note the war's lack of resolution, and, in their texts, concentrate on the investigatory process rather than on tidy resolutions and the spreading of false hope.

To create convincing texts, future noirists would need to tap into the culture at street-level. Arguably, it would be Vietnam war chroniclers like Michael Herr who, in substituting the language of survival for the phony street wisdom of past investigative fiction, set a precedent for future noirists. According to Herr, to effectively monitor the war, one need possess a working knowledge of history; counter-insurgency tactics; the relationship between war and drugs (the use of LSD and the appearance of high-grade marijuana such as Thai-stick, and its influence on troops and the anti-war movement; amphetamines as an aid to combat; and the proliferation of heroin – Saigon was the transfer point from the Burma opium fields); the music of Jimi Hendrix; and the writing of Thomas Pynchon. For the war was a cultural, as well as a historical construct. As the focus of world attention and a centre of blackmarket trade, Saigon would become, outside of Disneyland, the world's foremost tourist centre. Meanwhile, the war's harrowing narrative, and the attitudes of its participants, would allow crime writers to piece together the culture, create a comprehensible narrative, and, somewhere between flashback and oblivion, articulate the crime.

Robert Stone

With its concerns – the politics of war, drugs, scarred psyches – and plot construction, Robert Stone's 1973 *Dog Soldiers* constitutes an early example of neon noir fiction. Adapted for the screen in 1978 by Karl Reisz (US title: *Who'll Stop the Rain*),[32] Stone's novel is as introspective as O'Brien's Vietnam narratives, and as dark and drug-obsessed as Herr's *Dispatches*. Moreover, its anti-heroic quest captures the mood of the post-Vietnam era in which soldiers were returning home to find the extent to which they and their country had changed. With a plot that moves from Vietnam to California, *Dog Soldiers* takes place in the early 1970s, with the new left all but burnt-out, and heroin – imported, according to Stone, with the help of the CIA – replacing marijuana as the drug of choice amongst dealers and consumers.

Bearing in mind the amount of drugs consumed during the war years, *Dog Soldiers* reflects the transition between drug dealing as a small-scale activity and its emergence as a major capitalist venture. Moreover, it infers that, in terms of the production, distribution and consumption, drugs, as much as the war, linked America and Vietnam. Associating addiction with the same consumerism which, in the 1970s, would entice former political radicals back into the culture, Stone, who worked for the *Guardian* (UK) as a correspondent in Vietnam, depicts an already corroded society marking time before the energy crisis and the next phase of late capitalism.[33]

The novel centres on a triangle of individuals: Marge, a former anti-war activist, lives in Berkeley where, hooked on pharmaceuticals, she struggles to cope with life in a fractured society; her husband and war correspondent, John Converse; and the streetwise Hicks, who mules Converse's drugs back to the States. But, in the short time since Converse has been away, drug dealing has become so lucrative that even cops want to muscle in on the action. Admitting he has given Hicks's name to the CIA, Converse does not fully comprehend the dangers involved in bucking the system. Nor is he aware that drug dealing has become a government enterprise, a situation corroborated by Edward Jay Epstein, who, in *Agency of Fear*, reports that the Bureau of Dangerous Drugs and CIA agents, from 1968 onwards, were involved in selling heroin and protecting dealers.[34] By the end of the war, as corporations and organised crime were reaping substantial profits,[35] drug-dealing Vietnam veterans, such as Converse and Hicks, though possessing some sought-after skills, were doomed to failure.[36]

Planning to return to Berkeley, Converse is told by Hicks that, in the States, "it's got funny".[37] But Converse's ordeal – finding his wife has run off with Hicks and the heroin – becomes a survival test and a battle for a place in the post-Vietnam world. As well as being about the relationship between war and addiction, Stone's novel concerns the fag-end of the American dream as interpreted by the old and new left. Here no one fully grasps the meaning of their actions, nor the effect the war will have on American society. Like a nightmare from which they cannot awake, their journeys seem to go on forever: "I don't know what I'm doing or why I do it or what it's like . . . Nobody knows . . . That's the principle we were defending over there. That's why we fought the war."[38]

In Vietnam, this absurd *principle* is exemplified by the Great Elephant Zap, ironically described as "the last moral objection that Converse experienced in the traditional manner".[39] Believing the elephants are transporting North Vietnamese weapons and supplies, the Military Advisory Command decides to attack them:

> All over the country, whooping sweating gunners descended from the cloud cover to stampede the herds and mow them down with 7.62-millimeter machine guns. The Great Elephant Zap had been too much and had disgusted everyone. Even the chopper crews who remembered the day as one of insane exhilaration had been somewhat appalled. There was a feeling that there were limits. And as for dope, Converse thought . . . if the world is going to contain elephants pursued by flying men, people are just naturally going to want to get high.[40]

For many, the war had, in itself, become a drug, deranging those addicted to it to the degree that they perceive elephants as having joined the ranks of the enemy. And if you could not kill your quotient of gooks, you could at least set your sights on animals. Still, the "dissatisfaction remained and it was not loneliness or a moral objection; it was, of course, fear". Ironically, as far as Converse was concerned, killing elephants generated more fear and moral outrage than killing the Vietnamese: "Fear was extremely important to Converse; morally speaking it was the basis of his life . . . I am afraid . . . therefore I am."[41] Likewise, it is fear that sustains Converse and Hicks through the war and the novel. Not only is the Great Elephant Zap a surreal cause of moral outrage, but it is indicative of a double-take on reality that typifies subsequent noir fiction.

But the book's anti-hero is the Neitzsche-reading Hicks. Versions of Hicks will crop up in the fiction of James Ellroy, Eugene Izzi, Elmore Leonard and Daniel Woodrell. Pursued by crooks and cops, only to die along the border, Hicks, before his death, looks at the wall of a cave once inhabited by hippies, on which, like the "day-glow detritus of old highs", someone has written, "There Are No Metaphors". For the likes of Hicks and Converse would not be the only casualties of the war. Metaphor too would suffer, a lesson that future noirists would soon learn.

Newton Thornberg

Set a couple years after *Dog Soldiers*, Thornberg's *Cutter and Bone* captures the wound-gaping lassitude of those who came of age during that era. Published in 1976 and adapted for the screen in 1981 by Ivan Passer (retitling it *Cutter's Way*), Thornberg's novel eschews the traditional hardboiled style. Lacking a reassuring resolution or hope for the future, it centres on three survivors of the 1960s who, wrecked but not quite ruined, share a house in Santa Barbara: Cutter, a crippled and maniacal Vietnam veteran; Bone, a draft dodging corporate drop-out and sometime gigolo; and Mo, an agoraphobic alcoholic, and mother of a small infant. The novel turns on the murder of a young prostitute. Treating it as though it were another homegrown cover-up, Cutter and Bone take it upon themselves to investigate the matter. Making waves in the wrong places, their paranoia is seemingly confirmed when Mo and her baby die in a domestic gas explosion. Though, for the most part, set in Santa Barbara – here a more socially divided city than that portrayed by Ross Macdonald – the novel eventually moves to the Ozarks where Cutter and Bone travel in pursuit of a tycoon they believe is responsible for the three deaths. The book ends with Cutter strapped to a hospital bed, and Bone gunned down while driving back to California.

Thornberg presents Cutter and Bone as contrasting representatives of a once-promising era, now turned sour. Whether at odds or in alliance with one another, they constitute a bizarre but appropriate double act. Tanned and sleek, Bone knows he should, by rights, look more like Cutter, who sports missing body parts and a smile like the rictus of a scream. To Cutter, Bone is simply an "ideological blob".[42] But from Bone's perspective, "You had to know Cutter . . . to understand the savagery of his despair, that it precluded his responding to any idea or situation with anything except laughter . . . His mind was a house of mirrors, distortion reflecting distortion."[43] Berating and manipulating others by virtue of his appearance, behaviour and battlefield memories, Cutter runs on a mixture of despair and cynicism. However, Bone and Mo also suffer, each in their own way, the effects of the war. Living in an alcoholic haze, and dependent on Cutter's disability cheques, they, like so many others, have been burnt-out by the activities and paranoia of the era. As Bone puts it, "Inside we all limp."[44]

Cutter and Bone's pursuit of Wolfe, a wealthy capitalist and noted hawk, takes place at a time when corporate America, following the energy crisis, was regrouping to maintain, via debt and globalisation, its grip on the economy.[45] Like a crusading investigative reporter, Cutter insists society has the right to know about criminals like Wolfe: "The story was not so much about Wolfe personally as about the general new breed of 'conglomerates.' "[46] Of course, Wolfe is guilty, though not necessarily of the particular crimes Cutter has accused him of committing:

> "I don't like this motherfucker Wolfe and . . . all the movers and shakers of this world, kiddo, because I saw . . . the people they moved and shook . . . the soft white motherfuckers . . . come slicking in from Long Binh to look us over . . ., see that everything was going sweet and smooth, the killing and the cutting and the sewing up, and then they'd grunt and fart and squeeze their way back into their choppers and slick on back to Washington or Wall Street or Peoria and say on with the show, America, a few more bombs will do it, a few more arms and legs. And . . . one fact was always the same . . . it's never their ass they lay on the line . . ."[47]

In fact, Wolfe is the same kind of criminal found amidst the pages of countless crime novels. Like Carter in Stark's *Point Blank*, he calls the shots from behind a desk. When Bone balks at the plan to blackmail Wolfe, Cutter justifies crimes against criminals, and, like an intellectual version of Stark's Parker, attacks the logic that prevents Bone from acting:

> "Since, according to you, there is no God, then it follows that our so-called moral law is man's invention rather than God's dispensation. It is an aspect of Rousseau's social contract, that's all, a convenient mechanism for greasing the gears of social intercourse, for doing business, for making trains run on time. Therefore it's relative."[48]

According to Cutter, Bone's way of thinking is no different from the logic used by Wolfe, the Pentagon, politicians and criminals to justify their crimes.

With a manic intelligence that can wear anyone down, Cutter finally convinces Bone. After all, there is always more than a grain of truth to what Cutter says. Recalling the photographs that appeared at the time of the My Lai massacre, Cutter outlines the typical response, and, in doing so, illustrates the process that makes humanity despicable:

> "I found out you have three reactions . . . The first one is simple – I hate America. But then you study them some more, and you move up a notch. There is no God. But you know what you say finally . . . after you've studied them all you can? You say – I'm hungry."[49]

While events such as My Lai, and the images sent back from the war, caused many to join the anti-war movement, it also helped numb the public to future state violence and criminality. Moreover, it would provide a protective layering regarding the gross indecencies of future crime fiction.

Despite his cynicism – a condition that has disabled him when it comes to political action – Cutter knows he must go after Wolfe. What begins as part-fantasy and part-prank becomes, after the death of Mo and her baby, an obsession. By taking revenge on this particular capitalist, Cutter can displace his anger and hard-edged ideological approach:

> Essentially [Cutter's] position was that even if . . . a cabal of
> enlightened socialists and egalitarians somehow came to
> power, and the longed-for millennium of benevolent
> despotism finally arrived, and even if the political technicians
> managed to repeal all the laws of supply and demand and
> somehow miraculously wrought a society of both plenitude
> and liberty, man would still be in a funk. He would quickly
> begin throwing bombs at his benefactors, and for no more
> complicated reason that in the dark, secret oozings of his
> entrails he was as mad as a hatter . . . a lover of crisis and war
> and pestilence.[50]

It's this same need for stimulation that, after the war, would affect the genre's protagonists, whose world-weary perspective would turn politics into an irrelevancy, as well as its readers, who would require an adrenaline rush for every occasion.

While his cynicism and intelligence have, in the past, made political action impossible, Cutter takes pride in being able to abstract himself from dangerous situations:

> One of [Cutter's] great strengths, he said, was his ability to
> objectify his own experience, to see it clear and dispassionate,
> a trick he'd used in Vietnam in order to keep his sanity. "You
> just sort of rise up out of yourself, you know, like a chopper
> . . . so you can look down all cool and unafraid and say, 'My,
> my look at that poor grunt about to get his ass zapped . . .' "[51]

It's a defence mechanism – more a sign of illness than health – that allowed soldiers in Vietnam to commit atrocities without feeling responsible. Likewise, it is what many murderers say – *It was as though someone else was committing the crime*. But the ability to investigate the culture, and take subsequent political action necessitates empathising with the victim as well as the perpetrator. It's only in this way that the narrative under investigation can be recreated.[52]

Despite her cynicism, inertia and agoraphobia, Mo has a less tenuous grasp of reality, and takes exception not so much to Cutter's maniacal plans as to the way he manipulates others: "Talk about newspeak", says Mo, "you're becoming a real past master, you know that? Nixon couldn've used you in the White House."[53]

Though Cutter knows that blaming one particular capitalist for the war, or for a crime, constitutes a dangerous over-simplification, he underestimates capitalism's response to accusations that might threaten profits. Even at the novel's conclusion, neither the reader, nor Cutter and Bone, know if Wolfe is guilty of the crimes of which he's been accused. After all, blame – whether for the war or for the murder – is difficult to apportion in a country where guilt appears so pervasive.

Cutter and Bone represents the legacy of Vietnam, and points to the future of crime fiction. Published as Jimmy Carter was about to assume office with the promise that he would heal the nation, Thornberg's novel would set the standard for future political crime literature. For this was still a period of public cynicism. Watergate, Nixon's impeachment proceedings, and the Congressional hearings regarding the CIA, would have come as no surprise to the likes of Cutter and Bone. Yet Stone's protagonists are too vulnerable for their own good. Cutter and Mo are dead. And Bone, having survived Vietnam, may or may not have survived its aftermath. Regardless of how they finish the novel, Cutter and Bone bear the burden of future noir protagonists, whose fate will be to investigate the culture whatever the cost.

James Crumley

"It didn't start with the Vietnam War, and it didn't quit just because we did. Maybe it started with Elvis mumbling jive to Ed Sullivan, and maybe it ended with the Arabs squeezing our nuts at the gas pumps. But somewhere in there, I swear, there was a time when we were free."[54]

Given the above quote and Crumley's fiction, one might be forgiven for thinking that, given America's history, the war might have been inevitable. So much a part of the era has the war become that it is difficult to separate cause and effect. Could Elvis, "mumbling jive to Ed Sullivan", have caused the war in Vietnam? Or was the war part of a process which began with Elvis and ended with an event that has yet to occur? Regardless of Elvis's contribution to chaos theory, the war constituted a defining moment for the nation, separating hawks and doves, poets and pranksters, and state narratives from their more inquisitive counterparts. Setting the war alongside liberal legislation and the creation of an oppositional culture, one notes the era's anomalies, including a set of circumstances that warped the nation and, through drugs, flirtations with revolution, half-baked survivalism, and a crime-oriented culture, became the corrosive sub-strata of Crumley's writing.

Rewriting the post-war era, Crumley would influence future crime writers, and create a new readership for noir fiction. Yet in 1969, when his *One to Count Cadence* appeared, Crumley had only just begun to read Chandler. Consequently, crime literature did not influence Crumley's first novel, which, in any case, bears a greater resemblance to Vietnam literature than to noir fiction. Nevertheless, *One to Count Cadence*, already showing signs of Crumley's honky-tonk bravado, was ahead of its time, predating the work of Herr, O'Brien and Hasford, and bridging past war novels by the likes of Norman Mailer and Joseph Heller with the new wave of Vietnam documentarists and future crime writers.

One to Count Cadence begins as Slag Krummel, a thoughtful Air Force Sergeant, is shipped to a military hospital. When Krummel's plane is shot down, the incident is officially called an aircraft accident because "Not even the American Congress was supposed to know we were in Vietnam . . . I didn't know

how many casualties the 721st had taken, but I had seen enough
to know that it had been bad. A plane crash. Shit."[55]

At the end of the novel, Krummel returns home. JFK has
recently been assassinated, and Krummel, in a state of culture-
shock and war-weariness, drinks himself across the Rockies.
Barely distinguishable from the protagonists inhabiting
Crumley's future crime fiction, Krummel is politically sympathetic yet, like many crime fiction protagonists, too cynical
to throw in his lot with his friend, Joe Morning, who has some
exciting plans of his own:

> "Man, I know you don't think the world is worth saving, and
> in a way, I agree, but I have to do something . . . I can't go
> back and march in peaceful parades and sing about freedom,
> man. I can't help register voters for elections that I think are
> meaningless. I can't work in the slums because I want to tell
> the people to arm, to burn the fucking country down, to screw
> the New Frontier and get what they can. Get their guns and
> run for the hills. But it isn't time for that yet. America is
> hopeless . . . People have to learn, property has to burn, blood
> has to run."[56]

In 1975, Crumley's second novel, *The Wrong Case*, appeared.
This despite the fact that, according to the author, "detective
novels weren't hot that year".[57] Caught between a desire to
write a hardboiled novel, and wanting to create an anti-genre,[58]
Crumley, in this novel, helped clear the field for future noir
fiction. Having filtered Chandler and Ross Macdonald through
the barroom libertarianism of country singers Hank Snow and
Willie Nelson,[59] Crumley, by taking into account the state of the
culture, makes one of the most significant revisions of private
eye fiction since Chandler's cynical parodies of Hammett and
the Black Mask school of writing.

The Wrong Case features private eye Milo Chester Milodragovitch, an aging veteran whose tastes, like Crumley's, run to
drinking and country music. In unravelling his story, Crumley
can make an ordinary investigation appear earth-shattering. Yet

the novel retains a political edge, and, by referring to the war, reinvents the process and meaning of private investigation. A first-person narrative, the novel's opening two sentences – "There's no accounting for laws. Or the changes wrought by men and time."[60] – state a theme common to Crumley and future noir writers: the confrontation between personal morality and crime. However, *The Wrong Case* shows Crumley still on tentative terms with the genre. And despite his revisionism, he is only half-right in referring to it as belonging to an anti-genre. For *The Wrong Case* follows an established narrative pattern. Meanwhile, the crime under investigation reflects back on the investigator. Quoting his friend, the poet Richard Hugo, "the only prisoner/is always in, not knowing what he's done",[61] Crumley doesn't hide the fact that his work is self-referential. He writes, "The real criminal thing that happens in *The Wrong Case* is simply a personal failure."[62] In fact, Milo's failure – he allows his emotions to cloud his judgement, which results in some unnecessary deaths and investigative misunderstandings, not least of which is Milo's inability to notice that Raymond is Helen's son – is simply that he doesn't have the perspective to see the overall narrative and its implications. This reiterates the myopia of private investigators, from Chandler's Philip Marlowe to James Lee Burke's Dave Robicheaux and Lawrence Block's Matt Scudder. After all, if detectives could see the big picture, their investigations would fall apart; and if their personal investigations were to evolve into political action, they would either turn themselves in or turn in on themselves. Nevertheless, Crumley, a product of the civil rights movement and a former member of Students for a Democratic Society, faced a common dilemma:

> I was ready for revolution at the point of a gun, then I realized I didn't want to kill anybody. It took the edge off my politics and I backed away somewhere in the 1970s. I stayed active in the Vietnam veterans against the war.[63]

Fortunately for readers, Crumley opted for the pen rather than the sword.

The Last Good Kiss, published in 1978, concerns another Crumley alter-ego, Texas Vietnam veteran C. W. Sughrue. Moving between private investigation and bartending, Sughrue – the rawer half of Crumley's tag-team of investigators – searches the Pacific northwest for a missing woman. At the heart of the novel is the drunken poet Trahearne, perhaps loosely based on Hugo. That Hugo had encouraged Crumley to read Raymond Chandler might account for Trahearne being the fall-guy of the novel.[64] As Crumley says, Trahearne's crime is "a sort of literary arrogance".[65]

Not that Sughrue is beyond committing his own type of crime. Having learned a series of dubious skills while in Vietnam, Sughrue can do a passable imitation of a psychopath:

> "[The] U.S. Army trained me at great expense in interrogation, filled my head with all sorts of psychological crap, but when I got to Nam, we didn't do no psychology, we hooked the little suckers up to a telephone crank – alligator clips on the foreskin and nipples – and the little bastards were a hundred times tougher than you, but when we rang that telephone, the little bastards answered."[66]

Vietnam also taught him the art of lying – useful for interrogations, investigations and writing novels. Though Sughrue admits,

> The only interrogation I had seen in Vietnam had made me sick, but I didn't remember if I had vomited because of the tiny Viet Cong's pain, the Vietnamese Ranger captain's pleasure, or my own fatigue.[67]

In 1983, Crumley's *Dancing Bear* recycles Milo Milodragovitch. Older and more cynical, yet still a romantic, Milo, despite having inherited family money, remains a working detective. As this first-person narrative illustrates, even a well-heeled private investigator can locate and apprehend toxic waste polluters. Yet, despite its subject matter and laudable viewpoint, *Dancing Bear* does not carry the same impact as his previous novels. Nevertheless it's superior to Crumley's next two outings, both of which would appear in the 1990s. Though *The Mexican Duck Tree*, the most dispersed of his novels, reads as though three separate narratives were fighting for control of the novel,[68] it still has some memorable lines:

> There are rules of behavior in America, rules of conduct, rules that can change your luck in a country based on the rules of luck. For instance, after forty, never go anyplace you've never been before. Except on somebody else's nickel.[69]

Unfortunately, the novel's use of Vietnam purely as a reference point threatens to become an anachronism, indicative of an unwillingness to come to grips with the politics of the present. While *Bordersnakes* features both Milo and Sughrue, their voices intertwining to some effect, it lacks the immediacy of his earlier work. Though it appears that the genre, having moved to greater extremes, has caught up with him, and even passed him by, one hopes that Crumley will rediscover the plot, reconnect with the culture, and produce fiction capable of moving the genre's boundaries even further afield.

George V. Higgins

When it comes to the relationship between dialogue and narrative, George V. Higgins would take noir fiction into unchartered territory, where language comes close to dictating plot. Not only does Higgins's dialogue approximate natural speech, but it sustains a straightforward narrative, one that is every bit as realistic as Vietnam war writers, much less past crime novelists. Though reminding one, at times, of early Nelson Algren stripped of the latter's sentimentality and narrative intrusion, Higgins is no proletariat-panderer, but someone conversant with speech and politics at all levels of society.

In depicting even the most insignificant of conversations, Higgins captures the mood of the post-Vietnam war era, and gives his characters the space to create their own stories. Interested in the politics of crime, as well as the crime of politics, this is one author who works hard to remove, as much as possible, the narrator from the narrative.[70] In doing so, he allows his characters to conduct their own investigations and make their own articulations of a narrative that might have begun with Vietnam, or with Elvis, but which will end only when the story has finally been told.

It was *The Friends of Eddie Coyle*, published in 1971, that would establish Higgins's reputation, and influence the likes of Elmore Leonard, teaching the latter "to loosen his style, get into the scenes more directly and 'use more obscenities' ".[71] By allowing conversation to assume various degrees of significance, Higgins extends the provinciality of his narrative, turning the plot into something more than a by-product of East Coast dialogue and character interaction. Few crime writers, or writers of any kind – Higgins is, in fact, reluctant to apply the term to his fiction[72] – would be so subtle, or so bold.

Though the reader, engrossed in a Higgins novel, might feel like an eavesdropper, it is a different variety of voyeurism than that which accompanies the reading of a James Ellroy novel. Akin to overhearing a series of conversations, with the added attraction of being able to discover their narrative impact, Higgins's realism avoids undue vicariousness. In fact, his narratives are often brain-numbingly ordinary. In *The Friends of Eddie Coyle*, the crime – Eddie Coyle is caught transporting 200 cases of Canadian Club – relates to something with which most readers can identify: how to provide for one's family in a time of relative scarcity. For Eddie cannot afford not to commit the crime, yet neither can he afford to go to prison:

"I got three kids and a wife at home, and I can't afford to do no more time, you know? The kids're growing up and they go to school and the other kids make fun of them and all. Hell, I'm almost forty-five years old."[73]

Willing to accentuate the humorous side of his characters, Higgins refrains from demanding that they run the usual narrative maze. Higgins's respect for his characters means that what passes for autonomy will, if successfully executed, overcome any plot-derived distortion. With characters so realistic they might be anyone's neighbour, the bottom line of Higgins's fiction is that crime permeates every echelon of society, and everyone is a potential criminal.

A former prosecuting attorney, Higgins argues a good case, driving home the message that criminals negotiate their transactions with the same communication weaponry that politicians use. For instance, in *Digger's Game*, published in 1973, an ex-con seeks a bar licence. To get it, he must obtain a pardon for a past crime, which means paying off the right people. Refusing to comment on the morality of the situation, Higgins implies that the world is based on such negotiations. While Chandler and Ellroy identify with the police, Higgins sides with criminals, which, of course, includes the police. Reluctant to separate the hunter from the hunted, Higgins ignores the standard Chandler narrative, and the latter's insistence on turning every piece of dialogue into a witticism. Rather, Higgins reduces the role of the omniscient narrator, minimalising expositional statements, narrative perceptions and descriptions. The opening sentence of *The Friends of Eddie Coyle* – "Jackie Brown at twenty-six, with no expression on his face, said that he could get some guns."[74] – sounds more like a script direction than an exposition. But the sentence is really a narrative ploy, creating a moment of respite before the conversational tidal wave begins.

With a career that begins prior to Watergate, Higgins lets his characters, with their tendency towards a Nixon-like logorrhea, incriminate themselves. Yet he does not judge them, nor claims

NEON NOIR

that justice can be served. After all, Coyle is punished for a
betrayal that is beyond his control. Indeed, it causes him to lose
his ear, a vital body part in Higgins's world. So Eddie's ability to
function in a criminal world has been reduced,
his deafness turning him into a victim of half-truths and
betrayals.

Yet Higgins's characters maintain a swagger and a tenuous
moral code. Striving for a degree of dignity, it's Scalisi's
girlfriend, Wanda, not Coyle, who turns the narrative and turns
in her boyfriend. But this occurs after Scalisi – "a bad bastard
from the word go"[75] – insults Wanda in Coyle's presence. When
Wanda stomps out of the room, Coyle can only rub his crotch
and commiserate with Scalisi, who says, "You ever get laid
without a lot of goddamned talk?"[76] Turned into a sex object,
Wanda explains why she draws the line at having the intimate
details of her life discussed with a third party: "How'd you like
it if I was to start telling the girl at the store about your prick
and what you like me to do with it?"[77] Mirroring the angst of
men who have not come to terms with women, much less
feminism, Scalisi responds by slapping Wanda. Later, a still-
furious Wanda tells the local cop, Vardenais, about Scalisi's
bank accounts: "I don't think any of them are real people, you
know? I think they're all just him."[78]

Using Scalisi's own words to exact revenge, Wanda demonstrates just how thin the line separating truth and fiction can
be. Yet Wanda's conversation with Vardenais is not so much a
betrayal as a matter of taking the same liberties that Scalisi had
taken when conversing with Coyle. Thus Higgins's characters
are caught in a web of gossip, paraphrase and reported speech.
Though Wanda might lack scruples, her retribution cannot
compare to the personal crimes committed by Scalisi, including
his belief that Wanda's anger has to do with "all this Women's
Lib stuff or something",[79] or his willingness to collude with the
reptilian Eddie Coyle.

Scalisi is partly right. For *The Friends of Eddie Coyle* concerns
the end of an era, taking place as the war is coming to an end

and as feminism begins to make an impact on the culture. As Wanda says to Vardenais,

> "I said, they don't say very much in front of me, except my friend likes to talk about fucking me in front of his friends, he does that, its okay to talk about that. But otherwise they generally include me out of things, you know?"[80]

With its depiction of sleazy criminality, *The Friends of Eddie Coyle* juxtaposes social classes. Crime, according to Higgins, knows no boundaries. In fact, in Higgins's work, those who commit crimes are, more often than not, in professions the public perceives as dishonest – politicians, cops, and lawyers – but whose lifestyle it is meant to emulate.

Far from his best outing, *A City on a Hill*, published in 1975, is set in Washington DC against the collapse of the Nixon administration. Yet its topicality overshadows the fact that, rather than generating the narrative, the novel's conversation only generates more conversation. This is the corner that Higgins, if he is not attentive, can unwittingly box himself into. Filled with snippets concerning The Committee to Re-elect the President, McGovern, Muskie and politicians, real and imaginary, Higgins, sounding like a disillusioned New England liberal, examines the role of the media:

> "All information is valuable," Cavanaugh said. "It's a fact of history that there is such a thing as bad news. In the reign of a tyrant, the messengers who bring it are killed. In a democracy such as ours, I remain confident that its transmission is a service. I have bad news for you tonight. We are still in Vietnam. Shall the people who report that . . . be silenced? Or shall we return to Washington to put a stop to the arrogance of power which creates the news?"[81]

Likewise, Higgins's characters in *A City on a Hill* refer to the days of the Vietnam War protests, even if it's from the stilted and facile perspective of a group of Washington hacks:

"I met him at a Coalition meeting . . . back in '68. What the hell he was doing there I don't know. Of course it was never entirely clear to me what I was doing there, either, but there wasn't a single rock group in the place. I take that back: John Lennon or McCartney or somebody was there . . . They were all just the kind of people you'd expect to find at a Coalition meeting, the gawkers and the gawkees . . . No, what we were doing was demonstrating conclusively to Hubert Horatio Humphrey that the anti-war sentiment among the best people was so profoundly right that he was bound in conscience to go tell LBJ to get laid, and this meeting was going to do it."[82]

Though Higgins would go on writing novels through the 1990s, his work, over the years, has tended to recycle old themes, and, in doing so, parodies such astute and innovative novels as his 1983 *A Choice of Enemies*. Still one of the most perceptive novels about American political life, *A Choice of Enemies*, set in Boston, centres on Bernie Morgan, a Boston politician. Exuding corruption, Morgan, as Speaker of the House, builds his power base through the threat of physical violence. Consequently, Morgan seems "like a very heavy albatross around the necks of party stalwarts".[83] Here, after the Watergate scandal and on the eve of Ronald Reagan's election, politicians prove to be as corrupt as Eddie Coyle. When Frank Costello, the Speaker's adviser, describes the realities of legislation to Archambault, the latter says, "Fixing, in other words." Costello momentarily stops and says,

"Lobbying, . . . expediating, accommodating, adjusting: I've heard it called by lots of names. The names that sound evil are the ones used by the people at least temporarily unable to do it to their own benefit and to prevent other people from doing for themselves."[84]

Yet, as is often the case, a cynical protagonist like Morgan, who operates on the assumption that politics is a dirty business, has, in Higgins's world, more integrity than the ideologues who challenge him.[85]

Vietnam invariably informs Higgins's best work. Unfortunately, as the years progressed, Higgins would lose some of the edge that the war,[86] and the culture surrounding it, once provided. With a different era demanding new narrative choices, Higgins, always interesting, cannot help but rest on his laurels.

By the time *A Choice of Enemies* appeared a new era was well under way. After announcing that he would campaign on "the issues", Reagan sought to bury the so-called Vietnam syndrome through flag-waving, feel-good rhetoric and a series of foreign invasions. Like everyone else, crime writers would be caught in Reagan's holding pattern. Having utilised the angst generated by the war and its aftermath, the genre would manage to monitor the culture and articulate the era's crimes. Within a few years the Vietnam flashbacks would become a cliché, as though just mentioning the war could provide a protagonist with the necessary credibility to sustain a narrative. Soon new concerns would emerge reflecting the excessiveness, the inequalities, and the deregulatory policies of the Reagan era.

4

FIGURES IN THE MIRROR

Private-eye fiction, from Watergate to Whitewater: Lawrence Block, Stephen Dobyns, James Lee Burke, Sara Paretsky, Gar Anthony Haywood, Walter Mosley, James Sallis and George P. Pelecanos

Relying on a time-honoured structure, private-eye fiction, from the mid-1970s to the present, has sought to establish a discourse between past and present. Referring to the past while inhabiting the present, or inhabiting the past while referring to the present, detective fiction's special relationship with history has resulted in particular readings of the culture. Like figures in the historical mirror,[1] writers of detective fiction reflect the era, articulating its crimes while recollecting specific sites and situations. Accordingly, the writers discussed in this chapter have their own views of history, their own conceptions of the detective novel, and their own thoughts on the relationship between the two.

Though during and immediately after the Vietnam war, few detective novels were able to adequately deliberate upon the era's predominant crime, this situation would not last for long. Such events as Watergate and Nixon's subsequent resignation could not help but influence the direction of the genre. Meanwhile, in the mid-1970s, and taking place after a legacy of infractions, the Pike and Church Congressional Committees' investigation of the CIA and FBI attempted to assuage public concern and give, according to historian Howard Zinn, the impression that "the system was criticising and correcting itself".[2] Though the Church Committee's Senate report would be sanitised for public consumption, the Pike Committee, based in the House of Representatives, exposed a series of crimes, including the administering of LSD to unsuspecting Americans; assassination plots against heads of state; the introduction of the swine fever virus in Cuba; the destabilisation of the Chilean government; and the infiltration, monitoring and discrediting of political and cultural organisations. The implication was that these crimes had been committed by rogue agents and were not the result of state policy.[3] This redirection of the national narrative contributed to the recognition that further investigations would be necessary, if only on a private basis. With the Church and Pike investigations confirming past paranoia, conditions in the mid-1970s were ripe for the return of the fictional private-eye. Recalling the days of pulp culture, fictional sleuths would again find themselves tracking down clues and stalking America's mean streets, this even though they hadn't yet the courage to ask why the streets were, after all these years, still mean, and why, as investigators, they were striking poses similar to their predecessors.

Investigatory fiction's new lease on life can be traced back to Richard Nixon's war against opponents at home and abroad, his links with organised crime, and his corrupt campaign for re-election. For private-eye fiction always seems to flourish in periods of, or immediately following, government secrecy, duplicity and paranoia.[4] Thanks to Nixon, investigators were to regain their status, even if these investigators were, at first, journalists rather than fictional private detectives. In fact, Grub Streeters were to play a major role in obtaining significant, if surface, changes: Woodward and Bernstein's investigation would lead to Nixon's downfall; Seymour Hersh, of the *New York Times*, would be responsible for evicting the paranoid counter-intelligence chief James Angleton from the CIA; while consumer advocate Ralph Nader and his investigators would alter the practices of many US corporations.

Such events and conditions would lead to a resurgence of private-eye fiction by Ross Macdonald, Joe Gores, Ross Thomas,

Michael Collins, Robert B. Parker, Michael Lewin, Arthur Lyons, Lawrence Block, Joseph Hansen, Stephen Dobyns, and James Crumley. Additionally, investigative novels by Tony Hillerman and K. C. Constantine featured police detectives so marginally connected to the state as to make them more akin to private-eyes than state cops. The politics of publishing aside, the reemergence of fictional private-eyes during the mid-1970s also related to a desire to return to an era of recognisable signs. Hence many first efforts, like those by Roger Simon and Andrew Bergman, were, as exercises in nostalgia, little more than lightweight parody. Trapped in the past and struggling to make the transition from local to state crime, detective fiction would remain rooted in 1960s politics and the investigative atmosphere created by such journalists as Hunter Thompson and Woodward-Bernstein. Not surprisingly, investigative reporting would quickly fall out of favour. Two years after the Watergate story, *Washington Post* proprietor Katherine Graham, despite having the country's prized double-act in her stable, issued the following disclaimer regarding new investigatory fervour:

> The press these days should . . . be rather careful about its role. We may have acquired some tendencies about over-involvement that we had better overcome. We had better not yield to the temptation to go on refighting the next war and see conspiracy and cover-up where they do not exist.[5]

While private-eye fiction seemed poised to take the place of investigative journalism as the culture's main muckraking force, most writers had yet to locate the genre's radical possibilities, or realise that, though recalling the past, detective fiction has always contained the possibility of reinvention and regeneration.

While their situation differed from that of their predecessors, private-eye novelists by the 1980s still adhered to the genre's basic construction: namely, first person narratives which delineate the relationship between the private-eye's personal life, the culture and the crime. Occupying the centre of the narrative from which he or she dispenses witticisms and perceptions, the investigator solves the crime and restores a degree of public and private order. With state crimes so glaringly apparent, the problem facing private-eye writers in the early 1980s would be one of locating new boundaries, redefining the relationship between the private-eye and the state, and investigating the role of the investigator. Though a handful of hardboiled private-eyes, including Matt Scudder (Block), Dave Brandstetter (Hansen), Dan Fortune (Collins), Milo Milodragovitch and James Sughrue (Crumley), originally appeared in the 1970s, it would not be until the 1980s that the genre would be fully resuscitated.

Based on the traditional model, the private-eye of the 1980s no longer had to possess a witty response to every situation, nor be self-righteous or excessively moral. He or she need only possess the required investigative skills: tenacity, intelligence and an overview of the culture. Though few were to know beforehand the extent of the crimes committed during the era, a surfeit of private-eye novelists and detectives made their literary debuts around the time of Reagan's 1980 election victory. These included Stephen Greenleaf's 1979 *Grave Error* which introduced John Marshall Tanner; Jonathan Valin's 1980 *The Lime Pit* which featured Harry Stoner; Loren Estelman's 1980 *Motor City Blue* which introduced Amos Walker; Max Byrd's 1981 *California Thriller* which centred on Mike Haller; and James Ellroy's 1981 *Brown's Requiem*, a one-off private-eye novel which launched the career of one of crime fiction's leading practitioners.

So great was Chandler's hold on the genre that hardcore investigators from Amos Walker to Harry Stoner would remain in the Philip Marlowe mode. If the 1970s seemed like the 1940s, then the 1980s looked like the 1950s, as Reagan sought to reinvigorate the Cold War, attack organised labour, and initiate a series of deregulatory policies. It seemed like the pulp culture era all over again.

Another factor affecting the emergence of fictional private-eyes was the emphasis, during the 1980s, on dog-eat-dog individuality – in most cases, less a display of libertarianism than an excuse for adhering to extreme free-market policies. With rising unemployment, and growing disparities between the rich and the poor, it was the decade in which the freelancer emerged as a cultural phenomenon. Though, with rare exceptions, fictional private investigators have always been self-employed, the excesses of supply-side economics and the demands of the state would prompt a number of ex-police officers to become fictional private-eyes. Fed up with law enforcement and the inflexible relationship between law enforcement and the state, private investigation would prove a last best hope, and, as work, more satisfying than having to reinforce disparities created by free-market policies.

Given their employment prospects, it's ironic that many private-eyes seem unconcerned about bringing home a regular wage. Though some have alternative sources of income, others prefer a hand-to-mouth existence. Amongst the former is Steven Dobyns's Charlie Bradshaw, an ex-policeman who becomes a security worker. While the latter category includes Lawrence Block's Matt Scudder, who quit the police force after accidentally shooting a young girl. Now on his own, Scudder prefers doing favours for friends, saying, "Private detectives are licensed. They tap telephones and follow people. They fill out forms, they keep records, all of that. I don't do those things. Sometimes I do favors for people. They give me gifts."[6] Meanwhile, James Sallis's Lew Griffin begins by following a hand-to-mouth existence, but eventually finds more gainful employment. Even as an odd-jobber, Griffin would rather be dined at his clients' expense than bill them for his services. Hardly in the Philip Marlowe mode, these investigators, however tough or streetwise, are never more than ordinary. Yet, as victims of Reaganism, their uneasy entrance into the genre marks a shift in the private-eye's attitude to the job, the culture and the investigatory process.

Considering the pressures of their former jobs, and the exigencies of the era, it's not surprising that overly moral investigators end up enlisting in the *Twelve-Step Programme*. So much of a cliché has it become in detective fiction that some discerning readers must long for the moment when, for the sake of the narrative, ex-cops and former alcoholics like Block's Matt Scudder and James Lee Burke's Dave Robicheaux fall off their wagon, if not their high horse. Yet, taking abstinence and detection one day at a time, they are unable to stop being former alcoholics, just as they cannot stop being investigators. Addicted to the process, detection, like alcohol, has seeped into their system.

Despite this particular artifice, the likes of Block and Burke are too professional to court self-exposure or relinquish control of their narratives. Distancing themselves from their texts, they would rather recycle their prized protagonists. This despite the fact that there might well be a law of diminishing returns regarding the reappearance of any particular private-eye. Not only do consecutive narratives stretch believability, but, with each new book, authors must strike a balance between focusing on the culture and extolling the virtues of the investigating protagonist. An occupational hazard, excessive recycling has become an economic fact, dependent, in many cases, on the tacit desire of publishers and writers to create long-term money-spinners. Whichever way one looks at it, the private eye, in terms of effectiveness, style and job specification, is only as believable as he or she remains observant to the crimes of everyday reality.

Before discussing the likes of Block, Dobyns, Burke and Sallis, brief mention should be made of Mark Behm's novel, *The Eye of the Beholder*. This product of the early 1980s remains one of the few investigatory novels to significantly stretch the boundaries of the genre. Though a noirist, Behm cannot be strictly classified as a writer of detective fiction – as a screenwriter, he has contributed to such films as *Help* and *The Three Musketeers* – *The Eye of the Beholder* delves into a world of obsession, as an investigator, simply called the Eye, pursues a young woman who might be his daughter across America. Leaving behind a string of corpses and a series of discarded identities, the pursued, in Behm's novel, becomes as obsessed as the pursuer.

> The Eye took another picture. There was a funny taste on his lips, brassy. He wiped his mouth on his sleeve. His vision blurred. He tried to take a shot but couldn't see anything. He leaned against a tree, blinking and squinting. Jesus! the park was as dim as a void, and his fucking ears were ringing. He dropped the camera. He tried to spit, snorted and blew his nose. Was he bleeding? God, he had to take a monstrous fucking leak! . . . He unzipped with dead icicle fingers and squirted all over his trousers and shoes . . . The ice cream must have been poisoned! His cock was shriveling up. It vanished inside him![7]

The voyeurism of Behm's novel reflects the era's political passivity, and its obsession with dysfunctionality. Behm, born in 1925, is more concerned with psychological states than politics, more interested in pursuing crimes caused by dementia than solving crimes committed by psychos. In *The Eye of the Beholder*, the protagonist slowly but surely falls to pieces. No matter how much he pursues her, the Eye and his would-be daughter never connect on any level save that derived from accidental encounters. But then Behm is less interested in the incest angle than in examining the cause and effect of obsessional behaviour. As an investigation of private investigation, the Eye can only hope that his life might one day cohere.

As well as parodying the femme fatale-as-sublime-object, Behm's novel reinterprets the role of the private-eye and questions whether the investigator can still be considered an existential Marxist trudging the mean streets, or whether he has become merely an obsessed pervert who must clean up after the object of his desire. Owing more to pulp road fiction like Dan C. Marlowe's *The Name of the Game is Death* than to Hammett, Behm stretches the boundaries of detective fiction to breaking point. Following the corruption of belief, paranoia and the pursuit of one's obsessions are apparently all that remain. Not surprisingly, few have dared to follow in Behm's footsteps.

Though the proliferation of private-eyes in the 1980s suggests that the investigatory process had again become publicly expedient, the texts in which they appear remain mostly personal affairs, taking the investigator away from his or her normal life, but rarely from his or her private thoughts. Unlike the investigative reporter, the private-eye has rarely been an agent of social change; thus he or she remains cynical but honest. This inability to effect change often serves as an obstacle to the pursuit of his or her investigation. Though hardboiled detective writing constantly threatens to exceed its sell-by date, its longevity has been partly due to the way its anachronistic tendencies have been able to grease the wheels of the genre. In a literature whose independent, if not autonomous, protagonists walk a thin line between past and present, most detective writers find it difficult to move between the personal and the political. Yet, from Watergate to the belief that history is dead, there have been notable exceptions. An investigation of such writers, noting their idiosyncrasies, their relationship to history, and their response to the era in which they write, might indicate where the genre is headed, as well as where it has been.

Lawrence Block

In a career that spans four decades, Lawrence Block has produced a range of crime novels,[8] and at least two narratives – *Such Men Are Dangerous* and *The Specialist* – that relate to the Vietnam era. These days Block is best known for his series of hardboiled crime novels featuring Matt Scudder. Written from the viewpoint of an ex-alcoholic, these New York-based novels explore the dark side of contemporary society. Though Scudder, in the first few novels – *Sins of the Fathers* (1976), *Time to Murder and Create* (1977), *Eight Million Ways to Die* (1982), and *When the*

Sacred Ginmill Closes (1986) – is an excessive drinker, by the end of the 1980s, in novels like *Out on the Cutting Edge* (1989), *A Ticket to the Boneyard* (1990) and *A Dance at the Slaughterhouse* (1991), he has evolved into a coffee addict and AA habitue, haunted by memories of past crimes, barrooms and lost friends.

Having left his wife and the police force after accidentally shooting a young girl, Scudder's world is as lonely as it is tumultuous. Yet, as the years pass, his personal angst becomes increasingly clothed in middle-class armour. Enough, that is, for Scudder to look back with fondness on the benefits of working for the state. "There was a great security in being a cop," says Scudder, always eager to plumb the depths of his emotions. "I don't mean the job security, I mean the emotional security. There weren't as many questions, and the ones that came up were likely to have obvious answers, or at least they seemed obvious at the time."[9] One wonders if Scudder has forgotten that the morality entailed in working for the state exacerbated his drinking which, in turn, led to him shooting the young girl. Not surprisingly, Scudder seeks redemption for his misfiring, and, though not a Catholic, lights candles in various churches, before placing a percentage of his earnings in the coffers.

Because each novel revolves around his past alcoholism, one cannot help noting the degree to which drinking affects Scudder's investigative work. While, in the early novels, drinking helps Block's protagonist detect and solve the relevant crime, his post-alcoholic state now provides a perspective from which he can investigate the culture. So Scudder's presence at AA meetings offers him a moment's respite and the opportunity to view and comment upon the world. This despite the fact that going to AA meetings, where confession meets monotheism, seems no different from attending church. Likewise, Scudder, though attracted to the ethos of AA, finds its moral standards difficult to maintain.

By *Eight Million Ways to Die*, Scudder knows he must stop

drinking, but cannot understand why "anyone would think it a
good idea to stay sober in this city".[10] Scudder's drinking might
allow him to conduct his investigations from an unusual, but
effective, angle, but it also results in some unfortunate infractions. For instance, in the latter book, an inebriated Scudder,
unrelenting when it comes to murder, walks past a man in the
process of beating a woman. This determination not to get
involved would be anathema to Scudder in the 1990s.

In *The Devil Knows You're Dead*, published in 1993, Scudder,
investigating the murder of a man gunned down in the street,
has begun to view crime, not as a local concern – small-scale
and revolving around a small circle of friends – but as a sign of
the times. While Scudder is correct about the cultural role and
importance of crime, he hammers it home with such certainty
that one longs to draw one's own conclusion. Yet Block's tendency has become a common feature in contemporary crime
fiction, where extremism in the pursuit of vice has become a
literary virtue.

Significantly, *The Sins of the Fathers*, addressing the hypocrisy
of religion, appeared at a time when America was suffering the
first wave of born-again fundamentalism. So Scudder contrasts
his drinking problem with a crime committed by a tee-totalling
religious fanatic. Not surprisingly, when it comes to religion,
Scudder remains sceptical. Watching people go in and out of
the confessional, he concludes that "I thought how nice it might
be to be able to leave your sins in a little curtained booth."[11] But
when Scudder admits to having "lost the faith", he is not referring to religion but to law enforcement. Still, he remains a
moral relativist: "Good and evil. I have a lot trouble figuring
those things out."[12] Later, when he recollects that he once
planted drugs on a rapist-murderer who would otherwise have
gone free, Scudder asks himself "whether it was worse for men
to do the wrong things for the right reason or the right things
for the wrong reason?"[13] Needless to say, it's a question that
goes unanswered.

Reminiscent of Ross Macdonald's familial motif, *The Sins of the Fathers* describes an era delineated by the remnants of the war and the Watergate investigation. With Nixon about to be exonerated and President Ford a bumbling hostage in the White House, public morale stood at low ebb – a 1975 Harris poll reported that confidence in the military had dropped from 62% to 29%, in business from 55% to 18%, and in the President and Congress from 42% to 13%.[14] Thanks to a series of investigations, *the sins of the fathers* were being revealed with alarming alacrity.

A decade later, in Block's 1986 *When the Sacred Ginmill Closes*, Scudder's investigation remains as incisive as ever. Still inhabiting a noir world, the worst aspects of which he keeps at bay only with difficulty, Scudder says farewell to investigation as an adventure in inebriation. However, Scudder will become less interesting as he becomes increasingly moralistic. It makes one wonder if his drinking was not only a way of coping with 1970s America, but a means of loosening his mind enough to conduct his investigations. Once having viewed the investigatory process as an unconscious, intuitive and imaginative act, Scudder comes to take a more realistic, if less exciting, line, regarding it as a day-to-day process that owes more to induction than inspiration. One can only conclude that, if Scudder was an alcoholic during the tedious Ford administration, his sobriety during the Reagan years must have been partly based on the belief that its investigation would require a degree of lucidity.

After a period in which he can barely stand the company of others, Scudder's tolerance soon reaches saintly proportions. Likewise, in a genre known for its macho individualism, Scudder is one of the few private investigators capable of sustaining a long-term relationship. Not only does he discuss his cases with Elaine, his prostitute-girlfriend, but, reminiscent of Hammett's Nick Charles, he sometimes allows her to occasionally assist him in his investigations.

In the early novels, Scudder makes some interesting comments regarding the relationship between drinking, the art of detection and the detective's ability to read the culture. Still on the sauce, he informs a potential client that he is more expensive than the agencies, that he doesn't like writing reports or checking-in when there's nothing to say. Even setting a fee can compromise his newly acquired perspective:

> How do you put a value on your time when its only value is personal? And when your life has been deliberately restructured to minimize involvement in the lives of others, how much do you charge the man who forces you to involve yourself.[15]

Though he cannot produce a standard contract, Scudder's *modus operandi* remains clear: "You start any place . . . You don't always know until later what's useful and what isn't."[16] This even though Scudder's early investigations are affected by blackouts:

> I couldn't have been in too bad shape if I'd remembered to bolt the door. On the other hand, my pants were tossed over the chair. It would have been better if they'd been hung in the closet. Then again, they weren't in a tangled heap on the floor, nor was I still wearing them. The great detective, sifting clues, trying to find out how bad he'd been last night.[17]

Clearly a case of detective, investigate thyself!

Always self-effacing, Scudder is more forthcoming than most when it comes to demystifying the investigative process. When he was still on the force, he claims to have solved most cases in one of two ways: "Either I didn't know the answer at all until a fresh piece of information made itself instantly evident, or I knew all along who had done whatever had been done, and all that was ever needed was sufficient evidence to prove it in court."[18] Drinking might interfere with the process entailed in conducting an investigation for the state, but it did not affect Scudder's ability to concentrate:

> I took what I had and stared at it . . . , and all of a sudden I saw the same thing in a new light, and the answer was in my

hand. Have you ever worked a jigsaw puzzle . . . been stuck for the moment, and kept taking pieces and holding them this way and that, until finally you take up a piece you must have already held . . . a hundred times . . . ? And this time the piece . . . fits in a way that should have been obvious all along.[19]

Regarding the investigative process in this manner, Scudder's examination of the abstruse and the obvious leads to such cogent comments regarding the state of America as, "[That's] the American Dream. Steal from the boss until you can afford to open up in competition with him."[20]

But it's through conversational gambits that Scudder pursues his investigation. In *The Sins of the Fathers*, Tommy, a persuasive telephone salesman, is unable to sell his innocence to Scudder: "If we were doin' this over the phone, you'd buy what I'm telling you . . . It's fucking certain. Word for word, you'd buy the package."[21] Though Tommy hopes Matt's "high" will cause him to forget their conversation and his admission of guilt, Scudder cannot afford to feign amnesia.

Offering a mild antidote to the Reagan–Bush era's obsession with family values and one-dimensional morality, by 1990, when *A Ticket to the Boneyard* appeared, Block's fiction, though still effortlessly written, begins to wear thin. After all, Block must spend an increasingly large amount of time recounting past details, and so stretches to breaking point a moral framework that is, at best, cloaked in an uneasy relativism. At his AA sponsor's urging, Scudder takes comfort in *The Meditations of Marcus Aurelius*: "Whatever happens at all happens as it should; thou wilt find this true if thou shouldst watch narrowly."[22] But, in search of James Leo Motley, an old nemesis now murdering prostitutes, Scudder, making the rounds of the gay leather bars, is unable to maintain such narrowness:

[In] the Age of AIDS I found their atmosphere particularly unsettling. Part of this, I suppose, came from the perception that a large proportion of the men I saw . . . were walking time bombs, infected with the virus and odds-on to come down with the disease within months or years. Armed with this knowledge, or perhaps disarmed by it, it was all too easy for me to see the skull beneath the skin.[23]

A decent person who finds he must sometimes bypass the rules, Scudder, noting the effect prison has had on Motley, compromises his morality when apprehending him. Ironically, it is easier for Scudder to accomplish this as a private investigator than as a member of the police department:

> I don't need probable cause to search his dwelling, and I can enter the premises illegally without disqualifying any evidence I turn up. I don't have to read him his rights. If I get a confession out of him, they can't disallow it on the grounds that he didn't get to consult an attorney. I can record anything he says without getting a court order first, and I don't even have to tell him I'm doing it.[24]

After arranging the scene so it appears that Motley has shot himself, Scudder, referring to his sense of ethics, says, "[Here] I am playing God again."[25]

Block's later novels, such as *A Ticket to the Boneyard* and *The Devil Knows You're Dead*, demonstrate the extent to which Scudder's detective skills, now predictable, rely on coincidence and sheer doggedness rather than inspiration. Were Block's moralising narratives believable, they might be accused of excessive optimism. In the end, Block, though continuing to produce entertaining fiction, seems to have become, and perhaps always was, too slick for his own good. This not only cramps his critique, but it makes Scudder's confessional asides increasingly hard to sustain, particularly when addressed, in confidence, to a reader he does not know. Given the crimes of the era, Scudder's moral relativism pales into insignificance.

Steven Dobyns

Interested in narrative congruities instigated by the study of history, Steven Dobyns bases his work in Saratoga, New York, a town known for its racetrack and the fact that, as a 1930s resort centre, it entertained the likes of Franklin Delano Roosevelt. Though racetracks have often been a setting for detective fiction, Dobyns is less interested in the "sport of kings" than in its punters, touts, and professionals.

Significantly, Charlie Bradshaw, like Scudder, first appeared in 1976, when investigation had become a fact of life and politicians spoke about a nation divided by the Vietnam war. Yet Bradshaw's reluctance to investigate and his world-weary retreat into the minutiae of small-town manners can be traced to the decline in public confidence regarding the ability of mainstream politics to alter America's narrative. An established poet, Dobyns approaches the genre in a formal, but never formulaic, manner. Like Scudder, Bradshaw is a middle-aged divorcee who has come to regard police work as overly compromising. A burnt-out cop in *Saratoga Longshot*, by *Saratoga Swimmer*, published in 1981 – coinciding with Reagan's first year in office, the attempt on his life, and his resurgence in popularity – Bradshaw's obsession with crime threatens to become his undoing.

Another private investigator who leaves the police force for political reasons, Bradshaw will insist on solving crimes regardless of the consequences. Given this tendency, it's understandable that Bradshaw should be reluctant to take on a case. Yet his investigatory obsessiveness, coupled with his reluctance to investigate, comprise a contradiction common to fellow private-eyes like Block's Matt Scudder and James Sallis's Lew Griffin. This, given the politics of the Reagan–Bush era, is understandable. For some investigators were aware that delving too far into a case can be dangerous, bringing down the wrath of the state or the anger of one's employer.

Bradshaw's interest in history takes him outside the usual

Marlowe mode of detection in which an obsessional deliber-
ation on objects and habits is par for the narrative course.
Prefacing *Saratoga Headhunters* with a quote from Nellie Bly,
"Gambling is the atmosphere", Dobyns links speculation, investigation, 1980s free-market policies and Saratoga's raison d'être.
Meanwhile, Bradshaw focuses on Saratoga's criminal past,
recollecting early American outlaws like Black Jack Ketchum of
the notorious Wild Bunch, who would hammer himself on the
head with a gun butt whenever he made a serious mistake.
Commenting that Ketchum's arm was shot off in a train robbery,
Bradshaw says, "[What] he seemed to regret most was that the
subsequent amputation robbed him of the power to punish
himself for getting caught."[26] Could this also be a metaphor for
Bradshaw's plight? Or is he merely identifying with the criminal
class, and those who, like Ketchum, have had to "endure too
much"? Whichever, Bradshaw, stating an opinion that might
have been suspect had he remained a cop, prefers to side with
outlaws than with those who pursue them:

> Had any bandits managed to die of old age? The most famous
> was probably Frank James, but his thirty-three years of life
> after the murder of Jesse was a lonely and frustrated time. He
> had sold old shoes and men's clothing. He had tended horses.
> He had even appeared in Saratoga in the summer of 1894 to
> work as a bookie.[27]

Such insights, though appearing to be meditative interludes,
help shape Dobyns's texts, and are akin to Sallis's literary
speculations and Block's AA profundities.

Deploying quotes to plot the historical vectors of his fiction,
Dobyns, in *Saratoga Swimmer*, cites Henry James regarding the
condition of the town: "What society may have been at Saratoga
when its elements were thus simple and severe, I can only
vaguely and mournfully conjecture. I confine myself to the
dense, democratic, vulgar Saratoga of the current year." Here
Dobyns serves notice that he intends to investigate Saratoga's

lines of power, and discrepancies between the powerful and the powerless:

> Again, all his historical precedents were reversed. Although Charlie could name a hundred burglars and sneak thieves who had graduated from Marm Mandelbaum's burglar school at 79 Clinton Street in New York during the 1870s, he could not think of anyone, outside of a character in a P. G. Wodehouse novel, who had burgled his own house.[28]

In fact, Ackerman, the man found murdered in the swimming pool, had been Charlie's employer, and the person who had encouraged his interest in history. In Dobyns's world, there is always a link between a person and what he or she reads:

> Most recently Ackerman had begun to study Richard Canfield, the prince of Saratoga gamblers who had closed his casino in 1907 to concentrate on his art collection. Ackerman had been drawn to Canfield, because both men had freed themselves from the poverty of their youths by running poker games in their teens and early twenties. But while Canfield had gone on to build greater and greater casinos, Ackerman had turned to horses, giving up all other types of gambling which he claimed were close to robbery.[29]

In *Saratoga Longshot*, Dobyns begins by quoting Edna Ferber: "July and August there's nothing like [Saratoga] in the whole country. Races every day, gambling, millionaires and pickpockets and sporting people and respectable family folks and politicians and famous theater actors and actresses, you'll find them all at Saratoga." Thus the novel starts with an appreciation of the town's social mix. For Bradshaw, history is not dead; it's merely buried in books that few bother to read. Accordingly, Dobyns's protagonist spends much of the novel poring over a biography of Billy the Kid, even lending it to a cop who has the temerity to quote it back at him – "You know this book of yours, there's a sentence here that made me think of you. 'His misfortune was, he could not and would not stay whipped.' Ring any bells?"[30] In New York, Bradshaw gets his revenge when he tells the concerned cop, Driscoll, that the area they pass through was once the stamping ground of the Dead Rabbits, a gang who worked for Tammany Hall in the 1850s: "[It] was Morrissey who brought big time gambling to Saratoga Springs. Morrissey's Club House later became the Canfield Casino. Old Smoke used to tell people, 'No man can say that I ever turned a dishonest card or struck a foul blow . . . And it was Morrissey . . . who made horse racing fashionable."[31] While he often uses the past to make a point, at other times Bradshaw ruminates on the past so as to move from one point to another. In a bar awaiting the inevitable, Bradshaw's speculations – "[He] could name the banks robbed by Jesse James or the twenty-one men shot down by John Wesley Hardin. One of Hardin's victims had been a black policeman by the name of Green Paramour. Charlie thought that was one of the most beautiful names he knew."[32] – form a parallel narrative, one that clears his mind and lets him glimpse the larger picture.

Not one to court excess, Bradshaw is an observer as much as an investigator. To be effective at his job, he must court anonymity:

> He knew that part of the problem was that he neither looked
> nor acted like an officer of the law. Instead, he might be a
> vacuum cleaner salesman or a clerk for an insurance company,
> someone who rode buses and kept a canary, who put off
> buying a new pair of shoes. Although Charlie had spent years
> trying to achieve this effect, there was still the regret.[33]

Naturally, Bradshaw occasionally has second thoughts about maintaining such an existence. In countering the cult of the personality, anonymity might be politically correct, but it has its drawbacks. Like Matt Scudder, Bradshaw sometimes longs for the security that accompanies institutionalised law enforcement. Nevertheless, anonymity allows him a private life, one in which there is ample time to read. This is not as harmless a pastime as it seems; for, in establishing a relationship between crime and history, Bradshaw's investigation of the past will allow him to solve crimes in the present.

However, it's a mid-life crisis rather than an obsessional interest in history that, in *Saratoga Longshot*, helps Bradshaw make sense of his own time and place, and allows him to leave the police force. It's part and parcel of a case of downward mobility – an adventurous act in the midst of the Reagan era – which Bradshaw embraces when, in New York to find the son of a woman with whom he once had a teenage affair, he becomes involved with a twenty-three-year-old woman. Not exactly your macho womanising private-eye, Bradshaw, hoping the hormonal might be political, is so worried he won't be able to perform that, like an aroused speed-freak, he stays up all night spouting inanities. Momentarily forgetting that he is sterile, Bradshaw can't stop thinking that the person he is looking for might be his son. Consequently, he refuses to return to Saratoga until he can get some answers and sort out his life. Though New York is an effective antidote to the claustrophobia of small-town life, it also makes Bradshaw aware of his own vulnerability:

> He was frightened of being beaten again. He was frightened
> of losing what he had achieved in Saratoga. But his fear
> embarrassed him. His decision to go or stay seemed a matter
> of morality, and it seemed wrong to be influenced by physical
> fear and economics.[34]

Influenced by economics as well as history, Bradshaw willingly sinks into the muck of his own marginalisation. Regarding the separation between ordinary punters and those upmarket habitues of Saratoga during racing season, Bradshaw says, "Money, jewels, you're almost blinded. I found myself thinking like a communist or something."[35] Though private investigation has always allowed detectives to make such extrapolations, it's a brave man who, given the hegemony of the

Reagan era, can say it. Driven by an obsession with the past,·
and a desire to do the right thing, Bradshaw's irrepressibility
turns him into a source of irritation to those unlucky enough to
be involved in his case. Above all, the Saratoga novels counter
the era's arguments regarding excessive state power, the imposi-
tion of a restrictive moral code, trickle-down economics, and
the short-circuiting of history.

James Lee Burke

In uncovering corruption and the misuse of power, James Lee
Burke's Dave Robicheaux has long been liberalism's answer to
private investigation. Following the usual vitae, Robicheaux is a
Vietnam veteran, an ex-alcoholic and ex-cop who, after questioning his job – "a microcosm of an aberrant world populated by
snipers, razor-wielding blacks, mindless nickel-and-dime boost
artists who eventually panic and kill a convenience-store clerk
for sixty dollars, and suicides who fill the apartment with gas
and blow the whole building into a black and orange fireball."[36]
– and a series of personal tragedies, decides to go freelance.
Despite his moralisms and tendency to repeat himself, Burke's
first two crime novels, *Neon Rain* and *Heaven's Prisoners*, would
represent a significant marriage of public and private investigation. Together they helped reinvigorate the world of
investigatory fiction.

Prior to *Neon Rain*, the Texas-born Burke had published
such promising novels as *Lost Get-Back Boogie*, *When I Lay My
Burden Down*, and a collection of stories entitled *The Convict*, all
of which owe as much to New Deal leftism as to modernism.
But *Neon Rain*, with its circuitous narrative, would be one of
the first contemporary detective novels to investigate and
criticise the politics of the Reagan era. Moving between New
Orleans and the bayous – Robicheaux is himself a Cajun – *Neon
Rain* makes use of Louisiana's cultural traditions. In doing so,
Burke revives the genre's time-honoured links with regionalism,
adding his name to the list of crime writers – James Ross,

Charles Williams, Jim Thompson, Charles Willeford and Sharyn McCrumb – who utilise the south as a setting for their crime fiction. In fact, one of Burke's strengths is his ability to convey a vivid sense of place:

> Oak, cypress, and willow trees lined the two-lane road; the mist still clung like torn cotton to the half-submerged dead tree trunks back in the marsh; the canebrakes were thick and green, shining in the light, and the lily pads clustered along the bayou's banks were bursting with flowers, audibly popping, their leaves covered with drops of quicksilver.[37]

Always accessible, Burke's prose can be as lyrical as it is truthful. Yet, when it comes to verisimilitude, Burke's plots do not necessarily match his sense of place or subject matter. Even his use of the Vietnam war, recollected with such effect in *Neon Rain* and *Heaven's Prisoners*, becomes overused and increasingly difficult to sustain. Ironical, given the importance of the war, and the fact that it was clearly the most formative experience in Robicheaux's life, one from which he gained a trade, an identity, and a sense of ethics. He makes this clear when speaking about viewing photographs of My Lai:

> I knew that I would always be caught in that lens, too, locked inside a frame of film that people would never be able to deal with, because to deal with it would require an admission of responsibility that would numb an entire nation.
>
> This is why the word *obsession* is a convenient one in the analytical vocabulary. We apply it to those who were trapped inside the camera, who can never extricate themselves from those darker periods of history that were written for them by somebody else.[38]

A straight-ahead hardboiler with literary leanings, Burke, in the late 1980s, was unique in producing quality detective fiction for a readership disgusted with the corruptions of the Reagan–Bush era. Yet Burke is not now nor has he ever been merely a propagandist. Rather, he encloses his politics within well-structured plots. This makes a novel like *Neon Rain* more cautious and evenly-crafted than the anarchic texts of James Ellroy and Jerome Charyn. More significantly, Burke's narrative control contrasts sharply with the lack of control Robicheaux, in the early novels, has over his own life.

Though Burke's examination of the excesses of the CIA, Latin American drug dealers and Nicaraguan Contras predates public knowledge of the Irangate scandal, *Neon Rain*, published in 1987, is as concerned with personal as much as national redemption. Battling the bottle as well as those carrying out covert criminal activities, Robicheaux, as a Nicaraguan Somosista gangster puts it, "talks like a Marxist".[39] Moreover, his investigations are aided by a lesson learned in Vietnam: "Never trust authority. But because I had come to feel that authority should always be treated as suspect and self-serving, I had also learned that it was predictable and vulnerable."[40]

Within a couple of years writers would be falling over themselves to join Burke in his critique. Aware of the importance crime fiction would have for male writers, as well as political dissenters, Burke places this particular literary permutation in its historical context:

> During the 1970s it was real tough for male writers. The country was involved in national self-recrimination . . . And I think the same social forces that elected Ronald Reagan are responsible for the return of interest in male fiction. Because Reagan represents, in a cosmetic way, a superficial set of male values . . . all that stuff that makes everybody's genitalia begin to hum! . . . What's dangerous about these kinds of people is that they vicariously revise their lives through the suffering of others.[41]

Burke's final sentence – a reference to writers who *vicariously revise their lives through the suffering of others* – implies that their writing – and this includes a certain type of crime fiction – tends to be voyeuristic, particularly regarding the portrayal of violence. At the same time, the above quote suggests that contemporary crime fiction, regardless of how one interprets the politics of voyeurism, has been, to some extent, a reaction to feminism, and a refuge for marginalised male writers.

Encouraged, and presumably influenced, by Charles Willeford – another marginalised male writer writing about marginalised male protagonists – Burke creates a character who must stay sober if he wants to make a coherent analysis of his situation and the world around him. With the uncovering of corruption connected to Robicheaux's drinking problem, Burke links the personal and the political, maintaining that his protagonist is "A moral man living in an amoral world." However laudatory his politics, Robicheaux's good and bad qualities – his morality and lust for revenge – are often at odds with each other: for "Robicheaux is a man who has to pay a lot of dues, has had to make some hard choices . . . [These] books are meant to be as much about one man's struggle with his demons as they are books about criminals."[42]

Like Scudder, Robicheaux is moral enough not to place blame too freely. However, he sometimes ventures one step beyond believability, allowing, for instance, a major force behind a drugs-for-arms scam to go free because the man is elderly and, having heard of his son's involvement in the My Lai massacre, has fallen in with the wrong crowd. At least it illustrates that, when it comes to meting out justice, Robicheaux is more flexible than Marlowe, and more politically aware than Scudder or Bradshaw. As Robicheaux, in proletariat mode, says,

[In] the real world we fry paupers in the electric chair and send priests to prison for splashing chicken blood on draft files . . . We deal with the problem symbolically, but somebody has to take the fall . . . If you were an administrative pencil-pusher, don't you think it would be easier to deal with a drunk-driving fatality than a story about a lot of right-wing crazies who are killing peasant villagers in Nicaragua?[43]

On the other hand, maybe Robicheaux hasn't noticed that *administrative pencil-pushers* don't send people to prison; they merely follow orders and do the paperwork. Indeed, it would be ironic if Robicheaux were found to be pursuing the wrong people. For Burke, believing "a lot of crime writing is superficial because it doesn't treat the problem of evil",[44] fervently believes that noirists should address moral issues as well as locate the real culprits of crime. The fact is, Robicheaux may not be as hardboiled as he would have us believe. For his critique seems to be based on religion as much as political ideology:

> It's the fundamental theological question: how do we reconcile a benevolent God with the presence of evil in the world? . . . When you deal with evil in a book your responsibilities as a writer are not decreased, they are increased. How do you explain pathological behaviour? Do people elect to be evil, are they environmentally shaped?[45]

Rather than regard most criminals as intrinsically evil, Burke believes them to be mostly buffoons, who might as well be turned loose. Meanwhile, real criminals – those "polluting the environment . . . , in the munitions industry, the people who are responsible for the . . . exploitation of the third world – never see the inside of a prison".[46]

Insisting that one accept Robicheaux's liberalism simply because he has paid his dues, Burke says, "The amount of compassion and empathy in a person's life is directly in proportion to the amount of suffering he endures."[47] A laudable and perhaps Christian view, but one that is not necessarily true – suffering may produce saints, but it also produces psychopaths. Or is it that Burke thinks his protagonist's personal history will make his anti-Reagan views acceptable to an imaginary *lumpen* readership? Whichever, Robicheaux's excessive moralising, though admirable, can be hard to take. Citing poet Robert Frost, Robicheaux reaches the following conclusions:

He said the fear of God asks the question, Is my sacrifice acceptable, is it worthy, in His sight? When it's all over and done with, does the good outweigh the bad, did I pitch the best game I could, even though it was a flawed one.[48]

However, Robicheaux realises it is impossible to pitch his best game while working for the state:

I knew absolutely that it was as dishonorable for a man to allow himself to be used as it was for him to use others. I also knew as a cop that the use of people, which is probably our worst sin, was considered the stuff of moralistic rhetoric by the legal fraternity.[49]

This is Robicheaux's bottom-line regarding his relationship to the state and to history. One realises that Burke's difficulties in locating new territory relates to his sentimentality. With his fiction, until recently, on auto-control, Burke has become entangled in his own narrowing narrative web. By the fifth Robicheaux novel, *A Stained White Radiance*, his critique and investigation threatened to approach parody. Though making a partial recovery, Burke's *Dixie City Jam* and *Burning Angel* have little of the urgency and political incisiveness that marked his earlier work. Burke must have realised as much, for he has recently returned to form in his 1996 *Cadillac Jukebox* and, to a lesser degree, in his 1997 *Cimarron Rose*.

In the former novel, Robicheaux, once again employed as a cop – this time in heart of Cajun country, New Iberia – extrapolates on politics in the Clinton era. Here the new Southern Democrats, though educated and liberal, are as corrupt as their predecessors. Burke's insights are accompanied by a more exacting narrative approach. He accomplishes this in various ways: by including other perspectives and expositional material that allows him to move outside the confines of a strictly first person narrative; by using inventive imagery – "He watched the [football] bounce and roll away in the dusk, as though he were looking at an unformed thought in the center of his head[50]" – by offering complex and believable psychological insights, such as Jerry Joe's dislike of Dave, caused by an unintended childhood humiliation at the hands of Robicheaux's father; and by moving Vietnam to the background of his narrative. Meanwhile, in *Cimarron Rose*, Burke forsakes Robicheaux for a Texas lawyer, Billy Bob Holland. A welcome and overdue change; that is, until one realises that his new protagonist is just Dave Robicheaux with a law degree. While one is left wondering how much the quality of his writing reflects contractual obligations, Burke has shown that he can produce entertaining and relevant critiques beyond the Reagan–Bush era. Whether he can progress from criticising a political faction to criticising a political system is another matter. Though the real criminals have not disappeared, Burke, writing at a time when a poll-mongering Democrat sits in the White House, has not quite created a narrative that addresses history's latest permutation.

Sara Paretsky

Had she been writing in the pulp culture era, Sara Paretsky might have made an intriguing Gold Medal author. Today, despite her popularity, Paretsky's books, however worthy, fail to measure up to her high-profile packaging and presence in what remains a predominantly male genre. Yet she and the likes of Sue Grafton once heralded a wave of feminist writers who promised to reinvent detective fiction, while critiquing its notion of the detective as hero-investigator.[51] Though now there are numerous female private-eye writers, the genre, despite its possibilities for reinvention, resists overt manipulation. Political though it may be, detective fiction requires complex characterisation and narratives that address the contradictions of everyday reality. Without a warped edge to her writing, Paretsky appears restricted rather than liberated by the detective novel as a form. This has resulted in work less critical, subtle and subversive than female pulp culture predecessors, such as

Dolores Hitchens, Leigh Brackett and Dorothy B. Hughes, who had a more difficult task: to subvert the genre and write for a mass market, a process that often entailed masquerading, in style if not name, as men.

Yet Paretsky has her virtues. Depicting Chicago's geography, demographics and incipient corruption, Paretsky reads her city differently from fellow Chicagoans Nelson Algren, James T. Farrell, Willard Mosley and Eugene Izzi. In updating the city, Paretsky's private-eye, V. I. Warshawski, no matter how predictable she might be, maintains her immigrant working-class perspective and empathy for the dispossessed. And when, in traipsing through the city, she stumbles over state crime, she will follow it to its source. Or so she thinks. After all, precinct captains, corrupt officials and small-time corporate directors are not quite the source of crime, but merely its manifestation. Regarding political corruption and her role as a private-eye in an age of rampant corruption, she says,

> I know working for myself beats a whole roster of other employers I can list. Still, being a private investigator is not the romance of the loner knight that Marlowe and Spenser like to pretend – half the time you're doing some kind of tedious surveillance or spending your day in the Daley Centre checking backgrounds. And a good chunk of the rest of the time goes to selling people on hiring your services. Often not successfully.[52]

Educated at the Chicago Law School, and involved in the underground abortion movement and freedom marches of the 1960s, V. I. is a leftwing feminist, pro-union and pro-choice. In lacking the investigator's usual flaw – though, in a predominantly male genre, being female might be considered as such – she is, in some respects, too good to be true. Yet, given her credentials, V. I. at least has the courage to admit she is often "truly scared".[53] Her fear seems well-founded, for once every novel she finds herself in the local hospital, staying long enough to overcome her passivity and recoup her energy. Then it's back into the fray with no holds barred. Like many detectives, Warshawski demonstrates a masochistic craving for danger. Says her friendly doctor, "I would ask that you not be reckless, Victoria. I would ask it except that you seem to be in love with danger and death. You make life very hard for those who love you."[54] And who does love Warshawski? Having extricated herself from a pre-feminist marriage, Warshawski is unattached and answerable to no one other than a network of women and an elderly man who lives in her apartment building. Consequently, she, like the traditional detective, is independent, yet, unlike the traditional detective, accountable only to a small socially-arranged group of people. An ideal situation, which, if nothing else, makes one aware of the fantasy element in private-eye fiction.

Like many crime writers, Paretsky would like to convince us that her narratives are not artificial constructs. Yet she never does so to the extent of encouraging unwarranted voyeurism. A laudable quality, but one that prevents Paretsky's protagonist from abandoning the moral centre of her fictional universe. Consequently, Warshawski treats the victims of crime with respect and pursues her prey in a dogged manner. So much so that, devoid of imaginative leaps and non-linear pursuits, her investigations are disconcertingly straightforward. Apparently, Warshawski has not yet realised that some crimes are solved by making abstract connections, or, as Scudder points out, by suddenly noticing the missing piece of a puzzle which, when put in place, makes the case cohere. For solving crime, like analysing history, can be a convoluted process, its investigation requiring the investigator to proceed at odd angles and to go off on unpredictable tangents.

Nevertheless, Warshawski maintains that her technique is akin to Julia Childs's cooking method: "Grab a lot of ingredients from the shelves, put them in a pot and stir, and see what happens."[55] Or the unravelling of a sweater:

I used to watch my granny take old sweaters apart so she could use the yarn on something new. She'd start with a shapeless wad, tugging at it here and there until suddenly she'd find the thread that would turn the wad into a long string. I'm hoping Cyrus has the thread.[56]

Because Warshawski and her investigations tend to be one-dimensional, Paretsky's narratives remain unconvincing. With a network of women aiding, if not abetting, the protagonist, those around her contribute little more than moral support. Consequently, Paretsky gives the impression that it is not so much history that has ended, as complexity, mass movements and the possibility of narrative permutation.

Nevertheless, Paretsky's investigations include information that male private-eyes rarely consider. For instance, while wondering what device Elena uses for birth control, V. I. realises the reason for an unannounced visit by her aunt when Warshawski was a child must have been because her mother's sister had been pregnant. Not something a male private-eye would have considered. Moreover, Warshawski, like Robicheaux, moves beyond the street crime, to the front door of corporate criminality. Though despite its violence, it's the former that V. I. prefers:

That's why I like city crime better . . . Someone bonks you on the head and steals your purse. They don't sit in boardrooms raving about the niggers in Chicago while they're sliding a million or two off the top from the company.[57]

As she monitors the culture, V. I. reminds us that, despite changing attitudes, she is still handicapped by working in a profession dominated by men:

Because I'm a woman in a man's business people think I'm tough, but a truly tough and decisive person would have headed back to town at that point. Instead I felt the tired old tentacles of responsibility drape themselves around me.[58]

Yet being female does not stop her from handing out some fairly rough justice. When a company's cover-up regarding chemical toxins almost results in the murder of her friend, V. I. becomes so outraged that, like Mike Hammer's lost cousin, she shoots the villain and attacks his elderly accomplice:

> Chigwell had stood next to Louisa's stretcher throughout the fracas, his hands flaccidly at his side, his head hunched into his coat. I went over to him and slapped his face. I meant it at first just to rouse him from his stupor, but my rage was consuming me so that I found myself pounding him over and over, screaming at him that he was a traitor to his oath, a miserable worm of a man, on and on, over and over.[59]

Reminding the reader that she cannot stop making investigations, she tells a client who wants her to halt her investigation that she is "not a blender"[60] that can be turned on and off. Consequently, she goes wherever her investigations take her, whether into the inner workings of the state or into the personal lives of the victims and perpetrators of crime. Yet, in the end, there is something that doesn't ring true about Paretsky's narratives. One suspects this is because she insists on following in Chandler's footsteps. In doing so, Paretsky seems to have accepted the myth of the private-eye as errant knight without any sense of obsession, satire or revisionism.

If anything, Paretsky's overly neat narratives fail to acknowledge that V. I. might have a dark side to her nature. As it stands, Warshawski's only idiosyncrasy is her compulsion to investigate regardless of what she might uncover. Yet her insistence in *Burn Marks* that politics, feminism and friendship do not excuse criminal activity indicates that Paretsky, like Burke, could afford to occasionally forget their soft-centred critique. For Paretsky's sense of morality creates its own narrative dynamic, while her politics are not all that radical, nor interesting enough to sustain her exposés. In the end, Paretsky's narratives drag history to a place in which progress is unnecessarily linear, and the culture is encapsulated to avoid morbidity, much less any impending catastrophe.

Gar Anthony Haywood

Setting his work in South Central Los Angeles, Gar Haywood has created a series of novels featuring African-American detective Aaron Gunner. An army veteran who once hoped to be a police officer, Gunner remains one of the more anonymous operatives in crime fiction. Bald, short, and overweight, Gunner, looking in the mirror, "thought of himself as an old man getting older".[61] Though, as the omniscient narrator points out,

> Gunner was not an old man, but his was a face of charm worn
> down by thirty-four years of exhaustion, a handsome
> parchment of flesh he carried like a ledger filled with dreams
> that had died hard and hopes never coaxed off the ground.[62]

Regarding Gunner's realistic and non-macho attitude to the rough-and-tumble of the job, one notes with some relief that "It had taken Gunner over a week of seclusion to convince himself that his manhood was not worth fighting for, that his pride was a luxury he could easily do without."[63]

Though the reader learns about Gunner's background in the first novel, *Fear of the Dark*, Haywood supplies less information as time moves on. Writing in the third person, he leaves the politics and polemics to those who cross Gunner's path. After all, for Gunner, "Introspection, as always, was a walk down the road to nowhere."[64] Consequently, incisive perceptions often come from unlikely quarters. Says a member of the LAPD Community Resource Programme:

> "Take one kid, male. Put him in a fatherless family of eight
> that lives in a two-bedroom bungalow full of roaches and bad
> plumbing. Give his mother a problem with the bottle and a

tenth-grade education, and send him to a school where the books are eleven years old and the teachers are too preoccupied with the prospect of getting shot to teach anybody anything. Give him a college-educated brother who can't afford to buy a two-bedroom home in Lynwood and then move a gold-laden, Four-fifty SL-driving crack dealer into the house next door. What you got, inevitably? Somebody that learns fast not to give a shit about tomorrow, that's what. A turned-off, tuned-out, full-fledged illiterate dying to take his dead-end future out on the whole goddamn world."[65]

Given the history of racism within the Los Angeles police force, few would question the reasons prompting Gunner to leave the department. The fact is, he was booted out of the Police Academy for punching an over-zealous defence instructor. However, in hearing why he wanted to be a cop, the reader can glean something of Gunner's politics:

He had no hang-up regarding power of the life-and-death variety; by the first month of a year-long stint in Vietnam almost seventeen years ago, he had killed enough people in the interests of "duty" to grow tired of the thrill forever. And as for the law itself, he was less than enamored by its credibility. Crime and punishment was a fine concept, perhaps, but in the real world he had never seen it work indiscriminately, which was to say he had never seen it work at all.[66]

While he seeks a sense of identity and a specific role in the "free-for-all that was civilian life", Gunner, having grown up in an era of African-American militancy, finds himself in a world where politics has been stripped of meaning:

He was living in an age in which conviction to causes was out of vogue and apathy was often confused with open-mindedness. If people took sides at all, they didn't talk about it, an abstention that left the world virtually impossible to dissect into finite philosophical factions. The only line drawn between men that remained indelible was the law. Corruption was blurring that line more every day – money *did* talk, and everyone, it so often appeared, was listening.[67]

Underestimating himself and his job, Gunner begins by maintaining that it's money rather than scruples that motivate him. Nevertheless, he is able to deliver a cogent critique regarding racism, the brutality of the free market and the failure of trickle-down economics. When a white policeman, paraphrasing LA's former chief of the DA's Hardcore Drug Unit, maintains that the black community hates the police as much as the Vietnamese hated American soldiers, Gunner tells him he's wrong: "I think you're confusing hatred with fear . . . These people are too busy being afraid of you to hate you . . . You've got them scared shitless."[68]

Certainly, Gunner is no cliché-ridden soul brother, for Haywood refuses to romanticise or stereotype his subjects:

Being made to feel answerable to the whole of one's own race was a burden few white men ever had to shoulder, yet it was a black man's birthright from day one. To wander off too far from the beaten path of conformity, daring to expand upon what some people insisted were the unalterable parameters of "blackness," was to purchase the guilt of treason, and for some that guilt could be so incessant as to be crippling. Gunner himself was no such victim, but he had felt the sting of the phenomenon more than once, enough to know its symptoms when he saw them.[69]

Given his pursuit of reality, Gunner's investigations invariably entail a personal awakening, one which reconciles law, order, and the rights of those living within the community. After all, Haywood is concerned with how society is constituted, and the ability of people to exist together, without sacrificing their self-respect: "Someday . . . the LAPD and the Black community would find a way to break the vicious cycle that was pulling them further and further apart . . . All the finger pointing would stop and the healing process would begin. It was not inconceivable."[70] Despite Gunner's humanitarianism, he knows that one person – whether cop or private-eye – can do little to change the system. Though his novels are critiques of Reaganism – "The greatest damage that he has done is to repopularize the approach to American capitalism that says . . . that in the interests of free enterprise you can go ahead and discriminate as you see fit."[71] – Haywood's work has moved beyond the 1980s, into the Clinton era, and a new type of corruption. Demonstrating a harder edge than Walter Mosley, and without the latter's penchant for confusing the mean streets with memory lane, Haywood is too political to be Clinton's favourite writer.

Nor is Haywood likely to sacrifice realism for literary acceptability. With a constantly evolving narrative, Haywood's novels are about the politicalisation of ordinary people. Gradually, Gunner arrives, in *Not Long for This World*, at an understanding regarding the reasons young blacks join gangs. Appreciating their despair, he realises what it means to be a gang member and part of a closely-knit community. Or as Mike Davis says, regarding the Crips, "the power resource of last resort".[72] In doing so, Gunner begins to regain a degree of self-respect. While at the beginning of the novel, Gunner says, regarding his investigation, "[To] do the job right, I'm going to have to get knee-deep in this gangbanging bullshit . . . and I can't stand the view of it I already have."[73] He ends the novel in the following way:

> Deliberately, he thought about drive-bys and baby-faced wannabes, killers without conscience, making hand signals for TV cameras, and walls and fences obliterated by overlapping layers of prideful, grotesque graffiti. He thought about crack and PCP, shotguns and Uzis and AK-47s, scars across beautiful throats and heavy black bellies – in short every bleak, soul-crushing, and heartbreaking aspect of the LA street-gang culture he could possibly imagine.
>
> And still, the pure, uncomplicated abhorrence he had once known for gangbanging would not come.

In circumstances less than ideal, an understanding of the present allows Gunner to comprehend a historical process and, in doing so, become part of a community from which he has been estranged.

Though they might lack the obsessiveness and skewed narrative drive that marks the work of other noirists, Haywood's fiction concerns the relationship between the individual and society. Willing to alter his perspective should it conflict with reality, Gunner moves from pessimism regarding the future to a guarded optimism. As documents of the late twentieth century, Haywood's fiction addresses present day problems with an urgency rarely found in contemporary detective fiction.

Walter Mosley

Though writing about the past, Walter Mosley's fiction invariably refers to the present, particularly the interregnum separating the Reagan–Bush era from that which would follow. The author of a series of evocative novels that recount the lost narrative of black Los Angeles from the late 1940s to the early 1960s, Mosley occupies the other side of the coin from his LA counterpart, James Ellroy. Less manic, less extreme, less fanciful, and, strangely enough, less overtly political than the demon dog of Los Angeles noir, Mosley, with his ambivalent protagonist, Easy Rawlins, constructs straightforward narratives centred on the street life and barroom jive of a Los Angeles that, until recently, had been erased from public memory. In a line of African-American writers that includes Chester Himes, Iceberg Slim, Clarence Cooper Jr, and Herbert Simmons, Mosley exploits the nostalgia for an era that, for obvious reasons, exists only in a series of rarely glimpsed artifacts. In depicting a period that has, by and large, escaped historical contextualisation, Mosley submerges his politics within texts whose ambiguity leaves ample space for interpretation.

If not for the hype surrounding his work, one might read Mosley differently. While his acceptability is based on his apparent lack of politics, Mosley – half-African-American and half-Jewish – writes about situations brimming with political content. In allowing ex-GI Easy Rawlins to use his blackness to disclaim involvement, Mosley suggests that, for an African-American in Los Angeles, mere survival might be, in itself, a political act. Heralded as the new Chester Himes, Mosley lacks the former's psychological complexity and bitterness.[74] Demonstrating only a fraction of the anger and paranoia that Himes conveys in *If He Hollers Let Him Go* or *Lonely Crusade*, Mosley is able to communicate a greater appreciation of the dynamics of cross-cultural relationships. However much he is pushed, Easy never relinquishes his humanity, nor allows his circumstances to prevent him from empathising with victims, whether of McCarthyism, the holocaust or racism.

Part of the post-war migration from Texas to Los Angeles, Easy has one overriding desire: to be an ordinary home-owning middle-class citizen. In seeking a space of his own, one in which he and his family can live, Easy is no different from many other new arrivals in the area. But it's only because he pursues this dream, and because he can find no other employment, that Easy becomes an investigator. More concerned with loyalty and friendship than politics, his struggle to avoid becoming another statistic of racial abuse leads to some strange alliances. Thus Easy finds himself on speaking terms with crooks, hustlers, the police, and respectable citizens.

Personifying the difficulties facing African-Americans as they attempt to climb the economic ladder, Easy, realising political posturing might only make his life more difficult, often feigns political ignorance. With a hint of irony, Easy, in *Devil in a Blue Dress*, maintains that, because his friend goes to church, he surely could not be lying. Though trying to remain politically ambiguous, Easy possesses an introspective intelligence. Playing on the difference between *reality* and *real*, he offers his personal critique on the relationship between history and reality:

I didn't believe in history, really. Real was what was happening to me right then. Real was a toothache and a man you trusted who did you dirt. Real was an empty stomach or a woman saying yes, or a woman saying no. Real was what you could feel. History was like TV for me, it wasn't the great wave of mankind moving through an ocean of minutes and hours. It wasn't mankind getting better either; I had seen enough murder in Europe to know that the Nazis were even worse than the barbarians at Rome's gate. And even if I was in Rome they would have called me a barbarian; it was no different that day in Watts.[75]

Quite a perspective, even for 1950. Though being a victim of racism and economic inequality tends to focus one's politics and sense of history. Having struggled for a modicum of protection, Easy knows he no longer has the street-level wherewithal to articulate a political position, or at least not as cogently as his friend Jackson – "[The] closest I ever came to knowing a genius." – who says:

"You got yo' people already hot a hold on sumpin', like money. An' you got yo' people ain't go nuthin' but they want sumpin' in the worst way. So the banker and the corporation man gots it all, an' the workin' man ain't got shit. Now the workin' man have a union to say that it's the worker makes stuff so he should be gettin' the money. That's like com'unism. But the rich man don't like it so he gonna break the worker's back."[76]

When Easy, a veteran of World War Two, comments that they must therefore be on the side of the communists, Jackson warns him off: "You ever hear 'bout the blacklist? . . . It's a list that the rich people got. All kindsa names on it. White people's names . . . An' if they name on it they cain't work." He goes on to tell Easy why neither of their names are likely to appear on that list:

"They don't need yo' name to know you black, Easy. All they gotta do is look at you an' they know that . . . One day they gonna th'ow that list out man . . . Mosta these guys gonna have

work again . . . But you still gonna be a black niggah, Easy. An'
niggah ain't got no union he could count on, an' niggah ain't
got no politician gonna work fo' him. All he got is a do'step
t'shit in and a black hand t'wipe his black ass."[77]

Perhaps Easy isn't apolitical, but merely trying to avoid an
unnecessary confrontation. Nevertheless, Easy's relationship
with the state is double-edged:

I've never really been what you would call a friend to the
LAPD. We were on speaking terms only because they needed
my help from time to time. And also because I used to be fool
enough to put myself in the way when somebody down in the
community was getting the short end of the stick.[78]

Though the latter is spoken some years later, while JFK occupies
the White House and Martin Luther King's career is at its peak,
Mosley writes about a pulp culture world, one which, with
hindsight, is a welcome antidote to Raymond Chandler's
xenophobic view of Los Angeles. While the latter would refer
to South Central as a dangerous and dark place, Mosley portrays
a complex community, one constantly infringed upon, whether
by the likes of Chandler, the LAPD, or white racists. Meanwhile,
Easy's bottom line is his unwillingness to tolerate any kind of
racial abuse. When a redneck calls him "boy", Easy calls him a
"cracker", and says,

I wasn't marching or singing songs about freedom. I didn't
pay dues in the Southern Christian Leadership Conference or
the NAACP. I didn't have any kind of god on my side. But
even though the cameras weren't on me and JFK never heard
my name, I had to make my little stand for what's right. It was
a little piece of history that happened right there in that room
and that went unrecorded.[79]

While, for white culture, the years immediately after World
War Two were a period of increased political militancy and

consumerism, for blacks it meant fewer jobs and an equally racist society. With his ambiguous relationship to the state, and dubious role as a landlord, Easy moves through the post-war years and various cultural shifts, including the paranoia of McCarthyism, the apathy of the Eisenhower years, and the optimism of the New Frontier. Though, as Jackson points out, McCarthyism affected few African-Americans – unless, of course, they happened to be politically active – these cultural shifts would still be felt in the black community, influencing activities and providing a backdrop to Easy's investigations.

Moving backwards to go forwards, Mosley implies that history is a mixed blessing. On the one hand, it appears to have no end, while, on the other hand, as the descendant of slaves, it has the most precarious of beginnings. Being part-Jewish and part-African-American has left Mosley with a twice-fractured sense of history, and an interesting relationship to the past. Though in Easy's world, cause and effect originate in distant sites of power, the telling of his story leads to a different reading of history, and hints at future cultural alliances and shifts. With an anger that is always simmering under the surface, Easy's edgy attitude is tinged with humour and humanity. Significantly, Mosley's books end with Easy reaching some kind of reconciliation with the world. As he says in *A Little Yellow Dog*, "I felt as if I was an astronaut who had completed his orbit of the earth and now I was pulled by some new gravity into a clean cold darkness."[80]

James Sallis

James Sallis's 1992 *The Long-Legged Fly* is the first in a series of highly original private-eye novels featuring African-American and New Orleans freelancer Lew Griffin. Having killed a man in the opening pages of the novel, Griffin's reputation sweeps through the city, leading him to make alliances with cops as well as criminals. With a poet's heart, Sallis's investigator uses his knowledge of the streets to become not only a debt collector

and private-eye, but, fluent in Louisiana French, a part-time
university lecturer in French literature, and, finally, a writer of
detective fiction. Though it sounds far-fetched, Sallis, a former
writer of science fiction, portrays Griffin's transformation and
multi-faceted existence with skill and subtlety.

Another former alcoholic, Griffin is involved in his own
private recovery programme comprised, on the one hand, of
meting out revenge and, on the other, of accommodating
kindred spirits. No ex-cop, Griffin, whose debt collecting technique is such that he often gives money to those he is meant to
collect from, is not averse to taking the law into his own hands.
Most intriguing of all, Griffin litters his investigative path with
references to writers – Thomas Bernhard, George Perec,
Raymond Queneau, Albert Camus, Chester Himes – who, for
the most part, do not write crime fiction. In creating a character
with diverse interests and depth, Sallis qualifies as one of the
few recent writers to add something new to the genre of
detective fiction.

Sallis's narrative also suggests a historical process in which
linearity exists only in micro-narrative units. With stories pasted
together for the sake of their internal rhythm and mood rather
than for the sake of narrative development, the direction of a
typical Sallis novel defies detection. True to his aesthetics, the
author balks when it comes to connecting the disparate strands
that comprise his fiction. As Sallis says, "When I read crime
fiction and detective stories, I read for the atmosphere and the
voice. I could care less about plot."[81] Meanwhile, a chance
meeting or thought might result in a previously unforeseen
narrative diversion and conclusion. For instance, *The Long-
Legged Fly* begins in 1964, with Griffin's infamous crime, moves
to 1970 and 1984 before ending in 1990 with the disappearance
of Griffin's son. Interestingly enough, after three novels, the
son's disappearance has been neither explained nor resolved.

Basing his narrative on association, Sallis can warp time
until it seems to bend back on itself. In a typical Lew Griffin
novel, the narrative is comprised of "setting up the expectations

of genre literature, and . . . standing them on their head".[82] So, in the opening pages of *Moth*, one locates the shell of the novel: Griffin's former girlfriend is dead, her daughter has become a drug addict who has given birth to a crack baby. But that narrative leads to other narratives. Implied in this is the notion that events, ideas, history, and existence do not proceed in a straightforward manner, and that fiction, as a form, can create as much as replicate reality.

In keeping with his concept of the novel-as-artifice, Sallis, a white man writing about a black protagonist[83] – purposely crosses cultures. Says Sallis,

> I had intended him to kill somebody . . . and spend the rest of the story making him human . . . I was 20 or 30 pages in before I realised he was black. Not only black, he's a black man who has tried, albeit inchoately, to turn himself into a white man, to live up to white values, at various times in his life. And they always collapse on him.[84]

In a nice twist, Sallis ends *The Long-Legged Fly* with Lew Griffin, in bed with concussion and cracked ribs, having already written his first novel, entitled *Skull Meat*, about a Cajun detective. What's more, he's eighty pages into his second novel, *The Severed Hand*. The latter book features, according to Griffin, a character based on the one-armed French surrealist writer Blaise Cendars. By now, the reader must surely have realised that nothing in a Sallis novel can be taken at face value. Moreover, Griffin has also written a novel called *The Long-Legged Fly*. But his version ends with the author forsaking his Cajun investigator for another fictional private-eye, named, not surprisingly, Lew Griffin, before segueing into Sallis's next novel, *Moth*. This even though Griffin, in *The Long-Legged Fly*, insists his next novel is *Black Hornet*, which, in reality, is Sallis's third novel. Countering the expository cliché of numerous detective novels, and establishing the artifice of the narrative, *Moth* begins with the same sentences with which Griffin ends

The Long-Legged Fly: "It is midnight. It is not raining."[85] Suddenly, the reader realises Lew Griffin has made up the entire narrative. Or has he? As Sallis says, "If you're not aware that you're being told a story, that it's artifice, then where have you been for the past forty years? That's what fiction has been doing."[86]

In *Moth*, Griffin, flitting between academia and the mean streets, puts forth his thoughts on the novel and history. After delivering a lecture on Queneau's *Zazie Dans le Metro* to his class at the university, the dean – or could it be merely that his name is Dean? – suggests to Griffin that life is comprised of conjunctions. Griffin replies, "More like punctuation, I think. Colons and exclamations for some, dashes for the rest."[87] In another instance, Griffin tells his students that time is always the novel's true protagonist. Though he's talking about novels in general, he could be talking about this novel in particular, one that Griffin-as-Sallis-as-Griffin has evidently written. Later, wanting to have his literary cake and eat it too, Griffin lambasts a critic who, in refusing to note the artifice of the genre, claims that *Black Hornet* is merely a record of the author's personal failures. This gives pause for thought: perhaps Griffin's claim that the latter is his third published novel is true, even if he is making the claim in a novel that Sallis, not Griffin, has written. Maybe this is just another time-warp – the result of Sallis's fascination with *Oulipo* writers like Perec and Queneau[88] – or a suggestion that the Griffin version exists in some future, as yet unwritten, text. Or perhaps it's just that, for Sallis, it is always midnight, a time for tall tales as well as home truths.

By the publication – in the real as well as fictional world – of *Black Hornet*, Griffin has become, like Sallis, an established writer of detective fiction. Though perhaps the slightest of Sallis's novels, it, even more than his past novels, concerns African-American politics. Here Griffin recalls meeting Chester Himes, whose ghostly presence influences the book. In fact, Himes has been a major influence on Sallis, to the point that Griffin's predicament is partly based on the plight facing Jesse, the protagonist in Himes's novel *The Primitive*. Likewise, Sallis compares Griffin and Himes:

> Like Chester, he's not really politicised. Chester is extremely apathetic; like Lew, he let decisions be made for him again and again, because he wouldn't act. This is where a lot of the rage comes from.[89]

As though revising his statement in *Moth*, Griffin, quoting himself, explicates his concept of history and his approach to the detective novel:

> Someone once said life is all conjunctions, just one damn thing after another. But so much of it is not connected. You're sliding along, hit a bump and come down in a life you don't recognise. Every day you head out a dozen different directions, become a dozen different people; some of them make it back home that night, others don't.[90]

Meanwhile, Sallis, reading Juan Goytisolo's *Realms of Strife* during a dark night of the soul, contemplates the relationship between memory, history and the narrative. He might as well be talking about his own fiction:

> Memory, Goytisolo writes . . . cannot arrest the flow of time. It can only . . . encapsulate privileged moments, arrange memories and incidents in some arbitrary manner that, word by word, will form a book. The unbridgeable distance between act and language, the demands of the written text . . . , inevitably and insidiously degrade faithfulness to reality into . . . artistic exercise, sincerity into mere virtuosity, moral rigor into aesthetics. Endowed with later coherence, bolstered with . . . continuities of plot and resonance, our reconstructions of the past will always be a kind of betrayal.[91]

But, for Griffin, there is no silence. Truth, coherence, and history: these are the themes that matter to him. Though in less capable hands these novels would be unbearably pretentious,

Sallis, influenced by crime novelists, poets and writers of speculative fiction, remains wedded to artifice, literature, politics, and investigation. One has to admire Sallis's seriousness as much as his playfulness, as he attempts to alter the genre, stretching its boundaries as few others have done. Caught between trying to engage his readers and conveying the notion that they are involved in a literary act, Sallis, well-versed in the history of pulp literature and the author of an excellent study of Goodis, Thompson and Himes, must,[92] if his novels are to work, distance himself from the novel as a literary product, yet sustain the narrative by maintaining its element of suspense. Not an easy task in any genre, but particularly difficult in one filled with so many structural demands. More than most crime writers, Sallis demands something extra from the reader:

> Popular literature and popular art says that everything you believe is correct – you're a good boy for believing it. Real art says, as Rimbaud said, everything we are taught is false. Everything you believe isn't correct, and probably isn't even nearly correct, and why don't we think about that for a while.[93]

Still reluctantly courting linearity, Sallis's investigations are as original as they are incomplete. Involved in a process that is never less than thrilling, Sallis's fiction is as much a response to the notion that history has many angles, as to the belief that it is dead, or that, bereft of politics, private investigation is all that remains.

George P. Pelecanos

While Sallis deals with the relationship between time and history, George P. Pelecanos explores how the memory of the past can affect the present. His favourite protagonist and alter-ego is Nick Stefanos, an investigator whose personality and character deficiencies make him no different from those who read Pelecanos's fiction. While Griffin moves between high and low culture, listening to Cajun music and Delta blues, Stefanos maintains a predominantly low culture existence, working in bars and on showroom floors, listening to anything from New Wave bands to jazz. So compulsive a music listener is Stefanos that one could easily plot his emotional life by listing the music he plays. Both investigators drink and have problems with women. However, unlike Griffin, Stefanos has no desire to give up drinking. This and his refusal to be deluded by religion are, in an age of overly moral detectives, refreshing attributes. In fact, Stefanos's alcoholism and de facto atheism become major factors in his ability to investigate the culture and find the relevant crime.

Stefanos first becomes a private investigator in *A Firing Offense*, but only after he is relieved of his job at an electronic outfit called Nutty Nathan's. Yet, as a private investigator, he, like so many others in the post-Reagan era, remains only sporadically employed. Though he possesses some romantic notions about the downtrodden, Pelecanos never glamorises Nick's new position. After all, Pelecanos is quite specific regarding the artifice of the genre:

> When you read a hardboiled novel and it's not real you can
> tell right away. I can't abide by a guy who has a few shots of
> whiskey every night and then gets up and benches 400 pounds
> and goes and sees his luscious blond girlfriend. Drinking
> straight whiskey every night, you got a problem, man. A
> problem in all aspects of your life. What I try to do is create a
> guy who stays within those conventions in that he's a protector
> of society, yet could never really fit into it.[94]

It follows that Pelecanos avoids the stylistic excesses found in other writers of crime fiction. While, on the surface, his fiction might resemble that of Walter Mosley, the difference between them is one of historical context. While Mosley is immersed in the past, rewriting its narrative by filtering it through his cultural perspective, Pelecanos, like Haywood, stalks the present, finding space within its interstices to hammer out a hard-edged prose that is almost, but never totally, bereft of sentimentality.

When he does delve into the past, Pelecanos does so with a beguiling sense of nostalgia. As a character in *Nick's Trip* says, "It's easy to confuse being in love with just lovin' the memory of a certain time. A certain time in your life, I mean. When anything's possible, all the shit's out in front of you. Before the world beats you down."[95] Here a sense of nostalgia is essential to the narrative, for Pelecanos's fiction invariably concerns past relationships and their betrayal. As Nick says to Billy, his old high school friend, who hires him to track down his wife, whom he already knows is dead, "Our friendship – any friendship – it's the only thing that sticks. Everything rots, but that's always supposed to be there. You used it, man. You ruined it."[96]

Written in the first person, Pelecanos's novels utilise a cinematic technique that stops short of revealing every thought or plan of action. Unlike Lawrence Block's Matt Scudder, Stefanos does not automatically regard the reader as his confidant. Thus one is never sure when an apparently calm barroom scene will erupt into violence. Or in *Nick's Trip*, why, when matters seem to have been concluded, Nick telephones Billy to say that it's time they "settled up".[97]

Likewise, the reader can seldom discern how Pelecanos's novels will proceed. Occupying an almost believable present, *Down by the River Where the Dead Men Go* begins ominously, as though Stefanos's battle with the bottle will be his eventual undoing:

> Like most of the trouble that's happened in my life or that I've caused to happen, the trouble that happened that night started with a drink. Nobody forced my hand; I poured it myself, two fingers of bourbon into a heavy, beveled shot glass. There were many more after that . . . But it was the first one that led me down to the river that night, where they killed a boy named Calvin Jeter.[98]

Taking responsibility for his actions, Stefanos's drinking leads
him to some precarious places; and disperses his personality
enough to let him rethink who he is and where he is going.
Recovering from a blackout, a still drunk Stefanos finds himself
in his car:

> My wallet lay flat and open on the shotgun bucket. I picked it
> up, looked at my own face staring out at me from my District
> of Columbia license: 'Nicolas J. Stefanos, Private Investigator.
> So *that's* what I was.
> I turned the key in the ignition.[99]

It's drinking that pushes Stefanos to a place where, in *Down by
the River . . .* , he witnesses the crime. Other than its numbing
effect, alcohol allows him to find a place from which he can
view the culture.

Though he tries adjusting to cultural change, Nick would be
the first to admit that, though no sinner, he is no saint. And
when it comes to women, Stefanos's attitude is sometimes
suspect. He demonstrates this in *Down by the River . . .* , not so
much in meaningless sexual encounters as in the way he splits
up with his girlfriend. Because he does not want to stop drinking, nor stop her from not drinking, he decides to dump Lyla,
but this he does only after speaking to her father. Unfortunately,
Lyla, only slightly more of an alcoholic than Nick, has little say
in the matter. Nor does Nick see anything wrong in the two
men deciding her fate. Somewhat retrograde, particularly since
Stefanos, in a reference to his fathering a child with his lesbian
friend, Jackie, had, earlier in the novel, shrugged off a jibe
about his status as a spermbank donor.

Certainly, Nick would not be the first inner-city, working-
class male to have a problem when it comes to sustaining a
relationship with a woman. But at least he's aware of the
problem, and tries to deal with it. Regarding his relationship
with Jackie, Nick says, "As our friendship developed I began to
pat myself on the back for finally having a close relationship

with a woman that didn't involve sex. It had only taken me three and a half decades to learn."[100] He also has a non-sexual relationship with Anna, his co-worker at The Spot whom he corrupts in two ways: by introducing her to La Duke, a feisty investigator destined to inhabit the shadows of the novel; and, a deft hand with a cigarette lighter, by encouraging her to smoke more than is good for her. With the porno ring broken, Stefanos ends the novel by saying, "I lit a cigarette. I had my drink. This one started at the Spot."[101] One can only surmise that, after the fall of communism, smoking, drinking and atheism are the most subversive, if not romantic, things going. Yet, in staying within the confines of the genre, Pelecanos offers an accurate and appropriate response to the corruptions and tough-love of the Clinton era.

While he manages to convey the violence of everyday life – "It's amazing to me why there's not more random violence out there on the streets."[102] – Pelecanos has a sharp, and even slapstick, sense of humour, something which many crime writers, however much they strain for a wisecrack, lack. For instance, when Stefanos and his friends visit the porno film-maker in *Down by the River* . . . , each adopts a different guise, getting into their roles to such a degree that they lose themselves within them. And, in *Nick's Trip*, when Stefanos tries to find out about two hoods that have murdered his friend:

"What are they into? Organized gambling?"
   DiGeordano chuckled. "Not too organized, from what I hear. As far as bookmaking goes, they don't know shit from apple butter . . . "
   " . . . They moved their shops near a string of pizza parlors called the Pie Shack, and every one of the Pie Shacks got burned out. That can't be a coincidence."
   "It's not," he said. "But arson's not their source of income. Neither is gambling."
   "What is, then?"
   DiGeordano said, "Pizza . . . Gambling is their kick, and the business end of it just covers their losses. No drugs,

prostitution, nothing like that – just a bunch of hoods selling pizza."[103]

Taking a different tack, Pelecanos's 1994 *Shoedog* is firmly in the pulp culture tradition. Also about betrayal, it centres on Constantine, whose "strengths . . . his lack of emotion, the absence of a moral center – . . . made him a dangerous man."[104] With "two weird eyes that don't give two shits about nothin' " he hitches a ride with a man who involves the protagonist in an armed robbery. Having spent the last seventeen years abroad, Constantine, a typical alienated anti-hero, moves relentlessly towards his fate. As a loner who finds it difficult to sustain any kind of relationship – visiting an old girlfriend, he ends up raping her – Constantine finds, amongst the small band of crooks, a degree of friendship and mutual trust. At the same time, mirroring most work situations, Constantine develops an instant antipathy for the boss, a wealthy man who entraps those around him into committing crimes, from which he demands an unfair percentage of the profits.

The Big Blowdown, published in 1996, is unlike anything else Pelecanos has published. Bearing little similarity to the hard-boiled style of *Shoedog*, it amplifies the various Nick Stefanos novels. Though there is a character named Nick Stefanos in *The Big Blowdown*, this is not the Nick Stefanos of Pelecanos's previous books, but the private investigator's grandfather. In fact, the story of *The Big Blowdown* is previewed in *Down by the River* . . . when Nick visits his uncle – who isn't his uncle, but Costa, Big Nick's old bar-assistant. Regardless of the lineage of the two books, *The Big Blowdown* is a coming-of-age narrative about working-class life, one which begins in the recent past before moving backwards and forwards, to cover some thirty years in the lives of a group of men in Washington DC. Eventually centring on big Nick Stefanos and his tavern, *The Big Blowdown*, though written in the third person, gives the impression that young Nick Stefanos might be narrating the story. In doing this, Pelecanos uses the past to explain the present, and so provides background information regarding Nick's future peccadilloes regarding women, alcohol, his family, and the investigatory process.[105]

Pelecanos's most literary novel, *The Big Blowdown* turns into a cataclysmic confrontation between friends and enemies. But the title is also a reference to the atomic bomb, which pre-occupies Karras's girlfriend. Karras, a young Greek whose leg has been mangled by gangsters, tells Vera that dropping the bomb on Japan ended the war and saved countless lives, but he too, in his darker moments, ruminates on its meaning:

> And for a moment . . . through the clearing of the steamed window, he began to visualize this thing that Vera spoke of, this maelstrom of sound and flesh and architecture, hurtling toward him in one screaming, final rush. And for that one crazy moment, Karras had the peculiar wish to see this blowdown for himself. He knew with certainty that it might be pure and absolute horror. But he had the feeling that it could be something beautiful, too.[106]

Here Big Nick Stefanos is more a reference point than a protagonist. His bar becomes the spot to which the narrative moves, from which time the world will never be the same. In the final chapter, young Nick Stefanos appears riding in a car driven by his grandfather. He's listening to Elvis Presley. A new era is about to begin, and history has been kick-started into an already dangerous future.

Conclusion: One Man's Case is Another Man's Crime

The value of detective fiction lies in the fact that, regardless of the genre's tendency towards over-production, its narratives constitute a historical contour at street-level. Based on a tension between falsification and truth, power and powerlessness, the private-eye narrative searches for cracks in America's historical fabric, from which point it can locate places, stories and situations. Investigating the culture, these narratives move between micro and macro. This means that private-eye narratives can, if successful, bridge state and local crime, just as they can move from the personal to the political. As socio-historian, Perry Anderson, writes,

> Critical knowledge is to be found, not in the vain filibuster of macro-narratives, but in the modest commonplace books of the multitude – whose measure of freedom and responsibility is the only safeguard against the dangers which the diviners of post-history saw, as well as those they missed.[107]

For "commonplace books" – including, of course, detective fiction – reveal the cultural narrative and fabric of history at ground-level.

That detective fiction suggests a retrograde literary pursuit is its strength and its weakness. Written, for the most part, by those whose politics derive from concerns about the future, these texts necessarily address such finalities as the purported end of history, the corruption of ideology, the failure of meaning and various social conditions and issues associated with the coming of the millennium. Moreover, they look back on an age that, despite its promise, was tarnished from the start. Many of these writers might have been considered conservative, if not anachronistic, even in the 1960s, but, by locating the cultural crimes and by articulating the relevant signs, they discern a typically dystopic world, and an effective mode of attack. These are the parameters of the new investigation. Yet, as Anderson has pointed out, many have already arrived at:

> [Something] like a collective vision – glimpsed from many angles – of a stalled, exhausted world, dominated by recursive mechanisms of bureaucracy and ubiquitous circuits of commodities, relieved only by the extravagances of a phantasmic imaginary without limit, because without power. In

a post-historical society, "the rulers have ceased to rule, but the slaves remain slaves."[108]

The community of investigation continues simply because, at this point in time, there are few places left for the imagination to wander.

This and the urban environment – cracked, depleted, devastated and ruined – is that to which contemporary detective fiction addresses itself. Yet even though the investigation has yet to take place, the story has already been written, and, metaphorically speaking, can be located in other volumes. Likewise, the malaise remains displaced:

> For all the deliverance it brings, however, the conclusion of
> the story of human freedom has its costs. Daring ideals, high
> sacrifices, heroic strivings will pass away, amidst the humdrum
> routines of shopping and voting; art and philosophy wither, as
> culture is reduced to the curation of the past; technical
> calculations replace moral or political imagination. The cry of
> the owl is mournful in the night.[109]

Yet the crimes continue. And within the crevices, the bunkers and the warzones, the investigations which move between the public and the private, have become, since Reagan, as deregulated as they are excessive. Thus the genre strives to move backwards into the future.

5

EXTREMISTS IN PURSUIT OF VICE

An investigation of deregulated crime fiction: K. C. Constantine, Elmore Leonard, James Ellroy, Andrew Coburn, Andrew Vachss, Jim Nisbet, Daniel Woodrell and Vicki Hendricks

An overt display – at least as far as crime fiction is concerned – of political criticism, K. C. Constantine's *Cranks and Shadows*, published in 1995, examines the economic crimes of the Reagan–Bush era; specifically, the conditions produced by the era's obsession with deregulation and privatisation. Using a pseudonym – this is one author who opts for anonymity – Constantine, writing since the 1970s, begins his narrative in the following way: "But when President Reagan's economic policies began to trickle down to Rocksburg in the early 1980s, the usual rumors that had warmed up that election turned into something cold with a speed that jolted even the most cynical city employees."[1] A bold first sentence for a crime writer. As are the words of Rocksburg's mayor who, in the opening scene, tells Mario Balzic, the town's chief of police and the Serbo-Italian protagonist of numerous Constantine novels, that jobs in the police department will have to be cut. The mayor, claiming his decision has been prompted by national politics, lays the blame on past policy makers:

> "These presidents all talk a great game, Reagan, Bush and I have to include Carter in this too, because he came waltzing in there . . . talking about how it's Washington's fault and you just have to cut out waste and deregulate this and deregulate that and my god, who can't see how all that deregulation that

Carter started got us. You can lay the S&L mess right on
Carter's doorstep, I mean it took the thieves a couple years to
figure out what to do, and they just had a picnic under
Reagan."[2]

A portrayal of an ordinary working-class community,
Constantine's scathing attack on Reaganomics details the
extremes to which people are affected by public policies and
economic austerity. As such policies begin to bite, the citizens
of Rocksburg become increasingly edgy, their powerlessness
leading to situations both comical and dangerous. This becomes
apparent when the unemployed and eccentric Pete Christoloski
suddenly snaps. Taking his wife hostage, he refuses to untie her
until Balzic fills his prescription, gets rid of the newly privatised
rapid-response team that, unbeknownst to Balzic, has sur-
rounded his house and listens to his complaints regarding the
state of society. Tired of his wife belittling his lack of education,
and frustrated that his suggestions regarding the improvement
of Rocksburg have been ignored, Christoloski simply wants his
opinions to be taken seriously.

Balzic goes on to visit a number of Rocksburgians, only to
discover that each has an unsolicited opinion to express. It's
like the *Invasion of the Body Snatchers* in reverse, as the citizens
of Rocksburg suddenly realise the extent of their political
marginalisation. So powerless are they that Rocksburgians can
now be divided into two types: *cranks and shadows*. That is,
those whose opinions have become more extreme and eccentric
in direct proportion to their marginalisation; and those who
make deals, find loopholes and profit from deregulatory
policies.

The mayor, too honest to have much of a political future, is
not far wrong in his analysis. After all, Reaganism is said to
have begun during the Carter administration[3] when, in 1978, a
Congress two-thirds controlled by the Democrats endorsed the
President's legislative agenda – one that had been approved by
the Business Roundtable – that included a freeze on social

spending; higher interest rates; deregulating the airlines; and the partial deregulation of gas and oil prices, electric power generation, trucking, railroads, telephone equipment and banking. So Carter – "One of my administration's major goals is to free the American people from the burden of over-regulation"[4] – laid the groundwork for Reagan who, once in office, froze pending regulatory orders, attacked regulatory budgets, and appointed deregulators to head the Council of Economic Advisers and other agencies.[5]

Town crackpot Christoloski pinpoints the moment when Reagan's deregulatory programme became a political sledge-hammer:

> "But you know something had to change when them flight controllers went out and not even the damn pilots went out in sympathy. That's when I knew something was changed in America, and then that TV cowboy fired all those controllers and nobody made a peep – nobody!"

As for deregulation, Pete says,

> "Every chance [Pennsylvania steel companies] had to set up a mill in another country where they paid coolie wages, they done it. And they go on TV and they look you straight in the face and they try to tell you they're in com-pee-ti-tion with us."[6]

Naturally, when Rocksburgians feel the economic pinch, the town's silent majority cease to be quite so silent. Moreover, their reaction is indicative of the extent to which their opinions have gone unsolicited. Yet once Rocksburgians speak out, they demonstrate an intelligence that politicians and pundits invariably lack. As Pete goes on to say,

> "Those guys in golf carts, they need the commies. Man, they have to have 'em. Those commies, they justify everything these rich bastards . . . do . . . Build a steel mill in Korea, huh? That was to keep Korea safe from the commies. Piss on the three

thousand guys they put on the streets in Pittsburgh. And then the sonsabitches tell ya we can't compete 'cause the Koreans only pay their labor about a buck an hour."[7]

Though the deregulatory environment of the 1980s would comprise the background to crime novels by the likes of Carl Hiassen, Eugene Izzi and Andrew Vachss, there would be a dearth of narratives concerning specific deregulatory crimes, such as the notorious Savings and Loan scandal.[8] Whether schooled on the streets or on the cutting edge of investigative journalism, crime writers preferred to describe the general political atmosphere. Yet, as sleaze threatened to cause the collapse of the financial system, it would be difficult to ignore the dangers posed by deregulation.[9]

While deregulatory policies[10] relate to short-term profits, privatisation, rediscovered when business interests find it advantageous to liquidate publicly owned assets and demobilise state functions, is invariably explained in terms of efficiency. Rocksburg too has had its share of sell-offs, including the Tax Bureau, which, as a privatised company, now sells its services to local government agencies and schools.

However, there are few complaints, for most Rocksburgians, estranged from local government, are unaware that such policies exist. Nor do many know about the machinations that insured their implementation. Not even Chief Balzic, a man who prefers to stay clear of politics, can say when the decision to privatise tax collection was made. When he realises the seriousness of the situation, it is already too late:

> "I been thinkin' that everything I ever knew about this
> country, and who protects who and why and how, is . . . not
> what I think it is – or was . . . And the part that gets me, is that
> it's all legal . . . I mean, once the IRS gives 'em their blessing
> for an exemption from taxes, hey, they're home free. It's us
> saps, us schnooks that pay the taxes. And us schnooks – me,
> guys like me – we protect the bastards."[11]

Balzic is left fighting a rearguard action. When he argues against the privatisation of the police force, the mayor asks Balzic where he was when earlier privatisation policies were pushed through the town's council meetings. He tells Balzic the situation is even worse than he realises: "Hell, you don't want private police, you think the very idea of private police is an abomination, well what do you think those guys have? I'll tell you what they have. They have their own private government!"[12]

Just as the town's deregulatory policies have caused Rocksburg's citizens to express themselves in unusual ways, so too did Reagan's programme prompt crime novelists to express their discontent. Partly filling a vacuum created by the lack of a coherent political opposition, crime fiction sought to depict the tabloid reality of everyday life, from homelessness to trickle-down psychosis, from poverty to drug-addled paranoia, from child pornography and domestic abuse to serial killing.[13]

This would mean that artifice, once a necessary component of the genre, would be forsaken in favour of a realism hitherto unseen. Crime fiction was looking more like *true crime* literature, which, in books like Truman Capote's *In Cold Blood*, Norman Mailer's *Executioner's Song* and Joe McGinnis's *Blind Faith*, was exerting an increasing influence on the genre. This constituted a shift from the pulp culture era when *true crime* narratives seemed to emulate fiction (the likes of Thompson, Hammett, Lionel White, Harry Whittington had all written for true crime magazines). Suddenly, creating an artifact indistinguishable from reality became the preferred way to depict society and the conditions by which people are driven to extremes. Yet the desire to portray the consequences of the era's policies would lead to the notion that, to make fiction believable, writers must simulate reality, rather than allow, as in the work of James Ellroy and Elmore Leonard, the narrative to create its own reality.

As critics and literary novelists, wishing they could be so direct and accessible, began to heap praise on crime writers, it appeared that noirists had broken the barrier separating their work from serious literature. Though such praise threatened to depoliticise crime fiction, noirists continued to produce a number of highly charged texts. Moreover, in an era filled with various indicators, decoding a crime novel seemed an inviting prospect. In articulating the culture, the genre suggested that politics was being replaced by morality, the ideology of which had yet to be fully investigated. Though the era was not conducive to courting success *and* expressing dissident opinions, some writers, by depicting the pervasiveness of crime and corruption, were able to formulate a critique that avoided ideological categorisation. Consequently, a writer like James Ellroy could pass himself off as a right-winger, while producing texts that accommodate a left-wing perspective. For others, it was enough to match their style to the era's warped excesses. Hoping to map the cause and effect of violence, authors, as well as readers, were left searching for the ultimate crime.

Typified by its extremism regarding characterisation, structure and content, noir fiction began to stretch the boundaries of the genre, and alter the rules regarding what constitutes a crime novel. With all crimes and criminals fair game, the likes of James Ellroy, George V. Higgins and Elmore Leonard would produce fiction qualitatively different from that preceding it. No longer were writers tied to the romanticised cynicism of Chandler's private-eye. Yet such deregulation[14] would prove difficult to sustain, as cultural analysis, in lesser hands, would be lost beneath a series of sure-fire clichés – from protagonist-as-addled Vietnam veteran to sexually dysfunctional serial killers.

Moving to an extreme, crime fiction sought to portray a culture in which everyone is a potential criminal. Meanwhile, TV cops programmes like *Hill Street Blues* and *Miami Vice* tended to divide society into law enforcers and law breakers, while reinforcing paranoia regarding crime and the underclass. Sentimentalising middle-class life, they implied that at one time social classes and ethnic groups had accepted their lot and lived in a state of harmony. Unlike TV crime programmes, deregulated crime fiction, not having the same commercial responsibilities, and given the private nature of the literary experience, could forgo this sentimentalisation and criticise[15] the culture which produces such disparities.

Pursuing greater realism, deregulated crime fiction would also herald the end, save as pastiche, of the private-eye as a credible protagonist. Instead, it would concentrate on the deeds and misdeeds of cops and criminals. As James Ellroy, quoting Ed McBain, has said, "The last time a private-eye solved a case was never."[16] Freed from structural restraints, crime fiction's obsession with verisimilitude-at-street-level meant it could portray the underclass, ethnic groups and subcultures with greater reality. Libertarian in outlook, it could also afford to depict low-lifes and criminals with greater sympathy, and as displaying an intelligence equal to, if not greater than, the average politician and pundit.

The antecedents of deregulated crime fiction exist within a specific historical context. Thus Paul Cain's tough minimalistic prose is impossible to contemplate as anything other than an alienated product of the Depression. Like the Reagan–Bush era, the Depression created a set of circumstances in which extremist crime fiction could flourish. Violent and consciously lacking narrative reflection, Cain's single novel, *Fast One*, and collection of short stories, *Seven Slayers*, were harbingers of future extremist crime fiction. Moreover, Cain, like noirists of the 1980s, would refrain from commenting on the social circumstances and conditions surrounding his fiction. Of course, Cain's policy of non-intervention relates to an era when *objective realism* – camera-eye viewpoint, sparse dialogue and tough-guy action – was in vogue. Meanwhile, the reader, experiencing effect rather than cause, remains in the dark regarding motivation, and the degree to which historical, environmental or personal circumstances impinge on Cain's narrative.

With his investigations of obsessive psychological states,

Cornell Woolrich qualifies as another early extremist. Much of his warped but incisive work would also be written during the Depression. Indeed, it was a period in which his writing would, on a cognitive level, be forever stranded. In their 1962 study, *Le Roman Policier*, French writers Pierre Boileau and Thomas Narcejac cite Woolrich's novella *Rear Window* as the first example of modern crime fiction. They argue that, with Woolrich, the genre, now influenced by the cinema, began to foreground suspense rather than mystery. This would lead to turning the victim, rather than the investigator, into the central character. According to Boileau-Narcejac, Woolrich recognised that crime fiction demanded a metaphysical dimension and a narrative that could not be unravelled by mere fact-finding and reasoning.[17]

Another precursor of contemporary noir fiction, Patricia Highsmith's *Ripley* quartet demonstrates a cool anarchism, the likes of which would crop up in future deregulatory writing. In these novels, published over some twenty-five years, Highsmith portrays her killer-protagonist as an intelligent, likeable if snobbish individual, indistinguishable from any number of apparently normal and criminally sedentary individuals.

Citing her as the first crime writer to combine the modern detective story with elements of the psychological novel, Boileau-Narcejac suggest that Highsmith, in the *Ripley* novels, recognised that the villain had become the primary victim and the centre of the narrative, whose interventions are an attempt to make sense of a mystery in which he or she had become involved.[18] Though this narrative shift would be influential, Highsmith's novels, according to Boileau-Narcejac, tend to be overly psychological. Despite the fact that Boileau-Narcejac do not include such writers, nor extend their analysis any further, it would be the likes of Thompson, Willeford and Himes who, despite their extremism, would achieve the right balance, and realise the problem to be solved was metaphysical and a reflection of the political angst of the era in which they were writing.

All the excesses of the 1980s – conspicuous consumption, speculation, discrepancies between the rich and poor, drive-by killings, domestic and sexual violence, serial murder, the spectacularisation of law enforcement, and the increase in the use of hard drugs and hand weapons – can be seen in the era's crime fiction. While more recent novels, such as Newton Thornberg's *A Man's Game* and Peter Blauner's *The Intruder*, focus on middle-class insecurity regarding the family, the work of Eugene Izzi and Elmore Leonard displays a fascination with get-rich-quick schemes. Meanwhile, protagonists of such fiction, no longer necessarily good or moral, can be of any persuasion and point of view, whether criminals, cops, loners, schizoids, psychos, or members of disgruntled and marginalised groups. By the time Bush assumed office, in 1988, deregulated fiction, like its political and economic counterpart, had taken readers on a roller-coaster ride through hell. Through replication, crime fiction had become the new anthropology, investigating signs of entropy and excess, while testing the limits of acceptability.

Elmore Leonard

Writing crime fiction since 1968 when *The Big Bounce* was published,[19] Leonard has produced a series of novels as anarchic as they are crime-obsessed. Accordingly, his wise-guys, con-men, hustlers, and low-life criminals, who dream of the big score, only to betray one another, embody a view of the world that ensures narrative unpredictability:

> Guys at the top, Tommy said, you didn't have any trouble with. You could always deal with guys at the top. But little guys with wild hairs up their ass, there was no book on guys like that.[20]

Unlike the mayor of Rocksburg, Leonard, if he were to consider the subject, would insist that deregulatory policies did not begin with Reagan or Carter, but are part and parcel of corporate capitalism. However, in terms of style, Leonard displays none of the excesses associated with deregulated writing. Using few adjectives, adverbs, or lengthy descriptions, Leonard relies on a honed-down prose, idiosyncratic characterisation, smartass dialogue and incongruous plot turns.

Capturing the rhythms of urban life, Leonard's characters, always in search of greater status and wealth, will go to any length to commit a crime. Yet, in a genre that prides itself on plot construction, Leonard's story-lines are rarely integral to his work. It could even be said that Leonard has spent his career elaborating on the same basic plots.

Tough and tightly written, *City Primeval* exemplifies Leonard's narrative strategy. Published in 1980, as the stage was set for the first wave of Reaganism, it's a novel that avoids the era's easy moralisms. The title alone establishes the novel's subtext, with its implication that cities have become battle-zones, *primeval* sites where, to survive, one must be vigilant and capable of defending oneself.

Relying on media-generated urban myths, *City Primeval* revels in its non-literariness. For Leonard prefers to underplay the work entailed in writing a novel. Rather, he would like his fiction to be so smooth that readers forget they are engaged in the act of reading: "I don't want the reader to be aware of me writing . . . If you've developed your character adequately, the way the character speaks should be apparent. I used up all my adverbs when I was writing car catalogues for Chevrolet."[21] With expository passages kept to a minimum, Leonard seeks to convey the impression that his sleaze-ridden characters follow their own particular course of action: "What can happen, if a minor or no-name character shows he can talk . . . is he can shove his way into the story and get a more important part. Or he can get demoted."[22]

In *City Primeval*, Leonard depicts three interrelated but separate worlds: the legal system, in the guise of Judge Alvin Guy; the world of crime, personified by Clement Mansell; and, moving between these extremes, the world of law enforcement, personified by the Latino cop, Raymond Cruz. But no sphere of existence is any less criminal or moral than another. Meanwhile, the plot revolves around the standard Leonard theme: acquiring status and wealth amidst racial, sexual, and economic rivalry. Indicative of Leonard's approach, the novel begins with a narrative digression, one which separates the protagonist from his primary concern. With his girlfriend, Sandy, Clement Mansell is working a scam on an Albanian, Skender Lulgjaraj. One night, while tailing Sandy and the Albanian back to Skender's apartment, Clement is waylaid by a Lincoln limousine. Thinking the black man in the Lincoln is a drug dealer, Clement pursues the car, and, in doing so, passes judgement on its driver:

> He decided the guy was in numbers of dope and that's what the girl wanted, some spade with a little fag mustache, fine . . . The jig was driving his big car with his white lady; he didn't care who was behind him or if anybody might be in a hurry. That's what got to Clement, the jig's attitude.[23]

The man's appearance becomes a focal point for Clement's hostility: "The guy's hair . . . looked like a plastic wig, the twenty-nine dollar tango-model ducktail."[24] However, the driver turns out to be Detroit judge Alvin Guy. Unfortunately, Clement, not the most restrained of individuals, kills the judge and his white female companion. As usual, the misreading of people and situations pushes the plot, and foregrounds any incipient rivalries.

Likewise, *City Primeval* contains two divergent narratives: the scam regarding Sandy and the Albanian, and Judge Guy's murder. These are mirrored in the relationship between the sociopath Clement and the criminal family, which, through realignments of loyalty, sexual jealousy, racial rivalry, mis-readings of character, and differing responses to the criminal event, eventually collapses.

Interestingly, Leonard's plots are not about police detection so much as police comprehension. In *City Primeval*, the cops try

to piece together the narrative strands so they can predict the
next stage in the plot and the crime:

> "If it's robbery, why'd the judge pull in here?"
>
> "To take a leak," Bryl said. "How do I know why he pull in.
> But he was robbed and that's all we got so far."
>
> "It was a hit," said Hunter. "Two guys. They set him up – see
> him at the track, arrange a meet. Maybe sell him some dope.
> One of 'em gets in the car with the judge, like he's gonna
> make the deal, the other guy – he's gonna shoot through the
> window, his partner's in the line of fire. So he hits him
> through the windshield. With a .45."
>
> "Now you have the weapon," Bryl said. "Where'd you get the
> .45?"
>
> "Same place you got the piss he had to take," Hunter said."[25]

In this way, policing becomes hypothetical storytelling or textual
analysis. With the logic of the crime hidden to those outside
the criminal family, the police can only second-guess the
criminals. So they piece together a narrative to make sense of
the crime, the criminals, and the world they inhabit.

Setting his narratives in America's melting pots – Detroit,
Miami and Hollywood – Leonard populates his books with an
array of characters and uses vernacularisms that reflect a divided
society. Yet, as products of the melting pot, Leonard's low-life
characters constantly cross racial and class boundaries. While
Leonard is incapable of creating an uninteresting character, he
recognises the universal desire for subverting the culture, or, at
least, enjoying the thought that someone else might be
subverting it. In Leonard's world, the criminal is king. And
since, in *City Primeval*, Cruz-the-cop is partly criminal, he too
gains the reader's sympathy. That the world of crime should be
more interesting than the world of law and order, is as it should
be. After all, in the Reagan era, with government and white-
collar crime reaching pandemic proportions, small-time
criminals, doing their best to gain a foothold on the economic
ladder, share the aspirations of ordinary readers. More so than

those who govern society or uphold law and order. Besides, if those holding public office commit criminal acts, how much worse can petty criminals be? But lest the reader empathise too much, Leonard makes sure his criminals are no less immoral nor violent than his cops. Blurring these distinctions makes Leonard the most humanitarian of crime writers.

At the same time, Leonard's writing contains an unarticulated ideology. However, having reduced his writing to its essentials, it would take the skills of a literary archaeologist to uncover the contents of that ideology.[26] Suffice it to say that the author takes pleasure in the inventiveness and cultural necessity of crime. Because the criminal act, more often than not, goes wrong, Leonard invites the reader to side with his criminals and against the state. As in Lionel White's *Clean Slate*, the reader observes the criminal process, realising that, for Leonard's characters, crime is a desperate attempt to achieve economic and social autonomy.

While Leonard's fanciful portrayal of criminal life is convincing, other writers take a different line, pushing to an extreme the notion that they are recreating reality. But Leonard shows little interest in perpetrating this deception. Though feigning verisimilitude, Leonard's work, moving from hard-edged prose to film-script dialogue, is clearly artificial. Yet his sense of artifice gives his writing an added accuracy. So the confrontation in *City Primeval* between Cruz and Mansell bears the hallmarks of a western unhindered by cowboy moralisms:

Clement was saying from the kitchen, "That was interesting, that talk we had in your office. I never done that before with a cop . . . like seeing where each other's coming from. You know it? . . ."

He'll have something in his hand, Raymond thought.

". . . Yeah, that was interesting. Getting down to the basics of life, you might say. I mean our kind of life."[27]

Then comes the betrayal, the showdown, and the book's final sentences:

> Clement said, "I don't believe it . . . what did you kill me for?"
> Raymond didn't answer. Maybe tomorrow he'd think of something he might have said. After a little while Raymond picked up the opener from the desk and began paring the nail of his right index finger with the sharply pointed hooked edge.

The moral, if there is one, in *City Primeval* is as unclear as it is unnecessary. Is it that cops behave like criminals, and criminals behave like cops? Who knows? What is apparent is that, though constantly at loggerheads, cops and criminals – Cruz and Mansell – need each other to survive. The police need crooks to justify their existence. And vice versa. Morally ambiguous, Leonard's work, at least at the time of *City Primeval*, does not pretend to be anything other than pulp fiction, the primary task of which is to transport its readers from one point to another, and to provide a dash of paranoia to make the journey interesting.

While Leonard reads the culture as accurately as anyone, his characters are not quite so adept. Rather, they strut their stuff and search for definition, judging others according to an unstated code that entails dress, body language and speech. In *Gold Coast*:

> Elvin had looked at his reflection in the bedroom mirror and had to grin at himself, man, in that blue suit from Taiwan China and a bright yellow shirt with the collar spread open.[28]

Here surface appearances mean everything. And when it's time to go undercover, it's necessary to manipulate the code and hope it is sufficient to fool one's rival:

> He gave the handshake enough but not all he had. He liked the guy's sportcoat. He didn't like his maize and blue

Michigan tie, the way it was tied in a careless knot, the label side of the narrow end showing, *All Silk*. He had met millionaires before . . . He resented this one, the uncombed hair, the careless tie.[29]

The name of the game is fitting in, and going undetected. This means that anyone, if properly dressed, could be either a criminal or a cop:

He loved the old sportcoat because, for some reason, it made him think of Old Florida and made him feel like a native. (A Maguire dictum: wherever you are, fit in, look like you belong. In Colorado wear a sheepskin coat and lace-up boots.)[30]

Unfortunately for Leonard's characters, they never quite read the codes correctly. There is always something that gives them away. Their failure to read the culture is, in effect, their fatal flaw.

Around the time of *Glitz*, the rewriting of *Touch*, or the publication of his hippy crime novel, *Freaky Deaky* – "Living out there with the great silent majority. I know why they're silent, they don't have a fucking thing to say. I got into shoplifting just for something to do."[31] – Leonard, already with some twenty novels behind him, began to depict ever-more incongruous situations, characters and repartee. It's here that Leonard's work becomes more humorous and self-assured. This might be indicative of his success as a writer, the influence of a writer like George V. Higgins, or that, in the dog days of the Reagan–Bush era, there was no longer any doubt about the extent of corruption in high places or the cultural inevitability of crime. Whichever, Leonard, from the mid-1980s onwards, becomes a more complex writer. Even if, in doing so, he loses the unpretentiousness that had formerly placed him within the tradition of pulp, and therefore throwaway, fiction.

Set in Hollywood, Leonard's 1990 *Get Shorty* deconstructs the film world and, in doing so, establishes its relationship to the world of crime. The result is that Leonard's noir comedy joins F. Scott Fitzgerald's Pat Hobby stories, Nathaniel West's *Day of the Locust*, and Charles Willeford's *Woman Chaser* as one of the more perceptive accounts of Hollywood culture. By the time *Get Shorty* was turned into a film, its content contained the seeds of its success. Whereas *City Primeval* is a straightforward crime novel, *Get Shorty* indicates Leonard's interest in cultural and narrative incongruities: "You come in here, walk in the house in the middle of the fucking night? I thought you were some actor, *auditioning*, for Christ's sake."[32]

Here the ups and downs of venture capitalism are examined. At the airport to collect ten kilos of cocaine, the Bear compares the risks involved in what are essentially two types of venture capitalism:

> [In] the movie business you didn't worry about somebody getting turned to save their ass and pointing at you in court. You could get fucked over in the movie business all kinds of ways, but you didn't get sent to a correctional facility, when you lost out. The movie business, you could come right out and tell people what you did, make a name. Instead of hanging out on the edge, supplying highs for dumbass movie stars, you could get to where you hire the ones you want and tell 'em what to do; they don't like it, fire their ass. It didn't make sense to live here if you weren't in the movie business.[33]

Avoiding overt sociological statements, Leonard relies on editing techniques that juxtapose innuendo, misreadings and narrative drift. Chili, an eccentric loan shark, comes to Hollywood to collect a bad debt from a B-movie producer, Harry Zimm, but ends up investing stolen money in Harry's movie. Meanwhile, Harry is trying to sell a screenplay to Martin Weir, a Dustin Hoffman-type movie star. But Weir would rather play Chili in a movie about the latter's attempt to recover the money. Leonard's novel parodies Hollywood's reverence for anything that sells. Using drug money to ply his way into the film world, Catlett tells Chili they should write a script together. He explains how it's done:

> "You already learned in school how to write, didn't you? I *hope
> so*. You have the idea and you put down what you want to say.
> Then you get somebody to add in the commas and shit where
> they belong, if you aren't positive yourself. Maybe fix up the
> spelling where you have some tricky words. There people do
> that for you. Some, I've even seen scripts where I *know* words
> weren't spelled right and there was hardly any commas in it.
> So I don't think it's too important. You come to the last page
> you write in 'Fade out,' and that's the end you're done."
> Chili said, "That's all there is to it?"
> "That's all."
> Chili said, "Then what do I need you for?"[34]

Though Catlett reduces scriptwriting to its lowest common
denominator, the reader, recalling Harris's comments on
scriptwriting in Willeford's *The Woman Chaser*, knows his
description is no less valid than the clichés handed out to those
who pay exorbitant amounts of money to attend Hollywood
scriptwriting courses.

As reality and fiction merge into a recognisable glob, it
becomes apparent that Chili, like other Leonard characters, has
come to base his life on the movies. Though he has seen enough
films to give him a certain amount of critical awareness, Chili
still has problems when it comes to separating the real from the
representational:

> He could see himself in different movies Robert DeNiro had
> been in. He could maybe do an Al Pacino movie, play a hard-
> on . . . He couldn't see himself in ones, like say the one where
> the three guys get stuck with a baby . . . People like that cute
> shit, they went to see it. But, man, that would be hard . . .[35]

As Leonard says, "My characters are all playing roles . . . All
perhaps except the main character, and he'll notice this. And
he'll wonder: 'Who is this guy playing?' "[36]

Though his books beckon to be filmed – out of more than thirty books, twenty-seven have, as of 1997, been optioned or bought outright for the screen – *Get Shorty, Cat Chaser, 52 Pick-up* and *Rum Punch* (Tarantino's *Jackie Brown*) are the only Leonard novels that, as of this writing, have been successfully transferred to the screen. One reason for this is that Leonard's fiction is not necessarily plot-driven: "Plot to me isn't important. It just gets the people together . . . After the first 100 pages, that's when I have to stop and maybe do a little plotting."[37] Directors find it difficult to let the novels speak for themselves. After all, these apparent filmscripts-in-waiting contain a zero-level narration which drifts in and out of various interior monologues. This is a facet few film-makers have been able to co-opt.

While he insists he does not control his characters, Leonard's hidden hand invariably leaves its mark. With the rules of the genre asking to be broken, these self-enclosed texts conclude in a satisfyingly anti-climatic fashion:

> "What if," said Chili, "Leo hops on the railing and makes a speech. Says how he sweated, worked his ass off all his life as a drycleaner, but he's had these few weeks living like a movie star and now he can die happy. In other words he commits suicide. Steps off the balcony and the audience walks out in tears. What do you think?"
> Karen said, "Uh-huh . . ." Harry said he wanted a drink and Karen said that wasn't a bad idea. Chili didn't say anything, giving it some more thought. Fuckin' endings, man, they weren't as easy as they looked."[38]

In Leonard's 1991 *Maximum Bob*, the detective-protagonist, Gary Hammond, resurrected from the 1981 *Split Images*, also finds himself pulled in two directions: on the one hand, by his professional duties; and, on the other hand, by Kathy, his girlfriend, who, as a probation officer, pleads that he be more flexible. Hammond's inability to admit that an otherwise insignificant piece of garbage – a discarded pizza box – might be a valid piece of evidence, leads to his eventual death. But Kathy realises its importance:

> "If you have trouble seeing yourself walking in the Sheriff's office with a pizza box, let me do it."
> "Even if you could somehow place him at the house," Mr Methodical went on, "There's no way you can prove criminal intent . . ."
> "He was there," Kathy said. "I saw him."
> "You maintain you saw something, or someone."
> "Yeah, that's what I do, I maintain."

The pizza box becomes the crucial clue, one which allows Kathy to read the situation and connect the disparate elements: Judge Gibbs's relationship with his wife; a face seen inside Gibbs's house as a shot is fired; and Crowe's involvement in the conspiracy to kill the judge. While Kathy knows that to *maintain* is, in her business, the best one can hope for, the professional caution of Mr Methodical blinds Hammond to Elvin's role and contributes to his unpreparedness when Elvin comes to kill him. This is typical of Leonard's later books, which juxtapose what he regards as "feminine insight" with the ultra professional, predominantly male, mode of detection, one which can never quite manage to read the situation correctly.

The limitations of this male mode of detection reappear in the novel's resolution. Though Vasco is electronically tagged as a condition for his probation, and despite the fact that an unmarked car watches them, the criminals' house remains a centre for Vasco, his lover, Elvin and the prostitute Earlene. Yet it's also a place where crimes continue to be plotted. Surveillance might be a sign of state power, but, in an area within the area under surveillance, criminals are able to continue their facsimile of family life. It's only when Kathy, freeing herself from the confines of those watching the criminals, decides to leave the unmarked car and knocks on the door, that she is able to correctly read the criminal family, manipulate their rivalries, and expose their criminality.

Reading Leonard's work makes it apparent that, while deregulated crime fiction bears little relationship to *whodunits* or mysteries, it forms part of a tradition that stretches back to such writers as Thompson and Charles Williams. Considering that his fiction occupies a thoroughly non-literary space, Leonard might be too wily for his own good. Does he really have so little control over his work and his plots? And, even if one takes deregulation to an extreme, placing it alongside a laissez-faire libertarianism, can Leonard's work really be so democratic? For here is a writer who has the audacity to insist that his work is a world unto itself, the laws of which are apparently so deregulated that they cannot be controlled nor determined. Here speech is everything while linear development assumes post-modernist proportions. For Leonard suggests that he need only be carried away with writing, editing it at some point in the future. Whether this is an accurate description of how Leonard works is another matter. After all, with his background in advertising, Leonard has spent decades manipulating words and readers.

Leonard readily admits his main influence is neither Hammett nor Chandler, but Hemingway.[39] Thus Leonard, not wanting the reader to be aware of the writer's hand, has chosen to approach the artifice of the genre from a different angle than a writer like James Sallis. Certainly, Leonard's manipulation of the narrative voice, including the abstraction of the author's voice from the text, constitutes an effective and original form of artifice. Though it contains elements of proletariat fiction, particularly when it comes to cultural determinism, Leonard's writing never aspires to anything but lightweight entertainment. Investigating various milieux, and demonstrating a remarkable understanding of subcultures, Leonard consciously avoids creating anything of substance. His work, described by Ellroy as a "black comedy of manners",[40] is meant to be only what it is. This in itself constitutes a political position. After all, if everything remains on the surface, then anything can be said or portrayed. While over-intellectualisation, to Leonard, will always be politically suspect, his ability as a stylist exposes contradictions regarding the democratic nature of his work. However, Leonard is out to entertain. Which, in this context, might constitute the most extreme position of all.

James Ellroy

The quintessential neon noir writer, James Ellroy began his writing career in 1980 with his one and only private-eye novel, *Brown's Requiem*. The appearance of this book coincided with the publication of Leonard's *City Primeval* and Reagan's successful election campaign. Seventeen years later, Leonard is widely read, Reagan has Alzheimer's and Ellroy, once a petty criminal, drug user and alcoholic, has become crime fiction's top dog. Having long since ditched detective fiction and novels about serial killers (*Silent Terror*) for the sleaze of history, Ellroy is best known for his *LA Quartet* – *The Black Dahlia*, *The Big Nowhere*, *LA Confidential* and *White Jazz* – a series whose first book appeared in 1988, and which, taken as a whole, charts the history of Los Angeles, from 1947 to 1959. Yet even before the *Quartet*, Ellroy had produced a number of LA-based novels – *Clandestine*, *Because the Night*, *Suicide Hill*, and *Blood on the Moon* – as gruesome as they were emblematic of America in the 1980s. While *Blood on the Moon*, an otherwise straightforward narrative, is an invaluable account of how men perceive, and are threatened by, feminism, it reminds the reader that Ellroy's fiction takes place in a predominantly male environment. Taking his characters to the most extreme position possible, Ellroy delights in exposing their foibles and perverse fantasies. Whether Lloyd Hopkins, Buzz Meeks, Dudley Smith, or Pete Bondurant, the author drives his characters until they reveal themselves as total degenerates, by which time they have little alternative but to fall into their own nightmarish abyss.

While his fiction mythologises the past, Ellroy, going to any lengths to publicise his work, mythologises himself. Neverthe-less, Ellroy's desire for publicity hides an impressive ability to read the culture. In courting extremism, and dabbling in the pornography of violence, he has redefined what is acceptable in the genre. Not one to adhere to Elmore Leonard's minimalist approach, Ellroy has produced a series of obsessive, and sometimes self-indulgent, missives in which the words come in clipped and stinging onslaughts, as fevered as the characters he writes about. Meanwhile, Ellroy's writing style has become increasingly dependent on his two favourite modes of enquiry: tabloid journalism and crime reporting.

Able to descend into the slimier recesses of the culture, Ellroy has single-handedly altered the rules of the genre. Beginning with his 1995 *American Tabloid*, he has recently embarked on a series of historical, but no less criminally-obsessed, novels – the first being about the Kennedys – which entail complex conspiracies enacted by various armies of stooges. Arguably the most significant political reappraisal of crime fiction since Hammett's *Red Harvest*, Ellroy claims to have taken crime fiction as far as it can go, and so has opted to work against the public record, where the stakes are higher and the crimes assume greater meaning.

The need to evolve as a writer has been a constant factor in Ellroy's *oeuvre*, nowhere more so than in the *LA Quartet*. Beginning with the relatively conventional *Black Dahlia*, he ends with a gargantuan noir vision of Los Angeles, *White Jazz*:

> I pulled the trigger – *click/click/roar* – muzzle flash set his hair on fire.
> This scream.
> This huge hand snuffing flames out – stretching huge to quash that scream.
> A whisper:
> "We'll stash him at one of your buildings. You do what you have to do, and I'll watchdog him. We'll work an angle on his money, and sooner or later he'll spill."
> Smoke. Mattress debris settling.

Chick torched half-bald.
EVERYTHING SPINNING.[41]

In his *Quartet*, Ellroy, who consciously eschews Chandler's moral imperative, maps out the city's post-war boom. Here land development goes hand-in-hand with the rise of the cultural spectacle, be it the Hollywood film industry, or the construction of Disneyland and Dodger Stadium. It's also an era in which some men, unable to inflict their warped perspective, take out their frustrations on others, particularly women. Repelled and attracted by feminine difference, their world is turned upside-down when confronted with incongruities, whether Elizabeth Short's dismembered corpse in *The Black Dahlia*, the promiscuous female communist organiser in *The Big Nowhere*, or the prostitutes who have been surgically altered so they can double as movie stars in *LA Confidential*.

With a nightmare lurking beneath every dream, Walt Disney-clone Raymond Dieterling, in *LA Confidential*, builds the Disneyland-like Dream-a-Dream-Land, and makes animations for his son, who has grown up to be a psychosexual maniac. When those who inhabit Ellroy's fiction lash out, they, in their rage, seek to blind, if not dismember, their victims, who are, more often than not, female. So when Vogel, a cop in *The Black Dahlia*, contracts syphilis from a black prostitute, he takes revenge by visiting a Watts brothel where he ejaculates into the eyes of the women who work there. Meanwhile, when the body of Elizabeth Short, soon to be known as the Black Dahlia, is found, cut to pieces, it becomes fodder for tabloid journalism, and emblematic of the era. In fact, Short's dismembered state can be likened to a map representing the city's various subdivisions and points of exploitation:

A large triangle had been gouged out of the left thigh . . . the flaps of skin behind the gash were pulled back: there were no organs inside . . . the breasts were dotted with cigarette burns, the right one hanging loose . . . the girl's face . . . was one

huge purpled bruise, the nose crushed deep into the facial
cavity, the mouth cut ear to ear into a smile that leered up at
you, somehow mocking the rest of the brutality inflicted.[42]

Short's death pushes detectives Bleichart and Blanchard even
further into LA's underbelly. Moving from lesbian bars on
Crenshaw to Howard Hughes *fuckpads*, the two detectives are
aroused by Short's scented trail. When Bleichart tracks down
Short's alter-ego, he turns her into a Black Dahlia simulacrum.
Significantly, the novel ends beneath the famous Hollywood
sign, on a piece of property developed by silent film mogul
Mack Sennett and the land speculator who is also the simulacrum's pervert father.

If *White Jazz* is Ellroy's magnum opus of crime fiction, his
article, and subsequent book regarding his mother's murder is
his most personal piece of post-mortem prose. Looking at old
photographs of his mother, Ellroy admits everything:

> I thought I could touch the literal horror and somehow
> commute my life sentence.
> I was mistaken. The woman refused to grant me a reprieve.
> Her grounds were simple: My death gave you a voice, and I
> need you to recognise me past your exploitation of it.[43]

Written in the mid-1990s, "My Mother's Killer" informs and
embodies Ellroy's later novels. It's a moving and personal story
of his childhood, and how his mother's death affected him. A
reconciliation, a recantation, and a recollection – "That weekend
is etched in hyper-focus. I remember seeing *The Vikings* at the
Fox-Wilshire Theatre. I remember a spaghetti dinner at
Yaconelli's Restaurant. I remember a TV fight card. I remember
the bus ride to El Monte as long and hot."[44] – it's also a
deconstruction of the author's work and 1950s Southern
California culture.

Clandestine, published in 1982, would be Ellroy's first attempt at writing the history of his mother's death. It is also his first historical novel. Five years later *The Black Dahlia* appeared, taking the story of his mother and the history of Los Angeles a step further. The quote that appears on the book's opening page comes from the poet Anne Sexton, and forms the subtext of the novel: "Now I fold you down, my drunkard, my navigator,/ My first lost keeper, to love or look at later." Acknowledging the significance of his mother in absentia, Ellroy, in the novel's opening lines, dives into his subject matter: "I knew her in life. She exists for me through others, in evidence of the ways her death drove them. Working backward, seeking only facts, I reconstructed her."[45] Though Ellroy exploits his mother's death, it is an event that becomes his initiation into the textural history of Los Angeles, one that would alter his life and influence his writing.

In *The Big Nowhere*, a novel set against the Hollywood Red Scare of the early 1950s, Ellroy cites Joseph Conrad: "It was written that I should be loyal to the nightmare of my choice." Choosing to move into the darkness of post-war Los Angeles, Ellroy's destiny would be to recollect the nightmare that leads him back to his mother's corpse: "Part of him knew it was just a dream – that it was 1950, not 1941; that the story would run its course while part of him grasped for new details and part tried to be dead still so as not to disrupt the unravelling."[46] Like the author's pre-literary life, Ellroy's characters live in their own private hell, trapped between their dreams and the knowledge that they would be better off leaving events and emotions undisturbed. Likewise, *LA Confidential* starts with a quote from novelist Steve Erickson: "A glory that costs everything and means nothing." This reads as an apt definition of Ellroy's particular *obsession*: a series of grisly murders, the construction of a Disneyland-type theme park, the warped perspective of individual cops, and the twisted sexual habits of sundry politicians. While Ellroy continues to write about his mother's death, his journey is not as self-referential as the Erickson quote suggests. For Ellroy's narratives, concerned, as they are, with the era's seedy icons, are investigations of power and perversity at tabloid level:

> Press clippings on his corkboard: "Dope Crusader Wounded in Shootout"; "Actor Robert Mitchum Seized in Marijuana Shack Raid." *Hush-Hush* articles, framed on his desk: "Hopheads Quake When Dope Scourge Cop Walks Tall"; "Actors Agree: *Badge of Honor* Owes Authenticity to Hard-hitting Technical Advisor."[47]

Here Ellroy's narrative complexity seeps into the bones of the novel, as Captain Ed Exley, LAPD's Mr Clean, gains promotion simply because, in a 114-page report, he is the only person able to articulate the narrative, one that he, of course, has altered to his advantage. The corrupt Exley is not only credited with solving the "Nite Owl" murder case, but he has succeeded in burning the evidence, keeping the case files and money, saving the careers of his wayward colleagues, and assisting his father in his bid to gain the Republican gubernatorial nomination.

In the last book of the quartet, *White Jazz*, Ellroy, still combining police reportage, personal confession and smut magazine sensationalism, begins with a quote from Ross Macdonald: "In the end I possess my birthplace and am possessed by its language." *Birthplace, language* and *death*: these are the ponderables that drive Ellroy as a writer. Meanwhile the prologue marks out the parameters of guilt:

> All I have is the will to remember. Time revoked/fever dreams – I wake up reaching, afraid I'll forget. Pictures keep the woman young.
> LA, fall 1958.
> Newsprint: link the dots. Names, events – so brutal they beg to be connected. Years down – the story stays dispersed. The names are dead or too guilty to tell.
> I'm old, afraid I'll forget:
> I killed innocent men.

I betrayed secret oaths.
I reaped profit from horror.
Fever – that time burning. I want to go with the music –
spin, fall with it.[48]

The will to remember. No wonder Ellroy, after *White Jazz*,
forsakes the crime novel, just as he had forsaken novels about
detectives, serial killers, and vengeance-seeking cops. Yet Ellroy's
beginnings contain all one need know about the writer: that his
work is sanctioned by a will to remember and dream. The
crimes described in Ellroy's work come down to a single event,
and the author's subsequent sense of guilt surrounding it. To
explore that dark area, Ellroy deploys whatever is at his disposal:
memory, fact, fiction, autobiography and a language that moves
from poetry to obscenity. All so he can reconcile himself to his
conclusions: that he has *reaped profit from horror, betrayed secret
oaths,* while wanting to *go with the music* before he is consumed
by *time burning*.

Regarding Ellroy's world, it would be an understatement to say
that the past creates the present. A more accurate assessment
would be that the past has cursed the present. In this context,
nostalgia, often the province of crime fiction, becomes a sick
joke. In Ellroy's world, society cannot help but create murderers,
perverts and malcontents; while greed, sexual obsession and
violence are essential ingredients of the culture. With a literary
hard-on that cannot be hidden, Ellroy's deregulated and
sometimes anti-social prose reveals the unexpurgated version
of Los Angeles's corrupt narrative. On the downside, Ellroy
has, in an age of excess and simulation, spawned numerous
imitators who, responding to what they take to be the demands
of the market, operate under the illusion that the manic, if not
masturbatory, aspect of Ellroy's work can be easily co-opted,
and that the kind of violence Ellroy depicts can be arbitrarily
deployed.

As previously mentioned, it would be an over-simplification

to describe Ellroy simply as a right-winger. This even though Ellroy has described himself in this way.[49] In an interview Ellroy, when asked what his definition of right-wing might be, said, "More capitalist, free speech, libertarian type attitudes. Time has proved that communism stinks and it didn't work. It's like those guys in *The Big Nowhere* gradually get disgusted . . . and realize that the people they're investigating are no harm to America."[50] But what right-winger would conclude that Hollywood communists did not constitute a threat? Regarding the politics of Ellroy's work, LA urban archaeologist Mike Davis says the following:

> Quartet attempts to map the history of modern Los Angeles as a secret continuum of sex crimes, satanic conspiracies, and political scandals. For Ellroy . . . the grisly, unsolved "Black Dahlia" case . . . is the . . . symbolic commencement of the post-war era . . . concealing a larger, metaphysical mystery. Yet in building such an all-encompassing noir mythology . . . Ellroy risks extinguishing the genre's tensions, and, inevitably, its power. In his pitch blackness there is no light left to cast shadows and evil becomes a forensic banality. The result feels very much like the actual moral texture of the Reagan–Bush era: the supersaturation of corruption that fails any longer to outrage or even interest.[51]

Ellroy's work "feels like the actual moral texture of the Reagan–Bush era" because it *is* the moral texture of the Reagan–Bush era. After all, when Ellroy explores the past, he is, in fact, elucidating the present. To say that Ellroy's onslaught destroys the genre's tensions is to misread how the genre and the culture have changed. While the belief that Ellroy's *supersaturation of corruption fails to outrage or interest* the reader is akin to saying that the publication of the Pentagon Papers or the images sent back from Vietnam merely numbed Americans regarding the war. Though risking desensitisation, the Pentagon Papers and war photographs also caused many to join the anti-war movement. The level of corruption during the Reagan–Bush era obviously did numb the public – Reagan was, after all, the "Teflon President" – but the penny eventually dropped, and an incumbent President was defeated. Accordingly, readers of Ellroy's *Quartet* cannot avoid noting that the origins of political corruption are as perversely personal as they are political. The fact is, one cannot escape the era in which one writes. If nothing else, Ellroy, for all his noir deviancies, confronts the era head-on. Not only are his misreadings of history no worse than anyone else's, but, by focusing on warped obsession as a prime motivating force, he is, in all likelihood, closer than most to explaining how history works.

Because history is the prime mover, those inhabiting Ellroy's fiction become expendable. So, when his manic protagonists burn themselves out, as they invariably do, Ellroy disposes of them without a twinge of conscience. The twisted and tormented protagonist of his earlier novels, Lloyd Hopkins, is one such character. Too much a typical protagonist, his exit signalled the end, so far as Ellroy was concerned, of warped decency. Here avenging angels, no matter how right-wing and psychotic, are easier to eliminate than their devilish counter-parts. At least that is the case with the machiavellian Dudley Smith, whom the reader encounters for the first time some hundred pages into *Clandestine*, and who remains a constant presence throughout the *LA Quartet*. Through fear and manipulation, Smith – who "scared the hell out of guys who scared the hell out of guys." – builds a formidable power base. One of Ellroy's favourite characters, Smith is willing to kill, whether in or out of the line of duty. Personifying everything loathsome about law enforcement, he is, as Buzz Meeks, in *LA Confidential*, says, "smarter than everyone else". An old-school cop and racist, Smith carries a secret agenda the size of greater Los Angeles. Meanwhile, with a hand in everyone's pocket, he can alter his personality to fit the occasion; at one moment, pure Irish blarney, telling folksy stories about his family and offering fatherly advice to young police officers, while, at another moment, a hit-man for LA crime boss Mickey Cohen.

A minor character at the beginning of the *Quartet*, he ends up a major player, the personification of LA's noir narrative, and, within his twisted world, one of Ellroy's more moral characters.

Driven to extremes, Ellroy's protagonists are manipulated by both the era and the author. But unlike Leonard and Higgins, Ellroy, his work fuelled by private obsessions, is unlikely to suggest that his characters are capable of dictating the terms of his fiction. For Ellroy, protagonists are neither indispensable, nor capable of controlling his multi-layered narratives. Though autonomy has been a standard artifice in detective fiction, it becomes absurd when placed in the context of crime fiction. Strangely, Ellroy appears to be one of the few writers to demonstrate a willingness to take this proposition to its logical conclusion, driving his protagonists until they disappear from the page.

Fostering a mocking but desperate millennialism, Ellroy's nihilistic and manic prose snakes from one entropic nightmare to another. This ultra-deregulation is the opposite side of the coin from K. C. Constantine's anonymity and languorous investigation of small-town life. Coming from two different environments, Ellroy and Constantine are equally aware of the break-up of contemporary culture. The difference is that, while Constantine takes his time to explain it, Ellroy, a product of a helter-skelter society, writes as though explanations have become a waste of time and energy.

Though catering to sensationalism and maximum public impact, Ellroy, through excess and outrage, is able to shield himself from his audience. This allows him enough private space to reconstruct events, interrogating them until they crack under pressure. Whether investigating the Dahlia killing, the Red Scare, Mickey Cohen, Central Avenue jazz, the twisted life of Howard Hughes, or the machinations of the Kennedy family, Ellroy's interpretation is invariably personal and plausible. Turning his plots on how obsessive behaviour creates history, Ellroy, in reconstructing events, mocks the notion that coherence can be salvaged from a world built on the detritus of the past. Despite his fictional characters, their failings and embellishments, Ellroy makes no attempt to alter events, but only to reconcile himself to private nightmares and public facts. With his gargantuan ego and writing skill, Ellroy might be delivering even more than he claims.

Andrew Coburn

Writing about jealous spouses, extramarital affairs, corrupt practices, and murderous proceedings, Coburn investigates the impact of crime on middle-class suburban life. Like a noir pointillist, Coburn presents a tableau of criminal particularities, the overall picture of which he leaves to the reader's imagination. With his writing skills honed by a tenure as a political reporter, Coburn, whose first novel appeared in 1974, concentrates on those affected by crime, rather than on those who commit crimes. Possessing the nerve to be unfashionable, Coburn, now with some ten novels to his credit, remains an underrated writer.

Suffice it to say, if James Ellroy can make urban existence appear hellish, Coburn, forever pursuing the ordinary, can make suburban New England seem purgatorial, a place where inhabitants must linger before discovering if upward mobility will transport them to their paradisical home on the hill, or if, unemployed and mortgage defaulting, they must retreat to the ungentrified inferno of the inner city. With the inhabitants of Coburn's suburban world protected by tax scams and tasteful pergolas, violent crime occurs behind closed doors, in a neighbouring town or in someone's warped imagination. Demonstrating none of the stylistic flash associated with most contemporary crime fiction, Coburn's obsession with ordinary middle-class life gives his work an anthropological edge, as though he were sending back reports regarding a social class about to secede from the planet.

Neither a gentler nor kinder America than that depicted by other writers, Coburn's leafy streets house more than their share of white-collar criminals. So thin is the line separating law abiders from law breakers that the latter appear only slightly more immoral than the former when it comes to getting their way. For on these meandering rather than mean streets, autonomy is achieved through the accumulation of capital by fair means or foul. With inherited wealth breeding eccentricity and an array of tasty hors-d'œuvres, criminal activities and capitalist concerns are often indistinguishable. Able to hide their misdeeds within ledgers, loopholes, and delegated responsibility, those who populate Coburn's work climb the social ladder or exact revenge on those foolish enough to stand in their way.

A minimalist with a deadpan narrative, Coburn creates a claustrophobic world that is always slightly out of kilter. In his 1995 *Voices in the Dark*, a drifter confesses to having killed a sixteen-year-old boy. When the police express doubt about his guilt, the drifter puts himself in jail and, though the door remains unlocked, stays under auto-arrest until the investigation is well under way. Here, as in all of Coburn's books, the ordinariness of suburban life is as humorous as it is warped. Whether he has killed the teenager or not, Dudley is not the sort of person a peaceful suburban town wants in their midst.

> Morgan was glad of the distance between them. It seemed to lessen the tension, and he spoke in his coolest voice, "In this town we like our eccentrics harmless, not homicidal."
> "I go where there's a need."
> "What does that mean?"
> "I'm a professional," Dudley said, only part of his face visible. "A hitman."
> "You don't look like the Mafia to me."
> "I only do children. Reasonable rates."
> Morgan felt a greater weariness than before. Who is this man, he asked himself, and why am I listening to him?[52]

Typically, everyone suspects the stranger, for the suspicion of crime creates more paranoia than the crime itself. Meanwhile,

Coburn's depiction of various incongruities and intrigues reveal numerous skeletons hidden in the closets of otherwise respectable suburbanites.

In *Love Nest*, published in 1987, a prostitute is murdered, and the extent of small-town corruption and desire is revealed. Significantly, it was during the property boom of the 1980s that the seeds of the town's decline were planted.

> The Lawrence *Eagle-Tribune* . . . proclaimed that builders were changing the face of the town. "Developers," the reporter wrote, "are gobbling up the green, subdividing it, and erecting houses in areas that were once poultry farms, fruit orchards, meadowlands, pine groves, lovers' lanes, swamps, and gravel pits."[53]

Obviously, growth has its disadvantages:

> A plastics manufacturer was suspected of pouring poisonous waste in the Shawsheen River, and a maker of polyurethane foam for cushions and mattresses went broke and left behind a hundred or so barrels of deadly chemicals, which worried the fire chief because some of the chemicals were explosive. But, on the whole, few voices protested the town's economic development, which stabilised the tax rate while ballooning property values celestial to begin with.[54]

These suburban nightmares often recall the films of David Lynch, while, at other times, they are reminiscent of the alienated world described by Richard Ford in his *Independence Day*. Though Coburn constructs a similar landscape, he does so with less sensationalism than Lynch, and with greater intrigue, directness, panache, and humour than Ford. In *Sweetheart*, the local cop finds himself burdened by a broken marriage, bills and a dead-end career. When two young hoodlums murder the parents of a local Mafia head, the Mob's *capo* wants the cop to help him seek revenge. So "Sweetheart" becomes a double-agent. In Coburn's fictional universe, public deregulation does little to refine one's sense of morality, at least not when it comes to crime. In a conversation between a cop and an FBI agent, the latter, alluding to the effect of government austerity, says,

> "I wasn't always Bureau, you know. For a short time I was with the CIA . . . [But] I was a budget casualty. Saddest day of my life."
> "You seem to have landed on your feet."
> "I have that facility. I used to fight Communists, and now I fight scum of another kind."
> "Sounds like an obsession."
> "Everybody moves to his own music, Lieutenant. I imagine you move very nicely to yours – given the chance, that is. Out here, I suspect you march to a bored drummer."[55]

Here, as elsewhere in his fiction, Coburn's characters communicate at cross-purposes. Consequently, they cannot help but say more, as well as less, than they mean.

Published in 1980, at the onset of Reaganism, *Off Duty* centres on Frank Chase, an ex-member of the drug squad, who, subsidised by money stolen from a drugs raid, seeks a new life. After his wife discovers a corpse, word gets out that the head of the Boston Mafia has not taken the double-cross lightly. So the ex-drug squad member must leave his cosy suburban home and return to a world of crime. Meanwhile, at a local party, Frank is told by his neighbour Lee Gunderman how to survive in greener pastures:

> ". . . In a town like this it's a matter of style, quiet but subtle. The house you live in, and the neighbourhood – you're right on base there. What I'm talking about is personal style, the way you present yourself. You're *too* quiet, Frank. *Too* subtle. At parties – brag a little, hint at things. After all, you weren't just an ordinary cop. You were a detective . . . Karl said drugs. Sure. Talk knowledgeably about drugs and kids. People here are scared about that. Are you laughing at me?"

After Frank assures her that he is not laughing at her, Lee offers other hints on how to improve his "suburban smarts":

> "You went to Northwestern, right? No degree. Mention you have one. Who's going to know the difference? You can even make it a master's." She paused. "And flirt a little, I mean just to be sociable. It doesn't mean anything."

When Frank mentions that this could be dangerous, Lee tells him,

> "Parties are always sexual, beginning with the conversations. But that doesn't mean they end in orgies. First just enough to please the women and flatter their husbands. They'll remember you when it comes time to sell their houses."[56]

As is often the case, the dialogue, though polite, becomes increasingly caustic. Typically, Coburn's novels are filled with conversations which skirt around the subject. After all, when it comes to the niceties of polite conversation, touching the subject, any subject, is strictly forbidden. Meanwhile, here, as well as in his 1979 *The Babysitter*, professional and social roles are played with an inflexibility worthy of Orwell's state functionaries in *1984*.

Yet into this well-greased system, Coburn throws any number of spanners. In his 1990 *Goldilocks*, the crime boss of crime bosses is a beautiful female suburbanite, while Goldilocks is a gloriously handsome blond man who arrives in town, only to cause more than his share of mayhem. Thus Coburn turns the usual gender-based criminal hierarchy upside down. Published in 1984, *Widow's Walk* might well be Coburn's most wicked novel. When a gaggle of husbands misbehave – taking up with younger women or showing a penchant for spousal abuse – their bodies begin to appear, washed-up on the ocean's shore. Interesting for its slant on domestic and psychological violence amongst the middle class, *Widow's Walk* focuses on a group of independent women vacationing at the seaside in Maine. With time on their hands, they cannot help but observe a number of male indiscretions, including an episode in a bar where they witness a man heaving a drink into a woman's face. When the woman, pretending it's a joke, gropes for a napkin, the man inches it out of her reach. But these women are not likely to forget such infractions, and those who commit them:

> The next day they saw him on the beach, or rather he saw them. He sought them out. They lay long and flat on bright towels, and he, beetle-browed, crouched near them in brilliant swim trunks and let the hot sand breathe up his calves . . . They tried to ignore him . . . They swung onto their sides, their backs to him, which in no way discouraged him. Finally Pamela turned her sun-scathed face toward him, shoved the blonde hair from her eyes, and said, "Piss off."[57]

When the intruder refuses to leave, the women get to their feet and stride off towards the water. "He's digging his own grave,"[58] comments one of the women. It's a dry and ominous statement delivered by a woman who does not even bother to glance over her shoulder.

With crime a primary feature of small-town life, violence is kept at bay only because it sits uncomfortably alongside real estate deals, polite conversation and angst-ridden, but convivial, dinner parties. Without resorting to the clichés of the genre, Coburn's combination of crime and clean tablecloths makes him as incisive as he is unusual, while, in depicting ghettos of middle-class comfort, he suggests that criminal activity is not class-based, but endemic to everyday American life.

Andrew Vachss

The most bizarre of contemporary crime writers, Andrew Vachss has been publishing fiction since the mid-1980s, a period coinciding with trickle-down social conditions and concerns about dysfunctional families, recovered memory and child abuse. Addressing authentic and pressing social problems, Vachss' fiction relies as much on the artifice of romance literature as on the realism of crime fiction. Having created a series of ultra-violent but one-dimensional texts in which the ends invariably justify the means, Vachss, a New York lawyer specialising in juvenile delinquents and the maltreatment of minors, has even penned the text of a Batman comic book,[59] one in which the superhero, moving between Gotham City and Bangkok, crusades against the child sex industry. Like his comic book, Vachss's novels are written in a sparse and simplistic style. Meanwhile, his protagonist, Burke, seeks justice and settles old scores. Half-anarchist and half-survivalist, Burke possesses an array of weapons and a thorough knowledge of armed combat. Like Batman, his self-appointed duty is to rid New York of crime.

To assist him, Burke has at his disposal a creaking surveillance system, a dog – a Neapolitan mastiff described as "140 pounds of concentrated hatred for humanity"[60] – and a smorgasbord of accomplices, including a giant mute Mongolian warrior; a transsexual prostitute; an anti-Nazi genius who lives with a pack of wild dogs in the Bronx wastelands; and Mama Wong, who runs a nearby Chinese restaurant. Bordering the surreal, there are moments when, despite the subject matter, it is difficult to know if the author is conscious of just how exaggerated his characters and narratives tend to be.

Driven to extremes by a warped society, Burke – who, like Vachss, specialises in cases involving violence against children – might be advised to seek a sympathetic therapist. For Burke's paranoia seems certain to unhinge him. Arriving for an assignation at a local park, Burke is so paranoid that, though armed and dangerous, he repeatedly circles the park so as to not attract attention. Burke's paranoia even extends to his dog, Pansy – a name picked on the advice of a lawyer after Burke was hit with a $100,000 law suit when his last dog, a Doberman, decided on a takeaway dinner, homo sapiens style. Burke not only refuses to clean up after the dog, but allows it to use the roof as a toilet.

It's not that Burke is lazy, but he believes that dog shit keeps winos away – "Too many of them smoke in bed."[61] Adept at disorientation, Burke has trained his dog to respond to coded commands. So Pansy only eats when he hears the command *speak*. One might have thought this would have driven the animal crazy, but Burke's deviousness runs deep: "[If] you try to feed her without saying the word, you get to be the food."[62] Moreover, *crazy*, in this context, remains a relative term.

Burke's mental state is such that he videos everyone who enters his office, but not before checking them out through a circuitous process:

> I went through the back door to the fire escape and climbed out past the connecting window to the second office. I kept going until I was near the end of the building, where I had a periscope mounted to give me a view of the entire hall from the elevator on down."[63]

Even his money-making techniques are indicative of a precarious mental state. Placing adverts in mercenary magazines, Burke offers, for $10, ersatz opportunities to fight on foreign soil. He feeds the names of those who send him money into a primitive data base, and, after asking a small additional fee, sends respondents a recording of a speech by Adolf Hitler which, unbeknownst to the would-be mercenaries, is actually by Nazi-hunter Simon Wiesenthal. Burke's prize is that he can add more names to a list which he believes will be useful when searching for right-wing mercenary child abusers who missed Wiesenthal's spiel on their last visit to the Holocaust Museum.

Suffering from a lack of perspective, Burke, regarding his eccentric lifestyle, says, "People won't let you live the way you want to, but if you're strong enough or quick enough, at least you don't have to live the way they want you to. I live, though, no matter what."[64] And "This is my place – I survive here",[65] clearly with an emphasis on survive. Though he lives in his apartment rent free – he has done so ever since digging up some dirt on the landlord's son – Burke shuns luxury as though it were a communicable disease. So he carpets his apartment with astroturf, claiming it's easier to clean. As for communicating with the outside world, Burke, an inveterate freeloader, hooks up a secret extension to the telephone belonging to the hippy drug dealers who live downstairs.

Though Vachss would insist he is alerting the world to the evils that lurk in the heart of the Big Apple, his interpretation remains disarmingly naive. For example, one wonders how such a streetwise individual could associate child pornography exclusively with extreme right-wing paramilitary types. Hasn't it occurred to him that such a narrow view means other culprits will go undetected? Moreover, there are moments when Vachss's fiction might be mistaken for the very pornography he rails against. Though Burke insists he speaks with the voice of experience, he locks himself into the very environment he describes. Why else would he remain in the city? The truth is, once outside Gotham City, Burke would be like a shark in a goldfish pond. Consequently, his entrapment contributes to his strange view of the world.

As to what is wrong with today's society, Vachss offers an endearing but ridiculous recollection of the multi-cultural days of doowop. As though the magic of the music once made the culture cohere, Burke says, "Music was more participatory when I was a kid."[66] But today it is different:

> [Kids] don't seem to give a damn about music, they only envy the musical lifestyle – gold chains and limos and all the coke they can stuff up their noses. But the kids haven't changed . . . As long as you have cities you have people who can't live in them and can't get out either. As long as you have sheep, you have wolves.[67]

Other than causing one to speculate on whether the recent drop in New York crime might be due to a rumoured doowop revival rather than a tough-on-crime mayor, one realises that

Burke, unwilling to be a sheep, is fighting in the name of all good lamb chops.

Young at heart, Burke is a would-be superhero whose *banger* could, if only we could peek under the hood, be mistaken for a *Batmobile*. Wanting to give the impression that he is a taxi-cab driver, Burke believes his disguise will allow him to escape the scrutiny of others: "Driving a cab in New York is the next best thing to being invisible. You can circle the same block a dozen times and even the local street-slime don't look twice."[68] For, in tracking his prey, Burke is willing to pull any kind of scam: "As I got older and kept doing time I began to realize that maybe the counselor had been right – you do have to play the cards they deal you – but only a certified sucker or masochist would play them honestly."[69]

As for his style and approach to the genre, Burke works hard to throw his adversaries off-balance. His martial arts mentor tells Burke there is a style of fighting, called the Drunken Monkey, that resembles his way of dealing with fear:

> [The] object is to have the fighter so completely dehumanized that he operates purely on instinct. Max told me this style is not the best for doing damage to an opponent . . . But it's almost impossible to defend against because it's completely unpredictable – you can't telegraph what you don't know. Once my brain goes into full fear-response it's a lot like the Drunken Monkey . . . I may not come up with any good ideas, but if you tried to read my mind all you'd get would be vertigo."[70]

This, in effect, constitutes Burke's *modus operandi*. Meanwhile, vertigo is also the effect that Burke's actions have on the reader. And perhaps on Burke as well. For no amount of slapping the *Drunken Monkey* will make Burke walk to his office in a straight line. To throw his would-be opponents off the beaten track, he prefers taking the most circuitous route possible. Naturally this sometimes entails being conspicuous: "[You] stand out only if you don't look like you're watching, like in . . . Times Square. If you're tracking a man in that pit, the only thing to do is really gawk around and be obvious as hell . . . Then they only wonder what you're looking for, not who."[71] For Burke, in courting anonymity, wants to be conspicuous; otherwise no one would know about his battle against the forces of evil, much less his attempts at remaining anonymous. Such posturing characterises Vachss's fiction, and Burke as a protagonist.

Addicted to the inner city and a primitive concept of justice, Burke, in *Hard Candy*, prowls the Bronx, where he witnesses the horrors of urban life: wild dogs and seagulls fight over slabs of fat; "Blacked out windows in abandoned buildings – dead eyes in a row of corpses . . ." and "Whores working naked under clear plastic raincoats stopped the trucks at the lights."[72] Though the streets are "dirty, they've got a lot of vice on them, but they're not the kind of anarchistic places where there's no law".[73] One wonders if Vachss actually believes that anyone who questions a society obsessed by law and order necessarily sides with *lawlessness*? Or that lawlessness, in such places, might not be inevitable and understandable? One would have thought that an absence of lawlessness would be even more worrying. After all, it's not a question of why there is so much violence, but why, given the state of society, there isn't more violence. Whatever its level, and however one regards it, lawlessness can never be solved by a single individual, no matter how obsessive or moral. Moreover, not everyone inhabiting such places spends their time taking advantage of others. On the contrary, many, despite their circumstances, manage to live relatively ordinary lives. Yet because Burke operates outside the law and in a state of perpetual paranoia, this is beyond his comprehension.[74]

Vachss, who, like Burke, investigates the culture by using a cab driver's licence and a beat-up car, has created a series of well-meaning but one-dimensional and, in the end, solipsistic narratives which reflect the state of America during the 1980s. Obsessive, off-kilter, willing to go to any lengths, Burke falls prey to the very culture he criticises. In portraying society's ills – kiddie porn, snuff films, obsessive behaviour, rape, child prostitution – Vachss inhabits the extreme end of deregulated fiction. However, he should be given as much breadth as possible. For moral crusades can be frightening to behold. Fluctuating between romance and the tall-tale, Vachss's fiction depicts a society out of control. Here, with everything and everyone for sale, there is good reason to be paranoid. For no one escapes from Vachss's world unscathed.

Jim Nisbet

An eclectic extremist, Nisbet, born in 1947, acknowledges the influence of the Black Mountain poets as well as past pulp culture writers. Conscious of his extremism, Nisbet's stylistic eccentricities place him outside the formalism found in so much contemporary crime fiction. In fact, other than Thompson and Behm, few have dared to investigate delirium and derangement with such precision and humour. Unfortunately, as of this writing, much of Nisbet's work is out of print.[75] Given the nature of his work and ability to pick apart a culture steeped in excess, it is understandable that such a perceptive writer should have fallen out of favour.

Nisbet's writing invariably centres on reckless misfits and loners whose obsessiveness leads them into a series of horrifying situations. In *The Damned Don't Die*, the author transports the reader to Thompson territory, where nothing is as it seems, and everything is a reflection of itself. This, in 1981, some years prior to the revival of interest in the work of Thompson and other pulp culture writers. First published by Pinnacle books under its original title, *The Gourmet*, Nisbet's San Francisco-set novel features Martin Windrow, a private-eye and ex-cop. But the novel also concerns the inner life of a crime novelist. In the opening pages pulpist Herbert Trimble confronts the terror that preoccupies writers contemplating a blank page:

> The ecstatic moans from the apartment next to his kept
> Herbert Trimble awake, but they gave him, as he lay in bed an

idea for a story. It would be the best trash story he'd ever written. All he had to do was get up out of bed, walk to his typewriter, and begin. There was even a sheet of paper already in the machine; it was blank, and it was rolled down under the platen and back up about 3½ inches, just the proper distance from the top of the page at which to begin an opening paragraph.[76]

Is this what happens when a crime writer is forced to confront his own subject matter? "I've always wanted to skin a woman", reads a line on another piece of paper in Trimble's typewriter. It is as though Trimble's text is writing itself, and, in doing so, exacting a series of crimes over which he has no control. Meanwhile, a corpse is discovered next door. The dead woman, according to a neighbour, has suffered an agonising death, but the "pain was seducing her, and she couldn't stop it". Daring to venture into the Coburnian suburbs, Windrow eventually finds himself in a highly charged world of sex, violence and murder. Like other Nisbet novels, *The Damned Don't Die* deals with a world warped by desire and populated by characters seeking the final boundary. A "gourmet of sensations", this "nice, warped, psychotic tale"[77] depicts a fictional world that seems all too real.

Another novel about crossing boundaries and being stranded in a nightmarish environment, Nisbet's 1987 *Lethal Injection* concerns an alcoholic prison doctor who must execute a young black inmate by injecting him with a fatal dose of poison. The novel begins where others end, with the prisoner leaving his cell on Death Row to meet his fate. Reminding one of Camus' *L'Etranger*, Doctor Franklin Royce becomes so perplexed by the prisoner's indifference to his death – born out of anger rather than metaphysical disposition – that he wonders if he might have killed an innocent man. Yet Royce's skills are highly prized:

Anyone could hang a man, and quite a few people could pull a lever that released cyanide gas into an airtight room. A fewer number could probably electrocute a human; that was a job frequently botched. The half-burned corpus still twitching, requiring another thirty-second jolt of fourteen hundred volts, the lights dim again in the prison library ... But hardly anyone outside the medical profession could be found qualified to measure a lethal dose of poison and neatly prepare a man for the injection of it.[78]

So Royce sets out to discover the prisoner's story, only to find that fate and environmental determinism have combined to deal the young black man a hand from a crooked deck. And a criminal subculture that protects its own:

> [Gypsy] children were told not to point out shooting stars but to watch them silently, because each one represented the soul of a fleeing thief. If you pointed out a shooting star, a thief would be caught. So, what if you pointed out a satellite? Who would get caught? A crooked politician?
> Interesting legend. It meant the gypsies sided with the thieves, whoever they were. Thieves were good guys. Thieves were ... innocent? No, not innocent. Just good guys.[79]

Escaping the wreckage of his life – including a failed marriage and sinking medical practice – Royce is working in an era of Reagan's deregulation, when crime has, for many, become a necessity. Says a guitarist that Royce encounters, "Crazy is one thing, and thrift is something else. I been saving some of that Aid for the Totally Dependent money. I know ... you think that's impossible. After all, ATD's not all that much, and Reagan even cut it back. Still and all, we get by on the grace of God and miscellaneous felonies."[80] In Dallas, Royce uncovers a lifestyle that exceeds his experience or imagination. There he befriends those who rival the inhabitants of an Andrew Vachss novel. These include a tattooed pansexual psychopath, an Irish-Mexican heroin addict, and Colleen, a prostitute and one-time girlfriend of the man who has been executed. Royce becomes fascinated by her flawed beauty.

Faced with an inferno of horrific crimes and weird sex, Royce takes refuge in his supply of morphine. Eventually, Royce, like a perverse biographer, ends up reassessing his own bankrupt life:

> [He] wondered if life held anything more profound than monthly payments, overdrafts at the bank, unfair speeding tickets, a credit card scissored in two on a silver tray in a very nice restaurant, a life whose pecuniary rhythms sailed from troughs of embarrassment to peaks of anxiety and back again with no respite.
> Which is a bigger waste? A man born with a chance who blows it, or a man born with no chance who fights it? They're both losers in the end, aren't they?[81]

While Colleen thinks back on her life with her recently executed boyfriend, and how the world has passed her by, she talks as though she, if circumstances had been different, might have been a cultural critic or a writer of deregulated crime fiction:

> The idea of money was everywhere, but the actual stuff became more and more of a rumor about something other people had somewhere else. Friends started to sicken and die from unnatural causes . . . She couldn't really put her finger on when suffering had replaced fun as the ongoing environment, just like she couldn't put a finger on when junk became more important than anything else.[82]

Written shortly after the late 1970s Supreme Court decision to reintroduce capital punishment, a decree that threatened to turn executions into a spectator sport, *Lethal Injection*, in following the life of a dead man, might, like *The Damned Don't Die*, be one of the best novels Jim Thompson never wrote.

Death Puppet, published in 1989, begins when Mattie, a café waitress in a small town in Washington, has a one-night stand with Tucker, a travelling salesman. After a night spent indulging in a bizarre brand of safe sex – connected, oddly enough, with a tank filled with tropical fish – Tucker leaves in the early morning, his farewell a note that quotes Paul Verlaine's poem "Clair de Lune". Mattie, of course, has no idea who Tucker is, or the problems that will ensue. After all, she is a product of her surroundings:

> Indeed, as Mattie had learned long before, it was with interior landscapes, of other horrors or other beauties altogether, that this land most often clashed; and the petty battles fought by little men with monstrous machines – not the wind or drought or erosion – that most often defaced it.[83]

Here history and the dominant narrative threaten to scar the landscape and become an evil force, not dissimilar from that which imbues the stories of H. P. Lovecraft:

> She'd always entrusted her fate to its own vaguely benign historical course . . . and she exercised something of a mental shrug in deference to this spirit now. But then she veered close to the specter of despair that had raised its setaceous muzzle a little while ago, that she was mucking about with things beyond her grasp, and that if she didn't get a hold of herself . . . this land and perhaps some darker force would master her, swallow her up in an instant of mischief with a chortle, and leave no trace of her passage upon the earth.[84]

Despite her disposition, Mattie's inability, or unwillingness, to dominate nature has placed her on the wrong side of the historical fence. Interestingly enough, Nisbet cites Reisner's *Cadillac Desert* as a source book for *Death Puppet*. While Reisner's treatise concerns the corrupt and deadly politics of water, both books focus on the degree to which the environment has been manipulated by capital and human intervention.

As elsewhere in Nisbet's fiction, Vietnam figures heavily in *Death Puppet*. Unbeknownst to Mattie, the war has turned Tucker into a schizoid killing machine, reminiscent of Lou Ford in Thompson's *The Killer Inside Me*. The implication is that, though Vietnam was a defining moment in America's narrative, it was not an isolated event, but part of a historical process. In pointing to the politics and history of water, Nisbet suggests that the war was symptomatic of a greater malady. Nevertheless, it was Vietnam, rather than bad water, that turned Tucker into a killing machine and now causes him to hear voices which take him where few would choose to travel.

Nisbet's only book currently in print, *Prelude to a Scream*, published in 1997, concerns the theft of body parts. Stanley, who has cut himself off from humanity, visits a bar, gets picked up by a woman, only to wake up in San Francisco's Golden Gate Park, zipped into a sleeping bag and missing a kidney. Another Nisbet loner, Stanley eventually pursues those who removed his organ, only to find himself coming to terms with a world he has rejected. Nisbet, in following this urban myth,[85] constructs another evocative San Francisco-set narrative. Unusual for crime fiction, but not uncommon in a Nisbet novel, *Prelude to a Scream*, as well as delving into the world of medicine, is well-informed regarding ecological issues and poetry. As in *The Damned Don't Die*, Nisbet alludes to the act of writing. Having spent "six years wandering around Canada instead of allowing himself to be drafted",[86] Stanley is likened to a page that forms a text capable of articulating contemporary America: "It was the first time he'd actually studied the incision which, upon consideration, had the appearance of a lavender revision upon the white editorial of his neglected flesh."[87] This revision is part and parcel of a lucrative business, one that is perfectly logical given the parameters of cut-throat capitalism. Paranoid and with a single alcohol-drenched kidney, Stanley speculates on those who would take part in such an enterprise:

> They looked just like anybody else, right? . . . They were motivated just like everybody else – right? They stole kidneys because they wanted a bigger television? Because the rent went up? Because their guns required pricey silver bullets? Because they wanted to continue to breathe the perpetually fresh, blue, salt-tanged, increasingly expensive air of San Francisco instead

of the stale, brown, tangibly thick, if cheaper, effluent that passed for air in most of the rest of the world?[88]

As for the doctor who performs the operations, he is no different from a range of psychos found in any number of contemporary crime novels. Finding him in the process of *speedballing* while fucking his nurse, Stanley extrapolates on the doctor's maniacal snigger:

> It was the laughter of a man who'd always known that every-
> thing in the world had been put there either for his
> annoyance or for his amusement . . . Nothing was funny, and
> everything was funny, it was all up to him. It was the laughter
> of a man whose entire being had been subsumed by turpitude,
> who could not distinguish between pain or joy in others, who
> lived only for the depravity that he might deploy upon them.
> His philosophy would preach a freedom of indulgences . . . but
> he would believe in it only insofar as it enabled him to
> debase.[89]

But the final organ theft, the one that cuts his manhood down to size, is the only slice capable of making Stanley scream.

In combining horror and crime, Nisbet has laid claim to a particular literary landscape, one inhabited of late by the likes of J. W. Jeter (*The Land of the Dead*) and Marc Laidlaw (*The Orchid Eater*). Adept at indicating the relationship between absolute evil and saintliness, Nisbet plays upon the fears and phobias of his characters. In a Nisbet novel, one never knows what demons will be released, nor what personal apocalypse is about to ensue. Digging deep into the culture, Nisbet's fiction can be read as a satire regarding the corruption, excess, and pestilence of contemporary America. Creating his nightmarish narratives with an impish delight, Nisbet's dark humour, combined with an ability to distance himself from his fictional world, gives his fiction a perspective few other noirists have achieved. Though his books are full of casual sex and off-hand violence, Nisbet is the most literary and intelligent of crime novelists. That much of his work is out of print just might indicate how unsettling Nisbet's narratives can be.

Daniel Woodrell

Published in 1986, Daniel Woodrell's *Under the Bright Lights* is the first of three crime novels set in Saint Bruno, a small bayou town in Louisiana. The protagonist of Woodrell's first novel is Rene Shade, the local chief of police. Rene is also the main character in Woodrell's *Muscle for the Wing*, while *The Ones You Do*, also set in Saint Bruno, features Rene's brother, John X. Shade. Together these books form a trilogy whose subject is the push and pull existence of those living in a small Southern bayou town. But Woodrell's vivid portrayal carries none of the cultural tourism – no Cajun music nor French literature here – that peppers the work of James Lee Burke or James Sallis. For this is the land of the lumpen, and proud of it.

Full of wit, exuberance, and home truths, Woodrell's protagonists are unlike most contemporary crime fiction fodder:

> John X. Shade had long believed that the key to life was cue ball control, but lately his stroke was so imperfect on cue balls and life alike that his existence had come to seem far too much like the stark moral to a cautionary homily he'd chosen to ignore. He was in his sixties, a decade of his life had more miscues and comeuppances in it than he could construe as merely accidental.[90]

With its violence and white-trash morality, Shade's hand-to-mouth existence is as convincing as the author's portrayal of bayou life.

Undoubtedly, Woodrell's hardest hitting deregulated novel to date is his 1987 *Woe to Live On*. The irony is that the latter is more a western or war novel than a crime novel. Set in 1861 on the Kansas–Missouri border, *Woe to Live On* details the crimes committed in the name of the Civil War. In doing so, Woodrell implies that such violence has always been part of America's narrative, influencing values past and present. That Woodrell's novel is set in another century, should not disqualify it as a crime novel. If Walter Mosley and James Ellroy can delve into the past and write about post-war Los Angeles, and Elmore Leonard can write novels that are westerns without horses, then Woodrell must be permitted to stretch the definition of what constitutes a crime novel. For the crimes themselves are all too apparent: "It was not uncommon to thus meet enemies who had not been so in gentler times . . . Many debts were settled before they had a chance to be incurred, but thin-skinned fairness rarely crabbed youthful aim."[91]

In terms of violence, *Woe to Live On* compares favourably to Cormac McCarthy's classic western *Blood Meridian*. Though lacking the latter's baroque style, Woodrell uses language to heighten the novel's sense of violence:

> We all stood silent in the morning light, encircling the Federals. Many faces were sad, even squeamish, about the necessaries of the day. But several faces were poised with a hunger for the hot plate of revenge they'd been served. Lloyd and Curtin had been hung, then quartered and tossed onto the River Road to nourish varmints. The quartering was meant to disturb us, and in at least one case, it worked."[92]

Woodrell details the times and crimes of a deregulated and excessive era through the eyes of Jake Roedell, an initially innocent young man who rides with the notorious Quantrill and the First Kansas Irregulars. Once on the Kansas–Missouri border they commit various acts of gratuitous violence. Committed in the war's name, their deadly skirmishes are parodies of the real war taking place further to the east.[93]

What makes Woodrell's novel so contemporary is the way it conveys a noir-ridden sense of history, one that takes the reader from the 1860s to the present and a world in which ideology has been effectively plundered. Published not long after America's bombing of Libya, *Woe to Live On* communicates a familiar senselessness. While Woodrell's book, if read by war enthusiasts, might be mistaken for a homage to the glories of non-technological combat, few could misunderstand his insistence on detailing political policy down to the last command and body count.

Another writer influenced by Charles Willeford, Woodrell takes the measure of America's outlaw tradition, from Quantrill's Raiders to the Hell's Angels. His 1996 *Give Us a Kiss* is set in the Ozarks, where Woodrell has lived for a number of years, and concerns the lengths to which working people will go to stay afloat in contemporary America. This novel centres on Doyle, a writer bearing some similarity to Woodrell, who returns to his Ozark home only to become involved with his brother in a plan to cultivate marijuana. This leads to greater crimes, as well as problems with the law and iniquitous neighbours. Coupled with that narrative is the protagonist's search for a subject on which to hang his yet-to-be-written second novel. Like a rough-and-ready James Sallis, Woodrell portrays Doyle, incarcerated at the end of the novel, writing the story of the book one has just read. Thus the impression of autobiography, which, if nothing else, justifies the first-person narrative. This apparent merging of fiction and reality remains an artifice on which crime novels have long been based. Be that as it may, Woodrell's regionalism and use of history are exemplary, and, focusing on class and the messy aftermath of mindless armed conflict, a cogent critique of nationalism. In the end, Woodrell's macho approach to the genre and his manly attitude to writing as an art of self-defence is summed up by a quote prefacing his first novel, *Under the Bright Lights*, in which the author finds meaning in the words of former heavyweight boxer Joe Frazier:

> You can map out a fight plan or a life plan, but when the action starts, it may not go the way you planned, and you're down to your reflexes – that means your [preparation]. That's where your roadwork shows. If you cheated on that in the dark

of the morning, well, you're going to get found out now, under the bright lights.[94]

There are other writers who managed to ride the wave of deregulatory writing, or whose careers were kick-started in the early 1990s when deregulation, under the auspices of a Democratic President, had become a bipartisan political fact. Influenced by their predecessors, these writers also portray the downside of deregulatory policies. One such writer is Vicki Hendricks, whose novel *Miami Purity* was published in 1995. Though owing much to the liberating effect of feminism, *Miami Purity* reads as though it were written in a parallel universe where desire is the be-all and end-all of existence. It is also a novel whose deregulatory perspective – as though written from the viewpoint of a Jim Thompson heroine – is as original as it is satirical. In fact, it could be said that Hendricks takes up where Patricia Highsmith left off, except her vision is much pulpier and raunchier than Highsmith's could ever be. For Hendricks's obsessive novel contains a pastiche sexuality so extreme it borders on the ridiculous. Compare, for instance, Hendricks's line, albeit in a dream – "Her big tits were pointing up at him"[95] – with the macho Ozark honkie Woodrell, and his notion of bosom engineering:

> She left her chair. "Watch my tits." She settled to the floor, laid on her back, and her breasts dove toward her armpits like rabbits into holes. "These mamas are real – and that's how they really behave."[96]

As well as being one of the few crime novels to detail the dirty world of dry cleaning, *Miami Purity*, as a parody of how men think women think about men, might be said to have been written from the viewpoint of a woman imagined by a man imagined by a woman.

Significantly, Hendricks explains the novel and its web of duplicity by beginning with a quote from Sartre: "Passions themselves are freedoms caught in their own trap." Like Coburn's *Widow's Walk* taken to an extreme, Hendricks's novel concerns obsession and revenge. But, unlike Coburn's work, it concentrates on the habits of a slightly unbalanced woman in need of work and sex, but unable to put either in proper perspective. From the opening paragraph, the reader gets the gist of the novel:

> [I] picked up the radio and caught him across the forehead with it. It was one of those big boom boxes with the cassette player and recorder, but I never figured it would kill him. We were sitting in front of the fan, listening to country music and sipping Jack Daniels . . . and all of a sudden the whole world changed. My old man was dead. I didn't feel I had anything to do with it.[97]

Once out of jail, Sherri Parlay, a former topless dancer – "At thirty-six-looking-thirty, I was determined to get myself out of the dark bars and into the daylight."[98] – finds work in a dry cleaning establishment.

Obsessed with Payne, the proprietress's son, Sherri kills both him and his mother. She kills the former because he has been unfaithful, but kills his mother, Brenda, because, according to the unscrupulous Payne, she has, for years, been sexually abusing him. Not quite your average politically correct crime novel – Sara Paretsky would need to have served a life sentence in a backwater trailerpark before she could write something like this – *Miami Purity* contains a dark and subversive humour. Unable to say no to sex, Sherri spends the afternoon shimmying in a local bar when she should be celebrating at the grand opening of a new branch of the business. The novel ends with a hilarious and horrifying murder, as Sherri aims a gun at Payne and orders him into a dry cleaning machine.

> It was a powerful machine and it was clunking, working hard. His shoes were bumping the side, or maybe it was his head. I pictured his mouth open and the powerful cleaning fluid

filling his mouth, lungs, stomach – pooling in his ears, penetrating into his skin, burning through the tiny pipe of his cock, tearing its way like a knife up his asshole. He would soon be cleaner than any human ever got. His stench would be filtered and dumped with the toxic waste.[99]

Taking a decidedly different tack from other writers of deregulatory fiction, Hendricks is one of the few females to enter the genre at full force. Furthermore, her unique approach sets her apart from the likes of Patricia Cornwell, Poppy Z. Brite or Faye Kellerman. While Cornwell's work is interesting from a forensic point of view, it lacks the abandonment, wit, and style found in most deregulated fiction. On the other hand, Brite, despite her ghoulish interest in serial killers, remains a gothic fantasist rather than a crime writer. As for Kellerman, her frightening tales of orthodox Judaism, though capturing the mood of Southern California suburban Jewish life, remain ordinary in terms of structure. Having said this, her short story *Bonding*, with its Valley-speak hopelessness and sense of cultural breakdown, approaches Hendricks's noir sensibility:

> My friend and co-hooker came down with strep throat today and asked if I could service her regular johns . . . So I go down to the room she rents. It's a typical sleazebucket of a place – broken-down bed, filthy floor, and a cracked mirror. Who should I see in it but my father . . . To tell you the truth, I barely recognise his face. Then I realize he must have gotten a lift like Mom, 'cause his skin is also like stretched to the max.[100]

Nevertheless, Hendricks, for sheer perversity, remains on her own in this particular school of noir fiction. It remains to be seen what will become of someone possessing such an individual voice.[101]

At their best, writers of deregulated crime fiction reflect the paranoia one finds in contemporary America, whether in the inner city, suburbs or small towns. Though the statistics do not fully substantiate this paranoia,[102] the cultural discrepancies, economic uncertainties and the media's portrayal of violence have encouraged and perpetuated such fears. However one looks at it, the paranoia of everyday life is based on the effect of real policies. This post-mortem juxtaposition of fiction and reality brings us back to K. C. Constantine who, writing about Chief Mario Balzic, says,

> [In] all his years of trying to keep husbands and wives and parents and children from doing stupid things to one another, until this moment, he'd never been to a house where the paranoia factor was based on reality. Tens of dozens of husbands over the years had complained about somebody "out there" who was telling them to strangle the wife, shoot the dog, drown the sister-in-law, spill paint on the neighbor's cat, but this was the first time there was anybody actually out there. And the guys *out* there actually think they belong *out* there.[103]

Crime, like anything else, cannot be produced in a vacuum. For it is the culture that produces crime as well as crime fiction, its warp and woof reflecting the nightmares in which it luxuriates.

6

FROM MEAN STREETS TO DREAM STREETS

The portrayal of cities in contemporary noir fiction[1]

"The streets were dark with something more than night." (Raymond Chandler)[2]

Since its inception, noir fiction has depicted American urban life with unflinching accuracy. Born from a unique cultural mix – proletariat perceptions and muckraking instincts – such texts portray the city not as the site of the American dream, but as the epicentre of an all-consuming nightmare. Like moths to the flame, noirists, from Dashiell Hammett to James Ellroy, have been attracted to the city, viewing it as a malignant space, and the epitome of everything corrupt capitalism has achieved.

In its investigation of urban life, crime fiction has focused on the lone protagonist who, often wrongly accused, is caught within the narrative, and, to ensure his survival, forced to investigate the culture. The protagonist, part of the flâneur tradition – that is, an analytical observer and connoisseur of city life[3] – would permutate into the private investigator, who, though seemingly apolitical, bears the instincts of an existential Marxist. Searching for cultural clues only to uncover crime and corruption, the investigator possesses, as Chandler once said of a fellow detective, "a camera eye as rare as a pink zebra".[4]

To this day, Hammett's 1929 *Red Harvest* remains the template for the noir critique of urban America. A novel about incipient political corruption, it concerns a town called Personville – pronounced *Poisonville* by the local population. A canvas on which he will overlay his future politics, Hammett's novel, as an urban critique, precedes and eclipses the work of Raymond Chandler. While the latter is noted for his noirism, "Down these mean streets a man must go who is not himself mean, who is neither tarnished nor afraid", Hammett's protagonist, choosing a different line, dreams of pursuing a woman through a series of American cities. Once awake, the Op is able to connect dream and reality, eventually saying, "I have walked as many streets as I did in my dreams."[5] In suggesting the negotiation of urban America has less to do with fear or heroism than with the need to investigate, and the ability to imagine alternatives, Hammett's all-encompassing perspective helped radicalise the genre. Meanwhile, Chandler, parodying Hammett and the *Black Mask* school, had, with his British public school education and business background, a decidedly middle-class attitude towards urban life. Unfettered by ties to the genre's proletariat origins, Chandler, his witticisms soaked in an outsider's cynicism and paranoia, was free to interpret the culture with an accuracy hitherto unknown.

However, noir fiction's critique of the city would not become commonplace until after World War Two, coinciding with the rise of paperback fiction and the momentary politicisation of the workforce. Within a few years, McCarthyism, the Cold War, fears regarding the use of atomic weapons and a permanent wartime economy, made cities, more than ever, places of paranoia, conflict and anxiety. This would be typified in the writing of Horace McCoy, Chester Himes, David Goodis, each of whom sought to investigate urban life during the pulp culture era.

Noir fiction and films represent the city as a place of shadows, casual relationships and violence, where the discrepancies between the powerful and the powerless have become obvious. Shorn of a post-war political perspective, the contemporary urban protagonist cuts a ubiquitous figure as he or she moves through the urban landscape. Now a marketable commodity, noir protagonists inhabit TV adverts where, as the final consumers, they perambulate through centreless cities in which the struggle for survival has relinquished its place to style. However, present-day noir, with its portrayal of such subjects as crack cocaine, child pornography and domestic violence, is not so readily glamorised nor so easily co-opted.

If contemporary cities are battlegrounds, hardboiled noir writers have become akin to war correspondents, anthropologists and archaeologists, who test the culture as they dig amidst its wreckage. Invariably one opens a contemporary crime novel to find a city on the edge of a social, financial or environmental precipice, and the protagonist, tempted by urban corruption, in the midst of a personal or spiritual crisis. In James Lee Burke's *Morning for the Flamingos*, Dave Robicheaux must battle police corruption as well as the bottle, while admitting he can only perceive his identity in the reflections he sees in the eyes of others. Casting a new light on mirrored sunglasses, Robicheaux isn't alone in his angst. In an effort to atone for their sins, Block's Matt Scudder and Sallis's Lew Griffin, like tarnished boy scouts, forge their new identities by doing deeds for others. This, it is suggested, is the price one pays for working in a battle-zone without coherency, stability, or the luxury of a stiff drink.

With surveillance systems and security firms now amongst the most lucrative enterprises in town, inner cities have become virtual zones of repression. This in an era when employment in the private security industry has tripled over the last twenty years, making detective and protective work the twentieth fastest growing employment sector in the United States. In California today, there are 3.9 private security employees for every public security employee. By the year 2000, 73 per cent of the country's "protective employees" will work in the private sector, while only 27 per cent will work in law enforcement.[6] As home owners purchase weapons and lobby for Draconian zoning regulations, private security firms, guaranteeing a rapid response, have become the contemporary equivalent of the protection racket.

Says a motelier in Elmore Leonard's *La Brava*:

> "He gave me the pitch, all the protection I'm supposed to get
> for five hundred dollars. I ask him, against what? The guy
> says, "Well, let's see." He goes over to the door, looks out. He
> says, word for word, "Somebody could come and take a dump
> in your pool every night." . . . Not, he's gonna smash all my
> windows, he's gonna throw a bomb in, blow the place up, like
> they used to do it. Or even threaten to break my legs. No, this
> big blond-hair son of a bitch is gonna poo poo in my
> swimming pool."[7]

These days public and private surveillance have become
commonplace.[8] So much so that in Leonard's *Glitz*, the *eye in
the sky* mirrors the shifting perspective of the narrative, while
criminalising anyone in its path.

But who has time to monitor all these incriminating images?
And how, if monitored, can the images compete with multi-
channel TV? In Leonard's 1995 *Riding the Rap*, Louis watches
Donahue while, in the corner of the screen, he can see his
cohort Chip and newcomer Bobby fight it out as though part of
some cliché-ridden TV cop programme.[9] Apparently clued-in to
technology, Bobby realises he's being watched, so, after the
fight, he acknowledges the camera by urinating into the
swimming pool. After all, if one is on television, some kind of
performance is required. Though the viewer controls the image,
the person being viewed can, with their few minutes of simulated
fame, control the narrative, commit the crime and dominate
the space. In George Pelecanos's *Shoedog*, Constantine, caught
in the stable with the gangster's wife and thoroughbred horse,
stares into the camera and says, "He's got a thing about
protecting his investment." Constantine might be speaking
about the woman, the horse, or his own future involvement in a
crime organised by the person behind the camera. But Delia
assures Constantine the camera "is always on, but they're not
always monitoring it".[10]

Surveillance also functions as a cleansing device, ridding urban
centres and malls of potential criminals and those without
purchasing power. No wonder noir protagonists express
contempt for gentrification. For, in crime fiction, old sleaze
is preferable to nouveau commodification. In Block's *The
Devil Knows You're Dead*, Matt, regarding the semantics of class,
says,

> When it's a story about rising property values . . . then the
> neighborhood is Clinton. That's when they're talking
> gentrification and tree planting. When it's gunshots and crack
> vials, then it's Hell's Kitchen. Glen Holtzman lived in a
> luxurious high-rise apartment in Clinton. He died a couple of
> blocks away in Hell's Kitchen.[11]

In mapping the city and its political vectors, noirists reveal the
price society must pay for economic growth.

But an investigator's observations also depend on his or her
means of transport, which, as much as his or her relationship to
the state, can determine ideological orientation. While pulp
culture private eyes often *gumshoed* their prey on foot, most
contemporary investigators opt for the comforts of the car.
These days walking might be an act of defiance, or an economic
and spatial necessity. Temporarily testing public transport allows
Walter Mosley's Easy Rawlins to gain some valuable insights
regarding Los Angeles's black community:

> On the bus there were old people and young mothers and
> teenagers coming in late to school. Most of them were black
> people. Dark-skinned with generous features. Women with
> eyes so deep that most men can never know them. Women . . .
> who'd lost too much to be silly or kind. And there were the
> children . . . with futures so bleak that it could make you cry
> just to hear them laugh. Because behind the music of their
> laughing you knew there was the rattle of chains.[12]

Likewise, in New Orleans, Sallis's Lew Griffin maintains a

predominantly pedestrian existence. As does Lawrence Block's Matt Scudder, who constantly meanders Manhattan in search of an AA meeting, a cup of coffee, and a corpse. Always in confessional mode, Scudder admits he gave up drinking, driving and carrying a gun on the same day, realising, if he continued with any of the three, he would soon either kill himself or someone else. While in Pelecanos's *The Big Blowdown*, when Pete Karras borrows a car, he drives it with little idea of the finer points of automotive manoeuvring, much less its history.

Yet negotiating a city by car can prompt comments that might not have been possible had the investigator been on foot. Cars, if nothing else, offer a modicum of protection and, proportionate to speed and distance, can lead to some petrol-infested soundbites. In Loren Estelman's 1990 *Sweet Women Lie*, Amos Walker, a Detroit PI, drives through his city, reading it as though he were a member of Ralph Nader's hit squad. Referring to Detroit's unsightly industrial image, the incongruously surnamed detective observes the boundaries separating old from new. Noting the city's aging assembly lines, he comments on the Ford auditorium, which, he says, looks "like an air filter". Driving through the old section of town, he arrives at Outer Drive, once the boundary of the city "before developers . . . began a fifteen mile crawl northward, devouring trees and grass as they went and dropping concrete and asphalt behind them like manure".[13] Spoken while encased within a hunk of metal, Walker, protected from the rough-and-tumble of the Motor City, makes it clear that, in the new urban environment, everything is for sale, and every pedestrian, lacking the means to traverse the boundaries of the city, has become suspect.

Other than their resistance to the dominant narrative, what noir writers have in common is their use of language to express the dynamics of urban life, at the root of which is a feeling of displacement, regret and emptiness. An ability to communicate on the streets is essential to survival. Likewise, being linguistically *low-down* provides noir characters with a perspective and intelligence honed on the cutting-edge of society. In K. C. Constantine's *Always a Body to Trade*, a black drug dealer, speaking the language of the streets, is more informed than the mayor when it comes to the ins and outs of the city's politics. Meanwhile, a barroom conversation, based on the same urban intelligence, scotches any talk of how religion benefits the poor:

> "I'll ask you a simple question. What do you think of a father who lets his son be tortured to prove a point? And if you can explain the crucifixion to me any other way, I'll shut my mouth . . . A whole religion has been founded on that kind of torture."[14]

Street-level intelligence also figures heavily in the work of Chester Himes. In his novel *Blind Man With a Pistol*, urban renewal is regarded as just another infringement of public and private space:

> [Residents] bitterly resented being evicted from the homes where some had been born, and their children had been born, and some had married and friends and relatives had died, no matter if these homes were slum flats that had been condemned as unfit for human dwelling. They had been forced to live there, in all the filth and degradation, until their lives had been warped to fit, and now they were being thrown out. It was enough to make a body riot.[15]

Himes's view of a city within a city, in which ghettoisation supersedes segregation, is one in which the possibility of urban chaos is never more than an infraction away. Himes concludes that spontaneous violence, though understandable, is unlikely to halt the progress of racism and inequality; yet such is the paranoia of the state that, if three black men meeting together supposedly constitutes a riot, then a black man with a pistol must surely comprise a revolution. At the same time, the city, however one misinterprets it, is a place where the old must make way for the new. In Nick Tosches's novel, *Trinities*, a group of old-school mobsters gather to grouse about how they have allowed themselves to be marginalised by a new wave of young corporate criminals:

> "All them college joes with the degrees and the computers. Spreadsheets, venture capital, statutory mergers, cash-conversion cycles . . . They gave us this line of shit and we bought it. Leveraged buyouts. We got more leverage out of a fuckin' lead pipe than them and all their fuckin' mumbo-jumbo put together. But we bought it. We gave 'em the world on a fuckin' silver platter. It was us, not them. We're the ones who cut off our own fuckin' balls."[16]

As yesterday's dreams become today's nightmare, the crimes continue, making Raymond Chandler's remark that "There is nothing left to write about but death" seem, for addled godfathers, ghetto militants and deregulated crime writers, all too true.

Fallen Angel's Flight

As Chandler's noir nemesis, James Ellroy views death not as a literary artifice but as a final stop on a torturous and gruesome personal journey. In fact, *The Big Nowhere*, which comprises the title of the third volume of Ellroy's *LA Quartet*, might be a euphemism for death as well as for Ellroy's stamping ground. While the title recalls Gertrude Stein's remark regarding Oakland that "There is no there there", Ellroy's book is an investigation of a city whose surfeit of signifiers threaten to render it meaningless. By *White Jazz*, the final book of his *LA Quartet*, Ellroy can only view Los Angeles as a series of "fevered dreams". Revelling in icons that no longer exist, Ellroy exploits adolescent fantasies regarding money, sex, and crime. Meanwhile he replaces the Ozzie and Harriet view of the era with a grotesque parody that seethes with political corruption, unspoken conspiracies, Hollywood perversities, white-trash psychoses, Chicano sleaze and police racism.

Concentrating on the years between 1948 and the late 1950s, Ellroy turns the city into a memory theatre, recalling the past to amplify recent social and demographic changes. In fact, Ellroy's cataclysmic view of Los Angeles relates less to the 1950s than to the early 1970s when the city, particularly the downtown section, was at a low ebb and ripe for takeover,[17] exemplified by the evictions of residents from the famous Victorian sector known as Bunker Hill. An area brimming with history and nostalgia, it would be described by Raymond Chandler in *The High Window* and, more recently, by Edward Bunker in his novel *Dog Eat Dog*:

> Once upon a time, LA's famous Angel's Flight, a funicular railway, ran from Hill Street to what had once been Victorian mansions on top, although by his youth they were rooming houses. Now Angel's Flight was gone, as were the rooming houses, replaced by salmon and silver glass and aluminium shining in the hot sun of Southern California, somehow reminding Troy of the Emerald City in *The Wizard of Oz*.[18]

Having withstood geological shifts, these buildings would finally crumble when faced with the city's shift in financial power. Before long much of the exquisite shabbiness of LA, depicted by Chandler, James L. Cain, Himes and Ellroy, would fade into the past, replaced by glitzy foreign-owned skyscrapers.

LA's centrelessness[19] is crucial to Ellroy's fiction. Consequently, in *White Jazz*, Ellroy presents a multitude of identifiable urban points, each of which can be taken to represent a false centre around which the novel revolves. The most infamous of these is Chavez Ravine, where the Dodgers would be relocated after their move from Brooklyn. Soon to become central to the creation of the city's new image, the Dodgers would, as early as 1958, mark out a road of commodification equalled only by the 1956 construction of Disneyland. From its inception, the Dodgers' relocation constituted an economic point and source of prestige that promised to contribute to the city's notoriety. Turning his novel on this event, and the political machinations accompanying it, Ellroy illustrates the extent to which post-war Los Angeles is the result of conspiracies and political corruption.[20] Like the movement of water into the area, relocating the Dodgers to Los Angeles was, as Ellroy shows, a ruthless and noir-like activity.

Not all writers share Ellroy's apocalyptic view of Los Angeles. For Arthur Lyons, the city might be corrupt, but it is also a place in which redemption remains possible. Though he sets his work in the present, Lyons's moral centre and vernacular relate to the past. In *Other People's Money*, Lyons's protagonist Jacob Asch walks a thin line between urban compassion and intolerance:

> It had been two months since LA's Army of the Homeless had established a beachhead on the sands of Venice as a social statement about what the government was doing for the nation's poor. Along with the Unfortunate Regulars, however, had come a sizable regiment of winos, hypes, panhandlers, grifters, and other, less classifiable species of derelicti, the result being that those who had once come to the beach for fun and sun had departed for less socially conscious climes. The boardwalk – once jammed with tourists, joggers, bronzed and bikinied girls on roller skates, and Walkman-headed skateboard wizards – was now occupied by the Legion of the Damned.[21]

Wholesome if compared to Ellroy, Lyons portrays the dispossessed as a social problem, and contrasts their lives with those living in bourgeois uniformity: "All the commercial buildings ... had terracotta roofs, arched windows, and fake brick and stucco façades – what architects liked to call Mission Revival, and what I called Late Del Taco."[22] Finally, Tent City is blown away and Los Angeles can rest easy. Though Asch knows that fragmentation and entropy will, at some point, affect everyone.

Residents were calling it an act of god, which seemed to indicate that they did not buy the propaganda about the downtrodden being His favorite people. Personally, I didn't see it as part of any divine plan, but a lack of one. It was all a big cosmic crapshoot.[23]

Viewing the culture from the perspective of those enforcing the law, Joseph Wambaugh's *The New Centurions* concerns the five-year education, induction and indoctrination of three Los Angeles police officers. Wambaugh's world of law and order easily conflates with the city's recent history of racism, brutality, and corruption within the police department. Anything but politically correct, Wambaugh, a former police officer and one of James Ellroy's favourite writers,[24] does his best to give an accurate picture of the police at ground level, including how they view the communities in which they work. In a sense, Wambaugh's attempts to explain his gung-ho politics often make his work appear more politically correct than the novels of other, purportedly more enlightened, crime writers. As the three individuals go through training and establish themselves as police officers, they encounter the politics, prejudices and headaches that accompany the job. Written in the late 1960s, Wambaugh's novel depicts the changing face of Los Angeles, summed up by an elderly Jewish woman who has lived in Boyle Heights – once a Jewish neighbourhood, but which since has become predominantly Hispanic – for the past forty years:

"You should have seen Boyle Heights. Some of the finest families in Los Angeles was living there. Then the Mexicans started moving in and all the people ran out and went to the west side. Just the old Jews like me are left with the Mexicans now . . . We could have lived with the Mexican. An orthodox Jew is like a Catholic Mexican . . . Now look what we got. Reform Jews was bad enough. Now, Christian Jews? Don't make me laugh. And Mexican Baptisers? You see, everything is out of whack now."[25]

Driving down Jefferson, an older, more experienced officer gives a rookie a tour of his future division and an unpleasant lecture on the subtleties of the area's ethnic composition:

> "Almost all the citizens here are Negroes. Some Mexicans . . . Lots of crime when you have lots of Negroes . . . Ours are eastside Negroes. When they got some money they move west of Figueroa and Vermont and maybe west of Western. Then they call themselves westside Negroes and expect to be treated differently. I treat everyone the same, white or black. I'm civil to all people, courteous to none. I think courtesy implies servility. Policemen don't have to be servile or apologize to anyone for doing their job."[26]

The New Centurions ends with the Watts riots of 1965. Thirty years on, Wambaugh's novel reads like a distorted document whose time has passed yet whose spirit lingers on. Written before crime fiction had the nerve to cross class and cultural boundaries, Wambaugh's novel looks back to an era when drive-by killings and crack cocaine were mere twinkles in the myopic eyes of red-necked law enforcers. However, the world Wambaugh's police officers patrol is not beyond recognition:

> [Now] that night had come, the streets were filling with people, black people, and the building fronts shone forth. It seemed that every block had at least one bar or liquor store and all the liquor store proprietors were white men.[27]

Walter Mosley offers an alternative perspective regarding Los Angeles. His protagonist Easy Rawlins represents a character that hitherto has existed only on the margins of noir fiction. For Easy could have been the black man rousted by Philip Marlowe in a Central Avenue bar in the first pages of Chandler's *Farewell, My Lovely*. Or he might be one of the doomed men that Ellroy's cops obsessively pursue and persecute. Set in 1956, Mosley's *White Butterfly* is, time-wise, close to *White Jazz*. But the similarity ends there. Set in South Central, Easy, like Himes's protagonist in *If He Hollers Let Him Go*, can barely cope with the city's racism and the alienation it engenders. College educated, Easy belongs neither to the streets, nor to the black bourgeoisie. With his marriage falling apart, he finds himself on Bone Street – a euphemism for Central Avenue – frequenting clubs where, according to Rawlins, beautiful women drank with men while listening to Monk, Coltrane and Billie Holiday. By 1956, Easy tells us that most of the musicians that played on the Avenue have already left for Paris or New York, and the sidewalks are cracked and devoid of the promise which Central Avenue once held. Musician and cultural emissary Johnny Otis corroborates Easy's view:

> Central Avenue was our Harlem Renaissance . . . The history
> of rhythm and blues music in Los Angeles is inseparably tied
> to the development of the African American culture that
> formed and flourished in the Central Avenue area, that area
> that was fondly referred to by the people of the thirties,
> forties, and fifties as The Avenue.[28]

Not surprisingly, Mosley's perspective of Central Avenue differs from that depicted by Ellroy in *White Jazz*, in which his characters invade or sneak through the area, in search of criminals, drugs, or sex. To Easy, Bone Street is "local history":

> A crooked spine down the center of Watts' jazz heyday, it was
> four long and jagged blocks . . . Bone Street was broken and
> desolate to look at by day, with its two-story tenement-like
> apartment buildings and its mangy hotels. But by night
> Bones . . . was a center for late-night blues, and whiskey so
> strong that it could grow hairs on the glass it was served in.[29]

By 1956 South Central public space was rapidly changing – within a year even Wrigley Field, the black community's base-ball stadium, would be torn down. Yet Easy insists that the neighbourhood was once so open that even private spaces were semi-public. He describes a two-storey block-long stucco building renowned for housing black entertainers:

> People treated it like one big house. Most of the studio
> apartment doors were open. One door I passed revealed a
> man fully dressed in an antique zoot suit and a white ten-
> gallon hat. As I passed by we regarded each other as two wary
> lizards might stare as they slithered across some barren
> stone.[30]

Constantly infringed upon, Easy takes comfort in the fact
that he owns his house, has a degree of private space and some
protection from the white world. No wonder Easy, in future
books, seeks to acquire a substantial property portfolio. Or that
in the 1960s, he proudly notes the small changes that have
taken place in the black community:

> Southeast LA was palm trees and poverty; neat little lawns
> tended by the descendants of ex-slaves . . . It was beautiful and
> wild; a place that was almost a nation, populated by lost
> peoples that were never talked about in the newspapers or
> seen on the TV. You might have read about freedom marchers;
> you might have heard about a botched liquor store robbery . . .
> – but you never heard about Tommy Jones growing the biggest
> roses in the world or how Fiona Roberts saved her neighbor
> by facing off three armed men.[31]

Writing a few years later, Gary Phillips, in *Violent Spring*,
views the city from a post-Rodney King perspective. In
depicting the movers, shakers and opportunists in a
community where one ethnic group fights another over
whatever resources are available, Phillips moves the narrative
from the past to the present. Describing Central Avenue, his
African-American investigator, Ivan Monk, recalls that it had
once been "the cultural Mecca of Black Los Angeles in the
'30s through the '50s". However history has taken its toll:
"Now Central Avenue was home to mom and pop furniture
stores with names like Zuniga, and where Jack's Basket was

stands a branch of the Southern California Gas Company."[32] As for the future, Monk, unashamedly left-wing, puts forward the following possibility:

> LA might very well be lurching toward a Balkanized future, each ethnic group carving out its larger or smaller fiefdom ... The city might indeed become a low-rent Blade Runner, too beat and too broke to pay for the special effects.

However, given the right circumstances, Monk suggests an alternative ending, one in which there is a recognition that crimes committed to produce the economic miracle in South Korea affect criminal activities in Los Angeles. In this particular ending – one which exists only for the author and like-minded readers – disparate elements coalesce, and LA, contrary to the predictions of most pundits, becomes the "last possible chance for sanity in a world where the law of the pack ... had to be halted".[33]

Miami Vices

Miami is also known for its cultural mélange as well as its crime rate. Says Jewish hotelier Maurice Zola in Leonard's *La Brava*:

> "The neighborhood was taken over by junkies, muggers, cutthroats, queers, you name it. Cubans off the boat-lift, Haitians who had swum ashore when their boats broke to pieces, old-time New York Jews once the backbone, eying each other with nothing remotely in common, not even the English language. The vampires come out at night and the old people triple-locked their doors and waited for morning."[34]

Leonard's 1983 novel is a vivid portrayal of Miami's decaying Art Deco elegance and its contradictory elements. With the elderly – there for sun and low taxes – rubbing shoulders with criminals, Miami, despite the constant flow of capital in and out of the city and various attempts to spruce up the boardwalk, retains a seediness just this side of terminal decay.

Yet it's a city perpetually ripe for takeover. Says writer Joan Didion,

> Nothing about Miami was exactly fixed, or hard. Hard consonants were missing from the local speech patterns, in English as well as in Spanish. Local money tended to move on hydraulic verbs: when it was not being washed it was being diverted, or channelled through Mexico, or turned off in Washington. Local stories tended to turn on underwater plot points, submerged snappers: on unsoundable extradition proceedings in the Bahamas, say, or fluid connections with the Banco Nacional de Colombia.[35]

In Leonard's novel, Franny, a smart young New Yorker who sells cosmetics to retired women and longs to paint the beachfront buildings before they are torn down, deploys a modified version of Didion's linguistic shorthand, when she says to Joe La Brava, "The zoners are out to get us, man, cover the planet like one big enclosed shopping mall. We're getting malled and condoed, if you didn't know it."[36]

Unlike other cities, in Miami, linguistic and cultural assimilation seems beside the point. As *La Brava* illustrates, those who feel isolated or declassed by language in New York or Los Angeles invariably thrive in Miami. Leonard suggests this is because, in Miami, dependent as it is on the service sector, money is made by deals rather than by salaries.[37] When asked, in *La Brava*, about what Cundo the Cuban boat-lifter does for a living, Franny says, "What do you mean what does he do? He's looking for some kind of hustle, like the rest of 'em. They deal or they break and enter."[38]

With its unsavoury history – state corruption, discrepancies in wealth, disgruntled Cubans, Anita Bryant's anti-gay campaign, racism, right-wing politics and organised crime – it's hardly surprising that Miami should be considered the crime capital of America.[39] In fact, its reputation for murder and violence has become one of the city's primary attractions. Says Maurice Zola,

> "Two blocks from the Miami Beach Police station, they had over two hundred assaults, shootings, knifings, rapes, and ripoffs. You believe it? They got video cameras mounted on cement poles, close-circuit TV, so the cops can watch the muggings, the dope transactions, and not have to leave the station."[40]

This, after all, has long been the adopted home of criminals, from Al Capone to Meyer Lansky. It follows that, in Miami, entrepreneurs are truly appreciated. Or at least that is the gospel according to Maurice, outraged that the death of a ukelele-playing talent-spotter should receive more coverage than the demise of one of Miami's greatest *goniffs*:

> "Arthur Godfrey's on the front page of every paper in the country . . . Meyer Lansky gets two columns in the New York Times, he could a bought Godfrey. Arthur Godfrey gets a street named after him. What's Meyer Lansky get? A guy, I remember from the FBI, he said Meyer Lansky could a been chairman of the board of General Motors if he'd gone into legitimate business."[41]

Comprised of relative moralities, multiple trajectories and arbitrary but contingent social encounters, Leonard's fiction mirrors the modern urban experience. Intercut his terse narratives with newspaper headlines about tourist killings and riots in Liberty City, and it would be difficult to distinguish fiction from reality. Though the likes of Leonard could be criticised for stereotyping Cubans and African-Americans, racial discrepancies have long played a part in the creation of urban myths regarding crime.

While Leonard's perspective on Miami is that of a bemused outsider, novelist Carl Hiassen cannot afford such objectivity. It's because his relationship with Miami fluctuates between love and hate that his work contains a dark, and even slapstick, humour. In his first novel, *Tourist Season*, the President of the Greater Miami Chamber of Commerce chokes to death on a 79 cent rubber alligator. In *Skin Tight*, two tourists, walking on the beach, come across a corpse:

> As the thing floated closer, the young man began to wonder about his legal responsibilities, providing it turned out to be what he thought it was. Oh yes, he had heard about Miami; this sort of stuff happened every day.[42]

Instead of calling the police, the woman's first instinct is to take out a camera and photograph the corpse. It's a Kodak moment for the folks back home:

> "Otherwise no one back home will believe us. I mean, we come all the way down to Miami and what happens? Remember how your brother was making murder jokes before we left? It's unreal. Stand to the right a little, Thomas, and pretend to look down at it."[43]

Though tourists come to Miami to find proof of its media-based reputation, Hiassen criticises the city by portraying its worst qualities. Straining for every image, he depicts Miami as a final stopover, a place of excess where one laughs, deals or dies.

An Immigrant's Nightmare

If the discourse of Los Angeles can be said to be the product of social conditions and natural disasters – riot, flood, fire and earthquake – and the discourse of Miami can be located in a nexus which includes its immigrant community, political corruption, crime and the tropical climate, the discourse of New York turns on its historical presence and spatial organisation.[44] Though appearing, at times, to wallow in territorial despair, New York remains one of the few cities still accessible to the pedestrian. Here, a walker can still be a flâneur rather than a suspected criminal. Nor does one need own a car in a city subsumed by such architectural and human density.

Investigating the spatial aspects of New York, Jerome Charyn cloaks the city's urban myths in hyperbole, parody and grand gesture. With a crime writing career that spans two decades, Charyn has, since his *Issac Quartet*, redefined the genre, taking a route contrary to Leonard's gritty realism or Ellroy's gross extremism. Instead, Charyn's crime fiction revolves around his personal history of the city:

> My mother was Russian. My father was Polish ... [They] went from nowhere to nowhere, escaping one abyss only to come to a much deeper abyss. It would be nice to say that the children climbed over the parents' broken backs, but my language comes from their silence and inability to express themselves ... That's what New York is about.[45]

More interested in magic realism than verisimilitude, Charyn says, "The real relationship is between the author who is the criminal and the text which he or she juggles."[46] That is to say, Charyn, through transgression, conveys the manner in which urban space makes crime ubiquitous and necessary. His protagonist is his alter-ego, Issac Siddel. A product of New York, Issac, the chess-playing ex-Stalinist who loves baseball, ice cream, Hammett and Eisenstein, flits between law and disorder. Likewise, Siddel personifies the contradictions of New York, where Jews, Irish, Hispanics, and African-Americans inter-mingle, and where Issac-the-flâneur mutates into Issac-the-Golem with a tapeworm eating at his soul. Says Charyn about his city:

> The bones of a city are often inscribed on a people's back. Particularly in an immigrant town like New York, where whole populations arrived in phantom boats ... and if the country let them in, they toiled to earn their keep, made children, money, and died in the crush to become American. Both the

sadness and the vitality of New York come from the same engine: the greenhorn's desire to transform himself into some magical thing.[47]

Filled with guilt and self-doubt, Issac represents the cop-as-tarnished poet-of-the-streets. Issac, the reviver of dead memories and lost souls, whose greatest loves are his greatest losses, must sacrifice his blue-eyed boy – the ping-pong playing Manfred Coen – to satisfy his blood-lust and make the vertiginous streets minimally safer.

Noting the psycho-geographic origins of his fiction, Charyn admits the sentences he deploys are about loneliness and the final disconnection of the way we live and what we've become: "So New York becomes the deepest point in that well of loneliness."[48] These are tales of Gotham underdogs, Katzenjammer Kids and Krazy Kats who, like the Marx Brothers, are more criminally-minded than Dutch Schultz: "It's the explosion of sensibility that makes the city extraordinary. The rich may have built the towers, but the real fabric of the city doesn't come from them."[49]

Though working for the state, Issac often moves beyond its reach. Disappearing, he assumes a variety of disguises: from ranting criminal to whining prophet, from avenging angel to the pyjama-wearing manager of a kids' baseball team. Whichever disguise he adopts, Issac is a pitiful but courageous figure, illustrated by his many epithets: *Issac the Pure*, the *Pink Commish*, *Issac the Brave*, the *Rabbi* or the *Shit*. Above all, Issac, in search of meaning and cohesion, stalks the Big Apple as though it were the land of the dead:

"It's ungovernable . . . Psychosis is everywhere, in your armpit, under your shoe. You can smell it in the sweat in this room . . . we're all baby killers, repressed or not . . . how do you measure a man's rage? Either we behave like robots, or we kill. Why do you expect your Police Force to be any less crazy than you?"[50]

Published in 1994, *Maria's Girls* takes place around Sherwood Forest, a pastoral constabulary in New York's Central Park. In an age of austerity, education budgets have been slashed, while municipal politics and urban decay have made cops and criminals indistinguishable. Conveying the city's disintegration, Charyn is more concerned with articulating the mystery than solving the crime, maintaining that "In *Maria's Girls*, there's the appearance of solutions and the appearance of evidence, but the crime was there long before the book."[51]

According to Charyn, the reality of contemporary city life makes crime inevitable. In *Maria's Girls*, Maria Montalbán, the androgynous superintendent of lower eastside schools, finances his school budget by selling drugs and shuffling stolen goods. A teacher explains Maria's inner-city economics: "Steal from A to give to B . . . Supply and demand. We sell drugs so children can eat."[52] But Maria is only trying to survive in a cut-throat environment. Eventually, Issac, a helpless child in the presence of Maria's new realism, must agree with the relativity implied in Maria's style of management.

Able to "move to the rhythms of the city, and a focal point for its contradictions",[53] Issac can empathise with Maria's girls. "They're right to rebel," says Issac, "the whole system stinks."[54] For the city has become a place where "the worship of money is the only value". If that's the case, adds Charyn, "why not bring in the killer". However, in maintaining that the real killer is not the person who pulls the trigger, but his or her paymaster, Charyn gives urban crime a different twist. Issac expresses this when he tells the girls, "If you have to steal to feed yourself, then steal, but don't take any pleasure from it."[55] But this is a tall order in a city where theft, for Maria's girls, might be the only way they can pay for their education. In the end, Issac knows that no one can control the city. Says Charyn, "It's too powerful a beast . . . It doesn't matter if it's the Mafia or the FBI, they're all eaten up by the city. Issac understands that the most."[56]

One could say that crime fiction has become more violent and deregulated in proportion to its demystification of the criminal fraternity, particularly the Mafia, and its diversification into legitimate businesses.[57] Nick Tosches, a former music journalist, has written a number of novels regarding *family* values. Amidst racism and cultural claustrophobia, the characters in his *Cut Numbers* constitute an identifiable gallery of Mob types. This is the other side of the coin from Mario Puzo's novel of political intrigue, *The Godfather*. Scaled down to include low-lifes, small-time *capos*, and punk runners, Tosches's characters exist at the bedrock of organised criminality. These are the nephews and friends who might once have been associated with one of the five families, but, as loan sharks and fixers, must now scuffle for a piece of the action. In Tosches's 1995 *Trinities*, a driver, after shooting a dealer for no known reason – at least to the killer – outlines his career – now in its sixteenth year – and his relationship to those occupying the upper echelons of family power:

> He had run numbers and taken action, had handled jukebox routes and video slots. He had been purse-man in two precincts, had handled the Teamsters' dirtiest paperwork in three different locals. He had turned stolen bonds and guns, booze and cars. He had dispatched legbreakers, overseen gambling operations, dealt everything from counterfeit fifties to swag Mass cards. He had seen the inner beast of this world laid out before him in gross vivisection. And still there had been no passage from the realm of nickels and dimes; no green light, not from his uncle, not from anyone.[58]

More wrecked and ruined than the Mob members who inhabit Richard Condon's *Prizzi* novels, Tosches's hard men frequent bars and gambling dens in a permanent state of bewilderment. Out of touch with history, they display primitive but earthy attitudes. Yet they still manage to gain the reader's sympathy. Living in the past and existing on the fringe of organised crime, Louie, in *Cut Numbers*, picks up a woman whose name he does not know and walks her through a city once controlled by his forebears:

> She, the nameless one, spoke of being hurt in love, and he –
> heh, heh, heh – consoled her with the shoring wisdom of his
> soul . . . [A] little after one, they took a cab to Clarke's, on
> Third Avenue. Women, Louie knew, like going to manly
> places, especially those manly places where the men plucked
> between their eyebrows and sucked on little onions and olives.
> At least Clarke's . . . had good bartenders. It also had what was
> perhaps Louie's favorite urinal in all of New York – an ancient
> and marbled walk-in model that might have been designed by
> the great Zog himself.[59]

A flâneur, Louie "began walking toward those remembered things". But wherever he goes, he sees a deteriorating city:

> The ground beneath them was part of the hundred-acre
> landfill, a ghastly man-made desert of debris, that had just
> gotten underway the last time Louie was here. Like the World
> Trade Center, whose excavations had formed the landfill's
> base, the towering tombstones . . . destroyed what character
> and majesty this young city had. The Manhattan skyline, once
> a phantasmagorical monument to the New World's glory and
> greed, was . . . fast coming to resemble one of those sterile
> geometric *objets* around which rich faggots used to coordinate
> their décors.[60]

As the city provides less space, employment and facilities for its residents, crime becomes, for some, a matter of survival. While, for others, it becomes a source of paranoia.

Indicative of the culture's paranoia regarding crime is the fact that, in recent years, the biggest growth industry and the fastest growing public space has been that of prisons. In California, more money will be spent on prisons than on education.[61] More jails are being built than public housing, hospitals or schools. Rarely advocating overly stringent law and order policies, contemporary crime fiction portrays city spaces as only fractionally less secure or exclusive than penal institutions. Moreover, it captures the paranoia that leads to the purchasing of security at the expense of an evolving street-level culture. In Pelecanos's *Nick's Trip*, former convict Darnell says, regarding the degree to which Washington DC has changed, "Remember 1976, man? The way people acted to each other, everything – the shit was so positive . . . When I got out, in '88, it was a new world man. There wasn't no hope, not anymore – not on the street, not on the radio, nothin'. Nothin' but gangster romance."[62]

Even imaginary cities are depicted as potential dystopias. Jack O'Connell's *Box Nine* is an accurate portrayal of the discourse surrounding the politics of an imagined public space. Set in Quinsigamond, an industrial city loosely based on Worcester, Massachusetts, O'Connell's city, a modern version of Hammett's *Poisonville*, includes a quasi-bohemian quarter called the Zone, and a notorious inner-city area called Bangkok Park. The latter has a crime and mortality rate four times higher than anywhere else in the state, and a black economy whose GNP is ten times larger than the city's total budget. Ninety per cent of all drug trade in Quinsigamond takes place within a square mile of the Park.

The plot of *Box Nine* revolves around the introduction into the community of a new drug, *lingo*, which induces a state called the *rapture*. Published in 1992, at the tail end of the era's anti-drug crusade, O'Connell's novel features Lenore, a police detective who loves amphetamines, handguns and heavy metal music. Within this context, Lenore reflects contemporary urban concerns:

> Lenore no longer believes in God. She does not believe in an afterlife. She does not believe in some fixed code of divinely transmitted morality. She does not believe in turning the other cheek. She does not believe that the meek will inherit the earth. She now believes in power and persistence. In logic

and rational thought. In seizing what you need without regard
to the effect of your action upon others. She hides these
beliefs out of what she feels to be wise self-preservation, out of
the fact that if others knew her true convictions, it would
become pretty difficult to live the way she wants.[63]

Emerging from Quinsigamond's academic subculture, Dr
Frederick Woo, a lecturer in linguistics and language theory,
tells the police that *lingo*, though more addictive than heroin
and more deadly than crack, "could have a revolutionary impact
on fields as diverse as brain biochemistry and neuropsychology,
cybernetics, linguistics, all the semiological disciplines".[64] For
lingo goes straight to the brain, supercharging the areas where
language is produced. More incremental than *speed*, the drug
hits the user like a massive adrenaline rush. Able to turn an
idiot into a speed-reader, *lingo* has its positive side. But no one
pursues the scientific aspects of the drug, nor the idea that,
used in moderation, it might solve the city's education and
literacy problems.[65] Of course this might have something to do
with the drug's negative qualities. Because, once ingested, the
user's language skills increase until his or her speech turns into
a buzz, which leads to paranoid schizophrenia, homicidal rage
and, finally, death. Though clearly not for casual use, *lingo*
could be the ultimate urban drug, a more-than-potent leveller,
and the final linguistic *hit*.

With *speed* rendered redundant, the implication is that the
age of the flâneur has come to an end. In an era dominated by
instant communication, surveillance, automobility and
implosion, *stalking* has replaced *strolling* as the main urban
preoccupation. This has led to a heightened paranoia which,
according to urbanologist Sharon Zukin, reflects the disdain
for those who have inherited the cities:

As urban public spaces have included more strangers, those
who look and talk so differently they are considered "Others,"
the Americans who used them before have abandoned them,
leaving them to a generalized ethnic Other, a victim of the

politics of fear . . . [People] tend to think Others are criminals;
eventually, crime becomes a device, an idiom for thinking
about the Other.[66]

While one is left wondering if it was only *speed* that allowed
Woo and Lenore to overcome their fear of public spaces,[67] *lingo*
might well be the logical if fatal antidote to the privatisation of
public space.

O'Connell's narrative suggests the extent to which space has
been warped by political and economic considerations. To keep
in line with the changing urban reality, drugs – affecting speech,
thought and visual perception – have become necessary and
profitable. This is the price ordinary people pay for negotiating
the mean streets. In his 1995 *Skin Palace*, O'Connell, investigating the last vestiges of the city's underground culture,
including its flâneurs, notes how Quinsigamond's Gompers
Station has been ravaged by history:

> It's now a monument to entropy, an embarrassing hulk whose
> only purpose is to admonish the ego of a community. It's an
> arc of cracked and ash-caked vaulting walls, grand stairways
> that degenerate halfway to their destination into simple
> mountains of hacked-up bedrock, Greco-Roman columns that
> lie sideways in cinder beds and are covered with neon gang
> graffiti and now serve only as marble bull's-eyes for the spray
> of dogs and forgotten reprobates.[68]

If nothing else, noir fiction addresses the paranoia regarding
history's cruel arc. Constantine, in Pelecanos's *Shoedog*, cannot
quite adjust to the new urban reality. Back in DC after an
absence of seventeen years, he finds himself in a state of culture
shock: "It's like the young people don't know how to smile . . .
What the hell's going on?" His black partner-in-crime says,
"Simple, man . . . It's the end of the motherfucking world."[69]
Dependent upon a lack of definition and a degree of urban
chaos, crime fiction – from flâneur to stalker, from gumshoe to
TV surveillance man, from speed-freak to *lingo* addict, from

melting pot to balkanisation, from political sensibility to gangster romanticism – remains an accurate representation of the city's ever-changing landscape.

7

TURNING OUT THE LIGHTS

**Post-mortem aesthetics; the politics of serial murder
in the work of Thomas B. Harris and Bradley Denton;
pastiche noir; the future of crime fiction**

Without a sense of aesthetics,[1] crime fiction would be reduced
to a series of journalistic abstractions. Likewise, all crime would
be of equal significance. While the aesthetics of crime can be
gleaned from the term *copycat killer* or the idea of the perfect
crime, crime fiction, moving from reality to artifice, feeds off a
spectrum of illicit activities. Social anthropologist Elliott Leyton
corroborates this, maintaining that the most extreme crime –
multiple murder – "has become an increasingly fashionable
form of social art."[2] Competing against reality, crime fiction,
while reflecting the era, must seek ever-greater horrors and
facsimiles.

Thomas De Quincey's 1854 "Murder Considered as One of
the Fine Arts" constitutes an early recognition of the relationship between crime and crime fiction. "[The] tendency," writes
De Quincey, "to a critical or aesthetic valuation of . . . murders
is universal."[3] On the next page, he writes,

> [After] the personal interests have been tranquillized by time,
> inevitably the scenical features . . . of the several murders are
> reviewed and valued. One murder is compared with another;
> and the circumstances of superiority – as, for example, in the
> incidence and effects of surprise, of mystery, etc. – are
> collated and appraised.[4]

Appreciating the degree to which murder can whet the appetite of the reading public, De Quincey was arguably the first to link popular journalism and the crime narrative. Thus he suggested a genre that would entertain all manner of crime, and eventually include such writers as Poe, Dickens and Dashiell Hammett.

However extreme, crime fiction, in adhering to the laws of the genre, turns the fear of violent death into a narrative subtext while investigating the society from which that fear derives. Regarding the fear of becoming a victim, Ernest Mandel notes that "It is the nightmare that stalks the American dream as the shadow stalks the body."[5] Yet paranoia surrounding violation and violent death is often left unarticulated, subsumed by literary preoccupations and sociological discussions regarding crime as a means of gaining autonomy or climbing the social ladder. According to Mandel, "Reification of death is at the very heart of the crime story."[6] Recognising that even multiple murderers have a sense of aesthetics, Elliott Leyton says, "Their rebellion is a protest against their perceived exclusion from society, not an attempt to alter it as befits a revolutionary."[7] However one looks at it, violent crime, as an act of profit or power, is hierarchical, part of an aesthetic which gives crime the potential to alter the historical narrative.

Organised crime, and its pursuit of profit and power, has long been portrayed in crime fiction. After all, organised crime replicates the dynamics of corporate capitalism. Says Elliott Leyton:

> The wages of sin may be death, but the wages of organized crime are capital accumulation. Organized crime is capitalism freed from the bonds of penal law . . . Its particular mode of alienation leads to murder for business, to the business of murder as a source of profit, to, as it were disembodied murder, to the doubly alienated murder, the murderer without personal involvement or passion, the murderer for pure profit.[8]

However, in the fictional world, committing a crime for financial gain is seldom aesthetically pleasing. Hitmen, professional crooks or muggers are portrayed as committing crime from a sense of retribution or some twisted inner need. Profit is high on the agenda, but rarely to the extent that mercenary habits overcome romantic concerns.

For the collision of urban myth and reality invariably produces a by-product of political proportions. Moreover, those able to articulate the relevant urban myths – derived, more often not, from a literary, rather than police, perspective – hold the most interesting insights into crime. Suggesting it might be better for nihilistic psychopaths to roam the streets than for the "murderous liquidations of the totalitarian state"[9] to rule the world, Norman Mailer, in his 1957 essay "The White Negro", called on individuals to face up to the meaning of violent crime. While, in the midst of the Vietnam war,[10] Mario Puzo, author of *The Godfather*, links crime with the world around him:

> How are we to adjust to a society that drafts human beings to fight a war, yet permits its business men to profit from the shedding of blood? . . . [As] society becomes more and more criminal, the well-adjusted citizen, by definition, must become more and more criminal. So let us now dare to take the final step.[11]

Marking the intersection where fact and fiction meet, Puzo suggests a politicised genre, one which recognises the type of society created by a preponderance of state crime, and hypocritical notions regarding law enforcement.[12]

While a thin line often separates committing a crime from investigating a crime, both activities can be as subversive as they are complex. In John Straley's Alaskan thriller, *The Curious Eat Themselves*, the Commissioner, an Alaskan industrialist, causes the investigator to rethink his political agenda:

> "You want a one-class society? Why not a rich one? . . . It can be done, yes, certainly. Oil, gas, water, hell – even sunlight. There will always be something, and there will always be a hand on the spigot. We can do it. But what we can't do is give

up our position near that spigot, for without it" – he gestured around the room as if he were a huckster at a carnival and this was his illusion – "without it, there is nothing."[13]

For who knows what elements of humanism might lurk in the heart of the criminal, or what nihilism drives the investigator?

At the centre of much contemporary crime fiction is an end-of-the-millennium obsession with personality disorders, sexual deviancy and AIDS. Consequently, the cold-blooded but demented serial killer is often portrayed as a sexual deviant, his crimes akin to spreading a communicable disease. In Thomas Kelly's *Payback*, Butcher Boy, despite having killed thirty people while working for the Mob, denies he's a serial killer. "He thought serial killers were all weird fat guys from Ohio, places like that. Perverts. 'I'm a hit man.' "[14]

Could he be right? Murder historian Brian Masters maintains that "[All] crimes involving addictive murder have a sexual element to them . . . To [serial killers] killing is a paradoxical rebuilding of the self."[15] Combining intelligence with a need to explore the limits of pain and perversion, fictional serial killers are more likely to be descendants of *Psycho*'s Norman Bates than Dostoyevsky's Grand Inquisitor or Nietzsche's *übermann*. No matter how warped they appear, fictional serial killers personify a range of cultural clichés, from the masturbatory habits of introverts, to how maternal love – too little or too much – can turn an offspring into a psychopath. Since the cultural orthodoxy maintains that any activity outside the heterosexual *norm* constitutes deviancy, *abnormal* sexual pursuits, or the blocking of such pursuits, supposedly leads to criminal activity, whether murder, mutilation or the spread of sexually transmitted diseases.

The fear of becoming a haphazard victim of a violent crime formed a noticeable part of fictional crime narratives during the 1980s, an era that saw an increase in the number of serial killers and phobic attitudes regarding the spread of the AIDS virus. Moreover, paranoia regarding violent crime and AIDS have certain similarities. Both threaten to invade the system, whether personal or political. Both relate to fears of the *other* – whether immigrant, black, gay, recidivist or conspicuous loner. Both are spoken about in hushed or hysterical tones – this despite the fact that those considered culprits – homosexuals, drug addicts, prostitutes – count amongst its main victims. And both, we are told, are investigated by experts, working against the clock to find a cure, track down, and capture the instigators.

Like the silence surrounding the war in Vietnam, the subject of AIDS, during its early years, was seldom broached by crime writers. Yet it soon became a constant but peripheral concern. Though the genre has yet to investigate the criminalisation of AIDS, the subject most often takes the form of sexual paranoia, as in Tosches's *Trinities*: "Louie had known men hairless and purple-lipped from fruitless chemotherapy who had brokered deals for nuclear warheads, had heard of men dying of AIDS who had purposely infected others with needle or cock."[16] Or it stands as a sign of the times, as in Edward Bunker's *Dog Eat Dog*. Just out of prison, Troy and his fellow-criminal briefly discuss the matter as they examine Troy's fake driving licence:

"Yeah. It's his ID. We just changed the picture. He was a fruiter. He died in the Gay Men's Hospice. He had that bad shit."

"Cancer?"

"Cancer, my ass. AIDS!"

"Yeah, I know," Troy said. "You don't even like to say it, do you?"

"Scares me, man. It kills motherfuckers all kindsa ways. Some of 'em die horrible deaths. Shit growing in their throat, eating at their brain. How many dudes got it in the joint?"

"I dunno. I guess a few hundred are infected without bein' sick – "

"They will be somewhere down the line."

"So will all of us."[17]

With the potential to alter the narrative, AIDS has also changed the way its victims regard crime. In David Wajnarowicz's *Close to the Knives* two AIDS-riddled gay men move out of the ghetto of their concerns to discuss the politics and aesthetics of crime and one particular writer of crime fiction:

> "Stark . . . writes this . . . series of books about this guy Parker. They came out during the Vietnam war and during the Nixon years and [are] methodical accounts of . . . Parker planning these jobs . . . and never getting caught, and he was totally emotionless. The national attitude was: we hate Nixon and what he's done, what he did was all wrong, and yet these books were totally popular because people still had these fantasies of doing these totally anonymous crimes against the system. I have a real problem about that *still* – when I went out to California I was looking for somebody who wanted to do real jobs . . . I just didn't give a fuck at that point . . . I still have these fantasies: I try and think of places I can just go in and rob . . . Maybe I will someday, and if I do nobody'll ever fucking hear about it."[18]

The medical condition of the narrator adds to his not-uncommon fantasy, and his suggestion that the rise of contemporary criminal aesthetics, exemplified by Stark's fiction, corresponds to the corruption of an empire and the apparent demise of contemporary society. For the AIDS virus, by inducing paranoia and maintaining a degree of power over its victims, has, like crime, become part and parcel of the dominant narrative. It's indicative of an entropic condition that Giuseppe, an aging mobster in Tosches's *Trinities*, seeks to exploit:

> "The world will follow the streets to hell . . . And no one . . . will turn the tide. The question I'm asking you is this. Does your morality – call it whatever you want, your code, your principles, your sense of right and wrong, that scrap of something in your heart and soul that separates you from the beasts – does it allow you to make money from the business of

hell? . . . Given that there is no end to this plague, does whatever wisdom you possess lead you to side with your principles or your self-interest?"[19]

Before the up-and-coming Johnny can consider such a dreadful transgression, Giuseppe tells a story about seeing, as a child, an encrazed black horse crash through a glass storefront window. A single shot puts the bleeding and kicking animal out of its misery. But the horse is left in the street, its stomach bloating to twice its normal size. Before it's finally taken away, the horse's belly is ripped open with a crowbar. With pus gushing from the wound, the horse's rotting innards can be smelled a block away.

> "I think of this world now as a black horse running wild to hell, its body filled with disease. I think of seizing that horse for one terrible moment as it gallops towards those flames, riding it and looting all that is in the path of its destruction, then jumping off before being thrown and broken . . . Then I'll watch that doomed horse continue on its way. Nothing will have changed. The world will be no better and no worse. The only difference will be, as you say, *estetica*."[20]

With the world looking similarly pustular, criminals, whatever their aesthetics, make a final attempt to take what they can, and sometimes more than they need. While, at this point in history, one more crime is not going to make much difference, each transgression reflects the contradictions that make crime possible.

In considering the aesthetics of crime fiction, brief mention should be made of African-American writers like Donald Goines, Iceberg Slim, Charles Perry, Vernon Smith and Clarence Cooper Jr. Though they stand slightly outside the scope of this study, each writes about the *life* – that is, the world of crime, including hustling, pimping, dope dealing and surviving on the streets of urban America. Long ignored by the arbiters of mainstream literary taste, and only recently reintroduced to readers, they give an accurate and personalised overview of their particular world. Goines, for instance, wrote sixteen novels before he was murdered at the age of thirty-nine. *Black Gangster*, like a high-octane proletariat version of Chester Himes, is the story of a politically informed black *godfather* who ascends the ranks of organised crime:

> The winter wind had run most of the night people off the streets and into the bars and after-hours spots, pool rooms and greasy spoon restaurants. The neon lights beckoned them to the dim-lit places of entertainment that were their very existence. Many had been victimized, but still they returned, night after night, in search of fugitive pleasures. The dopefiends, whores, muggers and other parasites who earned their income off of them, moved with them through the shadows.[21]

Written in a pulpish style, Goines's novels, like the fiction of Iceberg Slim, are, stylistically speaking, the other side of the coin from Ricardo Cortez Cruz whose 1992 *Straight Outta Compton* contains its own criminal aesthetics. Set against a backdrop of violence and drugs, Cruz's writing – noir but not hardboiled – mixes avant-garde techniques with the politics and stylisation of contemporary rap music:

> Alondra bled real black blood mixed with 10W-40 oil and hard water as I walked down the street during the Rodney King beating. The LAPD kicked King's ass, causing him to let go of a bomb that hit me in the face. The coppers spat on him, insulted him, whupped his big head with their gas masks at hand and stuck black-eyed peas on King's face.[22]

This is noir fiction at its most extreme, the precursor of which might be the work of Clarence Cooper Jr. whose two 1960s novels, *The Farm* and *The Scene*, concern subjects he knew best – prison, drugs, and the streets. The latter book depicts a panorama of low-life characters, including cops, junkies, homosexuals, lesbians and whores. To junkie hustler Rudy Black, "The Scene's touch was like dead flesh",[23] while black Detective Sergeant Davis believes The Scene is just a heroin-infested place where "one out of every twenty or thirty voters is an addict or an occasional user of narcotics".[24] Though Cooper died of a drug overdose in 1967, his two novels, with their schizoid paranoia and obsession with violence, encapsulate the inequalities of post-war urban America. As African-Americans, the likes of Goines and Cooper have, regarding intent, historical presence, discourse and anger, their own sense of aesthetics. As Himes put it as far back as 1948:

> If this plumbing for the truth reveals within the Black personality a homicidal mania, lust for Whites of opposite sexes, a pathetic sense of inferiority, paradoxical anti-Semitism, arrogance, Uncle Tomism, hate and fear and self-hate, these then are some of the effects of oppression on the human personality These are daily horrors, daily realities, the daily experiences of an oppressed minority.[25]

Thus Himes outlined the aesthetics of a noir fiction that still fights for its right to investigate the culture. For crime has always been double-edged. Victims and perpetrators are often interchangeable. Consequently, by examining the artifice behind novels that address the politics of serial murder one can glimpse a society in extremis.

The Politics of Serial Murder: Thomas B. Harris and Bradley Denton

Constituting two widely read and culturally significant novels about serial killers, Thomas B. Harris's *Red Dragon* and *Silence of the Lambs* succeeded, during the 1980s, in taking police procedure and verisimilitude to unprecedented lengths. Page-turners that court extremism and manipulate the emotions of their readers, these novels appeared to replicate the politics of the Reagan era. Well-crafted and reductionist, they have become text books for cops and those unable to differentiate fiction from reality. In *Silence of the Lambs*, the heroine, like the protagonist in Kim Wozencraft's *Rush*, owes her professional position to the women's movement, yet would deny being part of that movement. In fact, given her individualism and lack of political consciousness, Clarice Starling can be read as a walking critique of feminism, the token woman who achieves results that exceed the expectations of her colleagues. Though vulnerable, Clarice solves the crime only because she is able to form a special relationship with Hannibal Lecter, a man who personifies Reagan's evil empire, save the fact that he's a warped killer rather than some vodka-swilling communist.

Though Lecter's cannibalistic activities signify the thick end of the era's deregulatory hacksaw, Buffalo Bill's handiwork, coupled with his homosexual dysfunctionality, would-be transsexualism, and the panic he engenders, suggest the onset, if not the homophobia, of the AIDS era. As the spectacularised equivalents of *Panic in the Streets* – a film whose subtext warned of the dreaded communist virus – Harris's books have become templates for future novels featuring serial killers, whether Ellroy's *Silent Terror*, David Lindsey's *Mercy*, or Michael Connelly's *The Poet*. Though one can imagine Harris's fiction influencing real-life killers, the increase in the number of serial killers during the 1980s had less to do with fictional creations than with social conditions, the increased presence and profile of law enforcers, and the recognition that serial killers are more common than previously thought.[26] Meanwhile, at the FBI training academy in Quantico – which Harris, researching his novel, briefly attended – the case of Ed Gein, on whom Buffalo Bill is based, is taught alongside Harris's book. With a thin line separating fact and fiction, Harris's novels have allowed former FBI agent John Douglas to conclude that "anyone can be a victim". Though obviously true, Douglas's edgy fervour has led to the kind of paranoia that contributed to the popularity of capital punishment, get-tough crime legislation, and false moral positions that coincidentally encourage racism, misogyny and homophobia.

In *Silence of the Lambs*, Lecter's advice leads Clarice to the culprit, and substantiates John Douglas's belief that incarcerated serial killers should be used to assist the FBI in their profiling procedures. Yet one wonders why, with their sophisticated technology and knowledge, only Lecter can explain the killer's motives? Interestingly enough, Douglas's profiling method, derived from interviewing incarcerated murderers, has not gained universal acceptance. According to Elliott Leyton, the interview, "as a data source, is a profoundly flawed instrument. When you interview a killer a long time after the event, he's got this whole act prepared and he'll tell you exactly what he wants you to understand".[27]

Long on detail, *Red Dragon* and *Silence of the Lambs* are, in the end, reactive texts, easily co-opted by the state. Accordingly, when Agent Douglas showed photographs of the victims of serial killers to actor Scott Glenn, the latter – "a pretty liberal guy"[28] who played Jack Crawford, a role based on Douglas, in *Silence of the Lambs* – became an instant advocate of capital punishment.[29] Perhaps playing the part of Douglas necessitated such a shift; but one would think the skilled actor or reader might be the person who can get through Harris's book with his or her principles intact.

Red Dragon begins with a quote from turn-of-the-century anthropologist Alphonse Bertillon: "One can only see what one observes, and one observes only things which are already in the mind." Regarding the novel's mode of enquiry – pseudo science under the auspices of deductive reasoning – it reminds one of the book's basic contradiction: the author controls a fictional investigator who claims to possess a body of knowledge denied to the reader. So Harris exploits the myth of the murderer as evil, obsessional, and intelligent. Incarcerated Lecter writes to the incapacitated Will Graham, certain the latter will understand his extremism: "We live in a primitive time – don't we, Will? –

neither savage nor wise. Half measures are the curse of it. Any rational society would either kill me or give me my books."[30] Without the resources the FBI agent has at his disposal, the reader must follow Graham into Lecter's murky world. Relying on Graham's investigative and interpretive skills, the reader cannot help but be manipulated by Harris's pro-FBI viewpoint.

Nevertheless, Lecter remains a fascinating antagonist. Here is a murderer who knows the relevant texts and can articulate his reasons for committing acts of gross indecency. One is reminded of fictionalisations surrounding the Leopold and Loeb case – Meyer Levin's *Compulsion*, Patrick Hamilton's *Rope*, and Joe Pagano's *The Condemned* – as well as real-life serial killers such as Ted Bundy and Ed Kemper. Countering Lecter's perverse genius, Will Graham, having entered the killer's mind, reads his adversary as though he were a difficult book. While in *Silence of the Lambs*, Clarice must compromise herself if she is to solve the crime. That Lecter should lead Clarice to the murderer substantiates his mental superiority and his sense of aesthetics. The inescapable conclusion is that Clarice and Lecter will one day settle down, exchange views, and find some kind of perverse happiness together.[31]

The aesthetics of Harris's books demand the reader accept the narrative as reality. But this pact leads to some dubious conclusions. Since suspending literary disbelief often means suspending political beliefs, readers might find themselves accepting the idea that technology and the psychological skills of the state are enough to solve society's problems regarding anti-social behaviour. Interesting as an insight into how the FBI works, Harris's books demand the reader collude with police procedure. Yet writers like Elmore Leonard, George V. Higgins, James Ellroy, Jerome Charyn and Joseph Koenig, in acknowledging – whether through humour, shifting perspective, historical trickery or hyperbole – the artifice of the genre, avoid any indication that they might be making a similar pact. Though crime fiction is dependent on a degree of street-level reality, the reader deserves to be reminded that he or she is involved in a literary, rather than pseudo-realistic, experience.

Rejecting the state's notion of morality, some authors forsake the procedural elements of the genre for straight-faced satire. At least that's the case in Bradley Denton's *Blackburn*, an intelligent take on a relatively overworked subject. In Jimmy Blackburn, Denton, recalling Jack London's protagonist in *The Assassination Bureau*, has created one of the few politically-motivated serial killers. Here the murderer is not only the novel's protagonist, but its primary moralist. Moving between realism and fantasy, Denton's novel is, by turns, hilarious and sad, simplistic and complex, democratic and psychological. Deploying a style that veers between comicbook exposition and gut-wrenching prose, *Blackburn*, as James Sallis has pointed out,[32] is part of that American literary tradition which colonises a genre narrative format to make a serious metaphysical inquiry.

Raised in Kansas, Blackburn, after each murder, moves to another town, restarting his life only to find himself confronting people who, according to the protagonist, do not deserve to live. For Denton's novel is a portrait of someone whose life consists of a series of infractions others have committed against him. Without love or luck, Blackburn, caught in a web of twisted emotions, cannot see the world as others see it. Unleashing his fury on those who take advantage of the weak and vulnerable, he kills, amongst others, a policeman, car mechanics who cheat an elderly woman, a man who commits adultery on his wedding day, a dog-killer, a militant anti-abortionist, and a fellow serial killer. Denton intercuts these scenes with vignettes that explain Blackburn's motives. It's not that Denton's protagonist wants to murder; rather, he's driven to it by the inhumanity of others. After a sadistic cop kills a dog who has chased a squirrel into a church, and before Blackburn stuffs the squirrel into the policeman's mouth and shoots him, he recalls a kaleidoscope of images detailing past hurts:

The dog was dead. Jimmy had tried to help it, and Dad had

made him drop his pants and had switched him with the fishing rod. The dog had killed rats, and Dad had shot it. The blind man had said that Jesus would help, but Mom had left, and the dog was dead. The dog had killed a squirrel, and Johnston had shot it. The blind man had not heard the voice of Jesus, had made it all up, had lied to him. Jimmy had swum in the pond with the dog, and now it was dead. Dad had hit Mom in the mouth. Jasmine had screamed at monsters in the night. Jimmy had hit the dog with a hammer so it wouldn't hurt. But Jasmine had seen. He had come into the church with the dog, and now it was dead. Jesus had not listened to him even though he was saved on Easter.[33]

The other side of the coin from Harris's straight-laced fiction, *Blackburn* appears closer in spirit to Bret Easton Ellis's *American Psycho*. At least that was what the blurb – "The novel that *American Psycho* should have been" – on the cover of the British paperback edition would have us believe. But even here there are some essential differences. Rather than being part of the genre of crime fiction, Ellis's novel, in terms of investigative perspective, is closer to the speculative work of writers from Huysman to J.G. Ballard, typified, as they are, by obsessive and anthropological detail. Even so, with murder and mutilation apparently a natural outgrowth of the era's cut-throat ethics, *American Psycho* remains an accurate investigation of 1980s culture. For Ellis's Bateman, unlike Blackburn, feels nothing, believes in nothing, and, other than what he acquires from style magazines, knows nothing. Celebrating his lack of substance, Bateman distances himself from his psychopathic activities by switching the narrative from first to third person:

[There] is an idea of a Patrick Bateman, some kind of abstraction, but there is no real me, only an entity, something illusory, and though I can hide my cold gaze and you can shake my hand and feel flesh gripping yours and maybe you can even sense our life styles are probably comparable: *I simply am not there* . . . Myself is fabricated, an aberration.[34]

Bateman's real-life counterpart is Joe Hunt, who articulated a 1980s paradigm in which the free market and mental superiority were used as pretexts for manipulating and allegedly murdering those he believed were preventing him from his profits.[35] That Bateman finally asks "Why?" is indicative of how the era ended: with a series of non-contingent crimes, a question mark, and the purported end of history.

But *Blackburn* goes further, requiring readers to question why they devour books about murderers, yet abhor the crimes of Patrick Bateman or Jeffrey Dahmer. Because Blackburn – closer in spirit to the *Unabomber*[36] than Joe Hunt – kills those who, in his opinion, deserve to die, the novel questions the morality of someone who, because of his circumstances, deigns to make such decisions. Confronting a fictional crime writer, Artimus Arthur, Blackburn says that, in creating a character who "understands the meaning of independence and justice, and who isn't afraid to act on that understanding",[37] the author has virtually written his biography. But Artimus tells Blackburn that he's a "lunatic who can't read his way out of a wet paper bag", because the man in his book is "[Worse] than a serial killer, worse than evil. He's *stupid*, which is the worst lunacy of all. The reader isn't supposed to sympathise with him. The reader's supposed to *loathe* him."[38] When Blackburn says that those murdered in Artimus's narrative deserved their fate, the author tells him that we're all horrible: "Trying to fight that isn't noble. It's *futile*. Why do you think I killed him off at the end, anyway?"[39] It's as though, in saying to the reader, *don't tell me you are actually identifying with Blackburn?*, Denton criticises the prurient aspect of his text, as well as anyone who dares to read it. Though when events turn violent, Artimus recants, saying, "I've always wanted to kill people . . . I've just never had the guts. So I write about it instead."[40]

Eventually Blackburn confronts his nemesis, the sadistic Roy-Boy. After trying to persuade Blackburn to join him in a life of crime, Roy-Boy entraps his would-be colleague: "You need to become aware of the superiority of my world, and to do that you've got to live in it a while."[41] Though abhorring the ethics it entails, Blackburn is forced to become a thief. Paraphrasing Artimus, Blackburn tells Roy-Boy, "You'd like to be evil . . . But you're only stupid."[42] Yet Roy-Boy is Blackburn's shadow. In killing him, Blackburn becomes his own final victim whose sole regret is not having killed his adversary sooner. For had he done so, he would at least have saved a woman from being brutally raped.

While on the run, Blackburn is absolved of his sins by Morton, a tramp who may or may not be a lunatic. Taking refuge in *Mortonism* – a kind of church of latter-day *pataphysics* – Blackburn believes he has finally found a religion free of hypocrisy. The book ends with Blackburn, his plight reminiscent of Gary Gilmore's, as a truculent but acquiescent victim of the state. A reader of comicbooks, Blackburn would rather be executed than live with the guilt of not having killed Roy-Boy sooner, much less having to pay for his crime by spending the next twenty years in Huntsville prison. Though an opponent of capital punishment, he does nothing to halt his execution. Given a lethal injection, Blackburn, as he descends into oblivion, tries out a string of epithets, before deciding on one that is sufficiently succinct and enigmatic to anyone unaware of his story: "*Green Lantern* isn't what it used to be."

Reading *Blackburn* necessitates questioning one's attitude towards murder, capital punishment and the state of American culture. Moving from rage to wish fulfilment, *Blackburn* constitutes an effective critique of Harris's FBI-pandering fiction. Not surprisingly, Sallis compares *Blackburn* to Nathaniel West's *Miss Lonelyhearts* and Blackburn himself to the genial psychopath in Jim Thompson's *Pop. 1280*. While Denton conveys none of West's bitterness nor Thompson's nihilism, his satirical eye is as perceptive as that of both writers. In the end, *Blackburn* is a parable of the new west, a place where junk food culture has collided with fundamentalism and family values. Unable to comprehend the culture, Blackburn turns into an avenging angel whose violence reminds us of society's fissures, and the fact that anyone, given cause, might be a potential killer.

Pastiche Noir

In Jack O'Connell's *Skin Palace*, Jakob, a would-be noir film-maker and son of Quinsigamond's most notorious gangster, gets rid of Felix, his low-life cousin, by persuading the latter's gang, the Roaches, to switch sides. As Jakob films his cousin's demise, the latter, pleading for his life, says, "This climax, beaten to death by the angry mob, it's derivative." Jakob laughs and pats his cousin's cheek: "You're a lowbrow schmuck, Felix. I'm a postmodern artist. I know all the images and I steal from the pool. It's all collage, cuz. Juxtaposition."[43]

Jakob's words might also be applied to crime fiction, which, in so far as it utilises already perceived elements of the genre, can be thought of as collage or its literary equivalent, pastiche. This is particularly true for well-read practitioners who lack cut-throat instincts and a criminal background. Seeking something new, their work is often marred by stylistic self-consciousness and the recycling of plots, protagonists, and urban myths. The problem for such writers is how to make pastiche coherent and convincing without resorting to excessive post-modernisms.

As Jakob implies, pastiche, in borrowing from other sources, suggests ridicule as well as simulation. According to critic Frederic Jameson, pastiche lacks humour and perspective, and is, accordingly, little more than unconscious parody.[44] Yet this view belittles a legitimate contemporary perspective that consciously steals from the past. As subtle simulations, Peter Blauner's *Casino Moon*, Stephen Hunter's *Black Light* and Steve Lopez's *Fourth and Indiana* – excellent novels they might be – aspire to parody, while the work of Vicki Hendricks, Bradley Denton or Barbara Neeley – her *Blanche on the Lamb* features a black domestic worker who observes and comments upon all that occurs around her – exemplify contemporary noir pastiche. While the former seem unaware of their place within the genre, the latter subvert various subtextual elements through humour, patchwork and perspective. Celebrating theft, deploying past stylisations and preexisting reference points, pastiche noir contains an inherent political critique, one capable of stretching the boundaries of the genre.

The problems relating to pastiche can be glimpsed in L. A. Morse's slice of pseudo-representation, *The Big Enchilada*. Published in 1982, it borrows from the Chandler–Spillane tradition, but its over-reliance on specific signs turns this would-be pastiche into an overly blunt parody. Aware of its place in the genre, Morse's novel ends up trapped in the claustrophobia of his expression. But at least the novel succeeds in ridiculing the macho aspect of the genre. Satirising preconceived notions regarding the private eye, Morse seems unconvinced about his ability to critique the culture, and so *The Big Enchilada* remains stylistically frozen in time. Meanwhile, the book's self-consciousness is such that it is unable to move outside the confines of its structure. Though light in tone, *The Big Enchilada* ends up as heavy an artifact as Poppy Z. Brite's *Exquisite Corpse*. Nevertheless, Morse's novel manages to illustrate the difficulty of manoeuvring within a stylised genre. Existing in an inflationary era, the protagonist, Vietnam vct Sam Hunter, finds that there are not many crimes worthy of his investigative skills:

> The law about no-fault divorces had cut into my business, and the same with all the computers they were using for credit checks. But it could have been worse. There were still nasty people who wanted dirty jobs done . . . And that was fine with me. The nastier and dirtier they were, the more I would charge them, and they didn't have any choice because I usually turned up just as much dirt on them. So I was working less, but my income was just about the same.[45]

Instead of trying to solve the problem of how the boundaries of crime fiction might be extended and the text turned into a critique, Morse reaches into the past and, acknowledging the limits of the genre, nullifies the expectations of the reader. Yet, at times, his humour suggests the possibility of disassembling detective fiction's time-honoured structure:

> Past the pulsating discos, the chic coffee houses, and the not-so-chic porno palaces, the sidewalks were a solid stream of the stuff that feeds off and is fed to the Hollywood dream machine. Pot heads, coke sniffers, hash eaters, speed freaks, skag shooters, bikers, draggers, racers, pimps, pushers, prostitutes, religious fanatics who have been saved, homicidal maniacs who never will be, yogis, Krishnas, Buddhists, Maoists, urban guerrillas, neo-Nazis, drag queens, butch dykes, leather boys, chain-mail girls, starlets hoping to be discovered, has-beens hoping to be rediscovered, and those who are there because there's no place else to go.[46]

Whatever its deficiencies, Morse's description sums up Los Angeles, crime fiction prose, and the investigator's place as a crumpled observer. Aware of the cultural signs, Morse spews them forth with more vehemence than even Chandler could have mustered. Unfortunately, *The Big Enchilada* often reads like a text languishing beneath the weight of its observations and points of reference.

Also addressing the politics of pastiche, Jonathan Lethem's *Gun, with Occasional Music* utilises Chandler's prose style to create something original, though not particularly subversive:

> The printed word had been dwindling in the news media, but it hadn't disappeared completely until a year ago, when it was outlawed . . . I double-parked and took a look at the paper. There were the usual captionless pictures of the government busy at work: the President shaking hands with the Inquisitor General, the congressmen shaking hands with the special-interest groups, the Governor shaking hands with Karmic Achiever of the Month.[47]

A hybrid of noir and science fiction, Lethem's novel points towards a possible direction of the genre. For the future of crime fiction will depend on its ability to plunder other genres, and its willingness to feed off various cinematic devices, even if those devices refer to past noir techniques. Like Jay Russell's *Celestial Dogs* and J. W. Jeter's Thompson-like *Into the Land of the Dead*, both of which add a bit of horror to their noir, Lethem's novel establishes a formal paradigm that relates to fanciful notions and media co-option of the genre.

Despite straying from its proletariat origins, contemporary crime fiction invariably retains an element of class-consciousness. Accordingly, it is the investigation, as much as the crime, that remains the essential element of the genre. With the future of noir fiction dependent on the perpetuation of crime, the aesthetics of the genre are such that without the need to commit crimes, there would be no need for cultural investigation. Fortunately for crime fiction, and its development, one cannot, at this point, foresee a society free of crime, nor one in which hierarchy has become irrelevant.

Indicative of changing times, recent noir fiction utilises, as one of its themes, the relationship between ordinary individuals who commit crimes and those involved in corporate crime. While the former deploy individual skills and street-nous, the latter depend on anonymity, technology, and capital. This is, for instance, the sub-text of Nick Tosches's *Trinities* or Pileggi's *Casino*[48] – adapted for the screen by Martin Scorsese – in which the protagonist reminds the reader that the Disneyfication of Las Vegas has been built on junk bonds rather than on Mafia vices such as drugs, prostitution, protection and gambling. This new type of crime, opaque and anonymous, could well affect the style and content of future noir fiction. But effective noirists, regardless of discrepancies between old and new crime, or changes in the urban and political landscape, will continue to extend the boundaries of the genre and address the relationship between the investigator and the investigated. However much it might replicate the present, the language and style of their fiction – rooted in the particularities of time and place – must also refer to the past. Addressing themselves to crime committed in the pursuit of wealth, power and revenge, noirists, regardless of cross-genre tendencies and notions of artifice, will not easily forsake the genre's time-honoured strictures and tendency to leave traces of its history. Likewise, given the state of society, neither can it help but critique the culture. That, after all, is its function. So long as crime, corruption, duplicity and secrecy exist, the genre, regardless of its various incongruities, will remain an integral part of the cultural narrative.

NOTES

I. Introduction: Skip-tracing the Culture

[1] "Chicago. A hardboiled crime writer is found hanged . . ." by Jay Rayner, *Observer*, London, December 22, 1996.

[2] See Thomas, "Body of Evidence", *Guardian*, London, January 28, 1997.

[3] "I didn't . . . know what it was like to be a citizen of Harlem; I had never worked there, raised children there, been hungry, sick or poor there. I had been as much a tourist as a white man . . . The Harlem of my books was never meant to be real; I never called it real; I just wanted to take it away from the white man if only in my books." Himes, *My Life of Absurdity*, Paragon House, New York, 1990, p. 126.

[4] Crumley, *One to Count Cadence*, Vintage, New York, 1987, p. 300.

[5] Of 1,043 major US companies covered in a late 1980s survey by *Fortune* magazine, 117 had been involved in at least one serious delinquency since 1970. The survey confined itself to convictions on federal charges, *nolo contendere* pleas and out-of-court settlements. Indicative of the extent of corruption at the lower level of US business was the rash of prosecutions for bid-rigging in the roadbuilding industry. In the first few years of the 1980s, federal prosecutors in twenty states obtained 400 criminal convictions resulting in some $50 million in fines and 141 prison sentences. By the early 1980s, over 100 companies had been blacklisted by the Pentagon for malpractice. Kidron, Segal, *The Book of Business, Money and Power*, Pluto, London, 1986, p. 161. In the late 1970s, organised crime's annual turnover in the US was estimated at $62 billion. When *Fortune* began publishing its list of the 400 richest families in 1982, included were at least three families of avowed gangsters – Meyer Lansky was eighth on the list. Mandel, *Delightful Murder*, Pluto, London, 1984, pp. 97–98. The borderline separating unscrupulous speculators, confidence tricksters and outright crooks grows ever-thinner, exemplified by the likes of Barry Cornfield, Robert Vesco and Michael Milken.

[6] As early as 1978, prior to crime fiction's recent rise in popularity, an estimated quarter of all fiction sold in Britain and America was crime fiction. Pavett quoted by Warpole, *Reading by Numbers*, Comedia, London, 1984, p. 44.

[7] *Pulp Culture*, Serpent's Tail, London,1995, attempted to place crime fiction written between 1945 and the early 1960s against the backdrop of the cold war and the era's cultural changes. Among the writers included in that study were Jim Thompson, David Goodis, Chester Himes, Raymond Chandler, Ross Macdonald, Dorothy B. Hughes, Dolores Hitchens, Leigh Brackett, Charles Williams and Charles Willeford.

⁸ "[Regardless] of whether you've ever witnessed a drive-by or freeway shooting, you live in the shadow of these acts. Public crimes with often arbitrary victims, they possess a psychic weight which plunges below our specific fears of hold-ups and murders, and ends up coloring our outlook on the routines of daily life, such as taking a walk after dinner." Ralph Rugoff, "Gun Rites," *Circus Americanus*, Verso, London, 1995, p. 65.

⁹ The middle classes, "who fled the cities because of their fear of crime, are far more likely to be killed in the suburbs. A study of the impact of cars on the quality of life in the Pacific Northwest found that more people die in suburban road accidents than are killed by guns or drugs." 16 out of 1,000 city residents faced the risk of injury or death due to either traffic accidents or crime, while 19.2 out of 1,000 suburban residents faced similar risk. Durning, *Guardian*, London, April 16, 1996.

¹⁰ Op. cit., Warpole. Though writing might be, metaphorically speaking, a criminal activity, a novelist, if successful, cannot, even if working on a novel seven days a week for two years, make more than the minimum wage. Even if one were lucky enough to make $20,000 a year on a novel that takes a year to write, that person, working fifty weeks a year, is being paid $7.14 per hour. If he or she works two years on a novel, they cannot hope to make anything near the national minimum wage nor meet the annual pre-tax average US income, which was, as of 1993, $19,800.

¹¹ From the jacket of Constantine's *Always a Body to Trade*, Hodder and Stoughton, London, 1983.

¹² Times were not so generous to pulp romanticist David Goodis and Charles Williams. Goodis died in 1967 following his retreat into bitterness, lawsuits and paranoia. His final novel was the posthumous *Somebody's Done For* in 1967. Williams would commit suicide in 1975.

¹³ Willeford, *The Woman Chaser*, Carroll and Graf, 1990, p. 11.

¹⁴ In just over a generation, the population of the US has almost doubled; per capita income has increased 1,000%; the total national product, as well as personal spending, has increased by more than 2,200%. Meanwhile there has been a global price revolution since World War Two of 300–600%. The dollar, which was halved in value from 1946–1969, was halved again from the mid-1970s to the mid-1980s, a trebling of consumer prices reflecting the worst inflation in US history. Now a majority of books in libraries have been published over the last thirty years. Edmund Wilson, in the 1930s, bemoaned having to choose which of 8000 annual titles he would review in *The New Republic*; these days he would have to cope with close to 60,000 titles. *The Nation*, March 17, 1997, p. 17.

¹⁵ In 1982, more than 50% of all mass market sales were accounted for by five publishers, and ten publishing firms accounted for more than 85%. In 1958, one-store, independent book firms sold 72% of all books sold by booksellers. By 1981, the four largest bookstore chains already accounted for 40% of sales. Whereas thirty years ago it took 2,500 copies at $4–5.00

of a first novel to break even, today the figure is at least 15,000 at $11–15.00 (numbers are obsolete by now). The effect of this is that the book buyer has seen his discretionary dollar greatly devalued. Ibid.

2. From Pulp to Neon

[1] Dates are mutable. In 1996, the US Senate's veteran's committee voted to fix the official start of America's longest war as February 28th, 1961, when the government claims American military advisers began accompanying South Vietnamese troops on combat missions. This was good news for those claiming the government had unfairly denied benefits to those serving before 1964. It also supports those who have maintained that the war was illegal, having been conducted, until the Gulf of Tonkin resolution in 1964, without congressional approval. This even though some 16,000 American troops had served in Vietnam before that date.

[2] But not the first televised war. That dubious distinction belongs to the Gulf War.

[3] Naylor, *Hot Money*, Unwin Hyman, London, 1987, p. 275. "The answer lay in the transformation of the international financial system, shifting it to a US-dollar standard and forcing the central banks of the major western countries to accumulate unwanted inventories of US treasury bills. One offshoot of dollar liquidity had been the emergence of the eurodollar and eurobond markets, and the proliferation of peekaboo financial centers, the foundation of the explosive growth of international bank lending in the 1970s." Ibid.

[4] A reference to soldiers who were treated leniently by military courts after killing Vietnamese civilians.

[5] "The conquest of the New World set off two vast demographic catastrophes, unparalleled in history: the virtual destruction of the indigenous population of the Western hemisphere, and the devastation of Africa as the slave trade rapidly expanded . . . While modalities have changed, the fundamental themes of the conquest retain their vitality and resilience, and will continue to do so until the reality and causes of the 'savage injustice' are honestly addressed." Chomsky, *Year 501, The Conquest Continues*, Verso, London, 1992, p. 5.

[6] A counter-terrorist programme of assassination and torture which, according to its director, eventual head of the CIA William Colby, was responsible for killing 20,000 people – citizens as well as enemy soldiers. See Valentine, *The PHOENIX Program*, Morrow, New York, 1990.

[7] Harold Bloom, in his landmark study of self-interest, *The Western Canon*, cites neither Hammett nor Chandler, much less Thompson or Ellroy.

[8] Few would deny that publishing is value-free, or that corporate interests do not play a role in what is published. While companies publish politically contentious books when they think they can profit from them, there was, according to Chomsky, considerable pressure

during the early years of the Vietnam war to marginalise dissenting opinion. It was during this time that large companies began to buy smaller publishing houses. Many of these small companies had been involved in publishing books expressing oppositional viewpoints. Since that wave of take-overs, publishing has become increasingly corporate, a situation that, according to Mark Crispin Miller, has altered output: "The slow course of an idea or vision through some subculture of thoughtful readers . . . is hardly possible when those who own the trade want only big returns right now. Thus have the giants shrunk the culture automatically, through that objective 'market censorship' . . . However, the giants have also shrunk the culture actively – by dumping, or red-lighting, any book that offers revelations irksome to themselves." Little Brown, bought by Time Inc. in 1968, is now part of the Time-Warner empire, and spends much of its money promoting coffee table books. Likewise, RCA's purchase of Random House in 1966. Under the auspices of Advance Publications, it has now become part of a $5.3 billion empire, and sinks its money into the likes of Donald Trump's *The Art of the Deal*. Miller, "The Crushing Power of Big Publishing", *The Nation*, March 17, 1997, p. 17.

[9] See Mangold, Penycate, *The Tunnels of Cu Chi*, Random House, 1985.

[10] In Mikal Gilmore's study of his brother, Gary, he says, "Instead of writing I preferred reading hardboiled crime fiction – particularly the novels of Ross Macdonald, in which the author tried to solve murders by explicating labyrinthine family histories." Gilmore, *Shot in the Heart*, p. 500, Penguin, London, 1994.

[11] R. Macdonald, *The Underground Man*, Allison & Busby, London, 1994, p. 241.

[12] Ibid., p. 8.

[13] In 1966, 27% of those with a college education favoured immediate withdrawal from Vietnam, while in 1970, just before the publication of *The Underground Man*, the percentage of those with a college education favouring withdrawal had risen to 47%. In 1966, of people with only a grade school education, 41% favoured immediate withdrawal. By September 1970, 61% of grade school graduates favoured withdrawal. In 1964, 53% of college educated people were willing to send troops to Vietnam, as opposed to only 33% of those educated up to grade school level. Zinn, *A People's History of the United States*, Harper & Row, New York, 1994, pp. 482–483.

[14] Op. cit., Macdonald, p. 94.

[15] Ibid., p. 231.

[16] J. MacDonald, *Dress Her in Indigo*, Pan, London, 1972, p. 25.

[17] Ibid., p. 26.

[18] Ibid., p. 60.

[19] Ibid., p. 70.

[20] Ibid., pp. 81–82.

[21] Ex-CIA agent John Stockwell estimates that two million people were

killed in the conflict. Stockwell, *The Praetorian Guard*, South End Press, Boston, 1991, p. 81.

[22] Op. cit., MacDonald, p. 170.

[23] Williams, *Don't Just Stand There*, Panther, London, 1966, p. 33.

[24] The Reagan administration did its best to rundown the Black community. "In its first year . . . it eliminated the Comprehensive Employment and Training Act programme . . . which ended 150,000 federally supported jobs; it cut by $1.7 billion the child nutrition programmes, designed to curtail urban hunger; it removed more than 400,000 families from the welfare roles. Within twelve months, the median income of Afro-American families had fallen 5.2 per cent before the 1980 figure and the number of Americans below the poverty line had increased by 2.2 million . . . for Black males aged 25–44, the rate of mental hospital admissions was almost three times higher than for white males . . ." Manning, *Black American Politics*, Verso, 1985, London, p. 104.

[25] Himes, *Hot Day, Hot Night* (reissue of *Blind Man With a Pistol*), Signet, New York, 1975, pp. 167–68.

[26] Thompson's suitability to write the novel is of less interest than speculation as to why the novel appeared in 1970, five years after the film's release, and past the moment when, given the heat of black militancy, it might have made its maximum impact.

[27] Polito and Macauley state that *King Blood* was written while Thompson was living in New York during the 1950s. If one compares the style of Thompson's 1950s writing with his 1970s writing, *King Blood* appears to belong in the latter era. Though it is conceivable that Thompson, while living in New York, wrote a treatment for *King Blood*, but did not write the novel until the 1970s.

[28] See Michael McCauley's *Jim Thompson: Sleep With the Devil* and Robert Polito's *Savage Art: a biography of Jim Thompson*, Knopf, New York, 1965. While James Sallis fails to mention Thompson's *Child of Rage* in his chapter on Thompson in *Difficult Lives: Jim Thompson, David Goodis, Chester Himes*, Gryphon Books, Brooklyn, 1993.

[29] Reiterating Thompson's thesis, *New York Times* correspondent C. L. Sulzberger wrote, "We lost the war in the Mississippi Valley, not the Mekong Delta." Op. cit., Zinn, p. 492.

[30] America's desire to expand and intervene can be traced to its origins, articulated in the nineteenth century policy of Manifest Destiny. In the 1845 debate on the annexation of Texas, editor John L. O'Sullivan, following ideas handed down from Franklin, Jefferson, Monroe, and Polk, became the first to use the term 'manifest destiny' in print: ". . . the fulfilment of our manifest destiny to overspread the continent allotted (sic) by Providence for the free development of our yearly multiplying million." Though the policy was cloaked in religious terms, the unimpeded movement westward had more to do with the railroad than New World theological inclinations. If the railway was to expand west, the desert had to be pushed back (a new meteorology based on divine

intervention was implied in the slogan "Rain Follows the Plow"), the Native Americans eradicated, the buffalo replaced by cattle, and, most important of all, the places through which the railway passed must be populated by people. During the four decades after the Civil War, 183 million acres – the size of California and most of Montana – went out of the public domain into railroad ownership. See Reisner, *Cadillac Desert*, Penguin, New York, 1993, pp. 37–51. Milner, "National Initiatives", *The Oxford History of the American West*, Oxford University Press, Oxford, p. 166.

[31] Thompson, *King Blood*, Sphere, London, p. 78.

[32] Ibid., p. 93.

[33] Invited to Paris by Rissient who hoped he might become the next Chester Himes, Thompson arrived drunk and soon wanted to return to the US. "Pierre Rissient lamented that Thompson could not seize the promise of his original 'sample', and Les Films La Boetie never pursued a film: 'That moment was the hinge, let us say, for his creative vitality. After that he was not able to write any more.' " Op. cit., Polito, p. 485.

[34] As a child, when Thompson came home covered in dirt, his mother would hold him up to a mirror and say, "Will you take a look at Mama's little black child. Where did your white mother get such a black son?" The working title of *Child of Rage* would be *White Mother, Black Son*. Ibid., p. 51.

[35] Thompson, *Child of Rage*, Blood & Guts Press, Los Angeles, 1991, p. 111.

[36] In his autobiographical *Bad Boy*, Thompson is less than truthful, claiming his father was in the progressive wing of the Republican party, when, in reality, he sided with the Jim Crow element of the party, and against the state's progressive governor. Polito, *The Savage Art*, pp. 39–40.

[37] "The bloodline of his 1930s Marxism circulates through all his subsequent fiction." Ibid., p. 279.

[38] Op. cit., Thompson, p. 107.

[39] Ibid., p. 44.

[40] Ibid., p. 46.

[41] Ibid., p. 49.

[42] Ibid., p. 150.

[43] Ibid., p. 178.

[44] Ibid., p. 179.

[45] Ibid., p. 229.

[46] Historian W. E. Woodward sums up the ethos of Thompson's *Child of Rage*: "The history of the American people showed that the westward movement went right on, regardless, over Indian land, Spanish land, Mexican land. Some day it would be Texas all over again . . . The American imperialists invented the grandiose term 'Manifest Destiny' to express their aspirations and to put land hunger on a lofty plane. Manifest Destiny was defined as an irresistible impulse in the racial life. Overlordship belongs by nature to the strong. They must not shirk

responsibility for the weak and servile peoples, for the Mexicans, Negroes, and Indians, however painful it might be to the dominant race. The white man's burden. Provided . . . that the weak and servile peoples possess fertile lands, mines, forests... Otherwise, the weaker races could shift for themselves. There is no use in trying to elevate people who do not possess anything worth taking." Woodward, *A New History of America*, Faber and Faber, London, 1938, p. 365.

[47] How substantial was Nixon's *silent majority*? While, in 1965, 61% of the US population thought American involvement in Vietnam was not wrong, by 1971, 61% thought American involvement was wrong. Op. cit., Zinn, pp. 482–83. The term *silent majority*, though credited to Richard Nixon, had been used earlier by Spiro Agnew – "America's silent majority is bewildered by irrational protest." Prior to that the term was used by Charles Lindberg, who, at a pre-World War Two rally, spoke of "that silent majority of Americans who have no newspaper, or newsreel, or radio station at their command", but who were nevertheless opposed to American involvement in the war against Europe unleashed by Nazi Germany and Fascist Italy. Hochman, Hochman, eds., *The Penguin Dictionary of Contemporary American History*, Penguin, London, 1997, pp. 487–488.

[48] See Chomsky, *Manufacturing Consent*, Pantheon, New York, 1988.

[49] Willeford, *Cockfighter*, Black Lizard, Berkeley, 1987, p. 26.

[50] Ibid., p. 30.

[51] Ibid., p. 65.

[52] Ibid., p. 121.

[53] Ibid., p. 131.

[54] Ibid., p. 125.

[55] Ibid., p. 125.

[56] Ibid., p. 217.

[57] Ibid., p. 218.

[58] Ibid.

[59] Ibid., p. 219.

[60] Op. cit., Naylor, pp. 25–26. Though a novel like *Dog Soldiers* addresses the micro-economics of small-time entrepreneurism, no crime novel has addressed the Vietnam war as articulated by Naylor.

[61] Ibid.

[62] Op. cit., Zinn, p. 466. Kennedy sent 16,000 military advisers to the region, many of whom would engage in military operations. Regarding US attempts to corner markets, Under-Secretary of State U. Alexis Johnson said, in 1963, "Why is it [Vietnam] desirable, and why is it important? First, it provides a lush climate, fertile soil, rich natural resources, a relatively sparse population in most areas, and room to expand. The countries of Southeast Asia provide rich exportable surpluses such as rice, rubber, teak, corn, tin, spices, oil, and many others." Zinn, pp. 465–67.

[63] Stark, *Point Blank*, Allison and Busby, London, 1962, p. 17.

[64] Ibid., pp. 125–126.

[65] Ibid.

[66] Ibid.

[67] Ibid., pp. 135–36.

[68] Ibid.

[69] Ibid., pp. 131–32.

[70] Ibid., p. 135.

[71] Ibid., p. 136.

[72] In November 1975, just after the publication of Gores's novel, Francis Ford Coppola's *City* magazine in San Francisco devoted an edition to their favourite son, Dashiell Hammett with articles by Gores, Warren Hinckle, private investigator David Fechheimer, and Hammett biographer William Nolan.

[73] Gores, *Hammett*, Macdonald, London, 1975, p. 17.

[74] "[Nostalgia], the San Francisco disease that clouds all vision and judgment." Herb Caen, cited by Christopher Reed, "Beating Heart of San Francisco", *Guardian*, February 6, 1997.

[75] These novels would provide their authors access to Hollywood. Bergman, for instance, would write *Blazing Saddles*, *Fletch* and *Big Trouble*.

3. Total Crime

[1] Spanos, *The Errant Art of Moby-Dick – The Canon, the Cold War, and the Struggle for American Studies*, Duke University, Durham, 1995, pp. 257–266.

[2] 2.6 million Americans were involved in Vietnam. If the war lasted ten years, the number of deaths equate to about 100 per week. This compared to the 300,000 Americans who died in a four year period during World War Two, or the 115,000 Americans who died from 1917–18 during World War One.

[3] Between 1970 and 1972, some fourteen per cent of soldiers tested in Vietnam were found to be addicted to heroin. "When faced with the threat of Army discipline (essentially, not being allowed to leave Vietnam) 93 per cent of those classified as addicts (and virtually all the rest of the users) managed to stop using heroin during their remaining months in the Army . . . From Vietnam the government was . . . able to obtain massive data about the behavior of hundreds of thousands of heroin users, and virtually none of the findings supported the hoary myth of 'drug slave,' or the addict who physiologically had no other choice than to do what was necessary to obtain a daily supply of heroin." Epstein, *Agents of Fear*, Verso, London, 1990, p. 188.

[4] Studies during the 1970s showed that 18 million former voters had dropped out of the electoral process. Only 23% of potential voters under thirty years of age participated in the 1970 mid-term election. In 1978, voter participation in the New York gubernatorial election reached a 150 year low – with only 38.5% of potential voters participating. Op. cit.,

Davis, *Prisoners of the American Dream*, Verso, London, 1986, pp. 224–225.
"As early as 1970, according to the University of Michigan's Survey
Research Center, 'trust in government' was low in every section of the
population. Classes differed in their apathy: of professional people, 40
per cent had 'low' political trust in government; of unskilled blue-collar
workers, 66 per cent had 'low' trust." After seven years of intervention in
Vietnam, public opinion in 1971 showed an unwillingness to come to aid
other countries. And 53 per cent of those polled by the University of
Michigan Survey Research Centre, in 1972, said the government was
being run by a few big interests looking out for themselves. Op. cit., Zinn,
p. 529.

[5] "Behind the theory lay the assumption of monolithic communism,
which is now seen to have been wrong." Ranelagh, *The Agency – The Rise
and the Decline of the CIA*, Sceptre, London, 1987, p. 468.

[6] *The Pentagon Papers* were released to the public by Daniel Ellsberg and
Anthony Russo in 1971. As Chomsky put it, the intellectual elite and
periodicals were "destroying the historical record and supplanting it with
a more comfortable story, transferring the moral onus of American
aggression to its victims, reducing 'lessons' of the war to socially neutral
categories of error, ignorance and cost". Op. cit., Zinn, p. 555.

[7] Secretary of Defense, Robert McNamara, in his memoirs, *In Retrospect*,
admits to knowing, as early as 1969, that the war could not be won by
"any reasonable military means", yet never said as much to the President
or to the public. Op. cit., Hochman and Hochman, p. 573. According to
aide Jack Valenti, President Johnson was unable to pronounce
Vietnamese place names, nor could he locate the country on a map. *Secret
History*, Channel 4, January 21, 1997.

[8] Incidents where servicemen rolled fragmentation bombs under the
tents of officers who were ordering them into combat, or against whom
they had other grievances. The Pentagon reported 209 such incidents in
1970 alone. Op. cit., Zinn, p. 485.

[9] "It isn't always easy, and it's never pleasant, putting yourself in these
guys' shoes – or inside their minds. But that's what my people and I have
to do. We have to try to feel what it was like for each one." Douglas,
Oishaker, *Mindhunter: Inside the FBI Elite Serial Crime Unit*, Heinemann,
London, 1996, p. 26.

[10] According to a 1952 National Security Council memo: "Communist
control of all of Southeast Asia would render the US position in the
Pacific offshore island chain precarious and would seriously jeopardize
fundamental US security interests in the Far East." And "Southeast
Asia . . . is the principal world source of natural rubber and tin, and a
producer of petroleum and other strategically important commodities."
The memo goes on to note that Japan depended on rice produced in
Southeast Asia, and communist victory in Vietnam would "make it
extremely difficult to prevent Japan's eventual accommodation to
communism". Op. cit., Zinn, p. 462.

[11] Op. cit., Spanos, p. 261. Quoting Rapaport, "Vietnam: The Thousand Plateaus", *The 60s Without Apology*, ed. Sayres, Stephenson, Aronowitz, Jameson, University of Minneapolis Press, Minneapolis, p. 139.
[12] O'Brien, *Going After Cacciato*, Flamingo, London, 1988, p. 255.
[13] Op. cit., Spanos, p. 32.
[14] Herr, *Dispatches*, Picador, London, 1979, p. 74.
[15] Op. cit., Stockwell, p. 80.
[16] *Encyclopaedia of the West*, Oxford University Press, Oxford, 1995, p. 428.
[17] Op. cit., Herr, p. 12.
[18] Ibid., p. 207.
[19] Ibid., p. 206.
[20] O'Brien, *If I Die in a Combat Zone*, Granada, London, 1985, p. 188.
[21] Ibid.
[22] Ibid., pp. 255–256.
[23] Ibid., p. 302.
[24] "No single quality of American culture is so distinctive as its continued assertion of the nobility and beauty of violence – a notion and a mythology propagated with excitement and craft in all popular cultural forms . . . This cultural predilection must have been immeasurably enhanced by the television coverage of the Vietnam War, which brought real bloodletting and killing into every American living-room, and rendered death sacred no more. Encouraged thus to act out their fantasies, our killers would come to find that their murderous acts would serve both to validate and to relieve their grievances." Op. cit., Leyton, p. 364.
[25] Hasford, *The Short-Timers*, Bantam, New York, 1987, p. 44.
[26] Ibid., p. 133.
[27] Ibid., p. 175.
[28] Ibid., p. 176.
[29] America's desire to expand and intervene can be traced to its origins, articulated in the nineteenth-century policy of Manifest Destiny. In the 1870s, Nebraska had its own Bureau of Immigration which rationalised its policies by citing the state's isothermal belts, i.e., longitudinal and latitudinal bands within which the most advanced muscular and mental development, as well as the most heroic achievements of invention and creative genius were supposedly produced. The most significant isothermal belt ran through Nebraska. While to the southwest, Colorado was populated by Spaniards and Indians. Op. cit., Reisner, pp. 37–51.
[30] "[Even] more unsuspected and irrecoverable are the forces that nerved and sinewed our industry and that still drive us toward the acquisition and consumption of more and more power. For what underlay our clearing of the continent were the ancient fears and divisions that we brought to the New World along with the primitive precursors of the technology that would assist in transforming the continent." Turner,

Beyond Geography – The Western Spirit Against the Wilderness, Rutgers, New Brunswick, 1986, p. 255.

[31] "It wasn't that the war would never go away; it would never come . . . we could never finally concentrate and focus that war. It was not a question of whether we should have supported it or not: we couldn't focus it, we couldn't realize it, either way, to stop it or continue it. That war and the intensity of drug usage are perhaps not accidentally parallel." Dorn, Edward, "Roadtesting the Language", *Interviews*, Four Seasons Foundation, Bolinas, 1980, pp. 92–93.

[32] Stone collaborated on two versions of the script before withdrawing from the project and subsequently disowning the film.

[33] 1973, the year of the publication of *Dog Soldiers*, saw the Pinochet coup in Chile, and the Chicago experiment – a testing ground for such policies as privatisation and deregulation that would become the mainstay of Reaganomics. It was also the year that economists Passell and Ross articulated trickle-down economics in their book, *The Retreat from Riches: Affluence and Its Enemies*. Herman, *Triumph of the Market*, South End Press, Boston, 1995, p. 40.

[34] Op. cit., Epstein, p. 105.

[35] According to Ralph Nader, the annual cost in the 1970s to the American public of illegal monopolist practices amounted to between forty-eight and sixty billion dollars. This figure was higher than the total annual turnover of US organised crime.

[36] "During the Vietnam War, the Golden Triangle, the contiguous parts of Laos, Burma, and Thailand, became the most important source of American heroin supplies. This after the fall of the French Connection in the early 1970s, when Turkey suppressed opium production, much to the joy of Southeast Asia warlords, whose opium the CIA was merrily flying to market." Op. cit., Naylor, p. 94.

[37] Stone, *Dog Soldiers*, Star, London, 1976, p. 27.

[38] Ibid., p. 305.

[39] Ibid., p. 41.

[40] Ibid., p. 42.

[41] Ibid.

[42] Thornberg, *Cutter and Bone*, Blue Murder, London, 1988, p. 25.

[43] Ibid., p. 26.

[44] Ibid., p. 22.

[45] "[It] was the staggering accumulation of 'stateless' dollars, arising from the US trade deficit and the OPEC price explosion, that provided the fuel for the debt-led industrial boom which swept the American, Mediterranean and East Asian borderlands from 1976–1980. This giddiest of post-war expansions was based on the export of metropolitan debts, magically recycled by the international banking system as credit money, to industrializing countries whose future export growth was, in turn, pledged as collateral." Op. cit., Davis, pp. 197–201.

[46] Op. cit., Thornberg, p. 94.

[47] Ibid., p. 91.
[48] Ibid.
[49] Ibid., p. 74.
[50] Ibid.
[51] Ibid., p. 157.
[52] "You have to be able to re-create the crime scene in your head. You need to know as much as you can about the victim so that you can imagine how she might have reacted. You have to be able to put yourself in her place as the attacker threatens her . . . You have to be able to feel her fear as he approaches her. You have to be able to feel her pain as he rapes her or beats her or cuts her. You have to try to imagine what she was going through when he tortured her for his sexual gratification . . . But just as difficult, I have to put myself in the position of the attacker, to think as he thinks, to plan along with him, to understand his gratification in this one moment out of his life in which his pent-up fantasies come true and he is finally in control, completely able to manipulate and dominate another human being." Op. cit., Douglas, Olshaker, pp. 174–175.
[53] Op. cit., Thornberg, p. 153.
[54] Crumley, "The Mexican Tree Duck", *Whores*, Dennis McMillan Publications, Montana, 1989, p. 5.
[55] Crumley, *One to Count Cadence*, Vintage, New York, 1991, p. 14.
[56] Ibid., p. 330.
[57] Crumley, "Introduction", *The Collection*, p. 11.
[58] Crumley, "Interview", *Whores*, p. 129.
[59] "If there is a legacy it seems to me I belong more to the Chandler side of things; what I do is different from what Hammett meant to do." From an interview with John Harvey, "Crumley: The Last Good Place", *Criminal Proceedings*, ed. Messent, Pluto, London, 1997, p. 152.
[60] Op. cit., *The Collection*, p. 7.
[61] The opening quote to *The Last Good Kiss*, *The Collection*, p. 259.
[62] Williams, *Into the Badlands*, Paladin, London, 1991, p. 150.
[63] Ibid., p. 151.
[64] Hugo is a poet and himself the author of an excellent crime novel, *Death and the Good Life* (Clark City Press, 1991). Though Crumley has said that Trahearne is based on Hugo, or even a younger version of himself, crime writer John Harvey suggests Trahearne is based on the poet-novelist James Dickey. While this might be the case, Harvey fails to note that, if a friend, Dickey, the author of *Deliverance*, was also a noted hawk during the Vietnam war, and so, politically speaking, Crumley's opposite. Op. cit., Harvey, p. 162.
[65] Op. cit., Crumley, p. 150.
[66] Ibid., p. 303.
[67] Ibid., p. 304.
[68] "[For] me, the mystery novel, the detective novel, is just something to hang the words on. I don't much care about the mystery itself . . . and in

that way I'm more like Chandler . . . [What] I'm saying . . . is that civilization doesn't work . . . And I think it doesn't work because societies and civilizations tend to reflect human failings and we are, unfortunately, all too human. And the other notion that there's a rational universe out there that you can figure out is, as far as I'm concerned, as nonsensical as believing in the risen Jesus Christ . . . I like to play with language and I like to embed jokes in the text, and I like to have a lot of things going on at one time . . . " Op. cit., Harvey, pp. 152–153.

[69] Crumley, *The Mexican Tree Duck*, Mysterious Press, New York, p. 78.
[70] An interesting comparison could be made to the writer of historical fiction, Paul Metcalf, who, in novels like *Genoa, Patagonia* and *Apalachee*, has removed the narrator from his fiction.
[71] Shelley, "The Detroit Spinner", *Life, Observer*, March 9, 1996.
[72] Op. cit., Williams, p. 205. Says Higgins, "A crime novelist writes novels about crime. I have never done that . . . I write novels with crimes in them, who didn't? Madame Bovary committed the crime of adultery."
[73] Higgins, Three Novels, *The Friends of Eddie Coyle*, Robinson, London, 1985, pp. 13–14.
[74] Ibid., p. 3.
[75] Ibid., p. 26.
[76] Ibid., p. 112.
[77] Ibid., p. 111.
[78] Ibid., p. 121.
[79] Ibid., p. 111.
[80] Ibid., p. 141.
[81] Higgins, *A City on a Hill*, Critic's Choice, New York, 1985, p. 145.
[82] Ibid., p. 166.
[83] Higgins, *A Choice of Enemies*, Robinson, London, 1987, p. 5.
[84] Ibid., p. 231.
[85] "Ideology . . . has come to be seen as a negative quality in political life. But the opposite of ideological zeal isn't pragmatic compromise. It is corruption . . . Kleptocracy tends to take hold on the morning after ideological optimism . . . Graft is what happens when politicians try to change the world and fail . . . [What] feeds political corruption is not genuine ideological commitment but jaded, cynical disillusion." Finian O'Toole, "Pulling Strings", *Guardian*, London, August 27, 1997, p. 17.
[86] Higgins avoided the war due to a bleeding ulcer. That the ulcer was brought on by the thought that he'd be sent to Vietnam is an incongruity deserving of a place in one of Higgins's novels.

4. Figures in the Mirror

[1] The phrase *figures in the historical mirror* derives from the final sentence of Perry Anderson's "The Ends of History", which concerns Fukuyama and the death of history: "Historical analogies are never more than suggestive. But there are occasions when they may be more fruitful than

predictions . . . Oblivion, transvaluation, mutation, redemption: each according to their intuition, will make their own guess as to which is more probable. Jesuit, Leveller, Jacobin, Liberal – these are the figures in the mirror." *A Zone of Engagement*, Verso, London, 1992, p. 375.

[2] Op. cit., Zinn, p. 542.

[3] "There were not so much rogue officers as obedient officers diligently following government's criminal orders." Cockburn maintains that the press leak regarding CIA infractions was the work of the CIA, to lay blame on rogue agents and Angleton and, in using "the episode as an object lesson in the folly of sharing secrets with blabbermouths in Congress", preserve the integrity of the agency. Alexander Cockburn, "Colby Had His Share of Dirty Tricks", *Los Angeles Times*, May 1, 1996.

[4] Nixon: "I want the North Vietnamese to believe I've reached the point where I might do anything to stop the war. We'll just slip the word to them that, 'for God's sake, you know Nixon is obsessed about Communists. We can't restrain him when he's angry – and he has his hand on the nuclear button.' " Ranelagh, *The Agency: The Rise and Decline of the CIA*, Sceptre, London, 1988, pp. 502–503.

[5] Cockburn, Silverstein, *Washington Babylon*, Verso, London, 1996, p. 3. "The chairman of the *Washington Post* was not alone among her fellow proprietors . . . in feeling that the time had come to cry halt . . . [The people] had seen institutions corrupted, politicians plying corporate leaders for bribes, and they were eager for change. It was the profound and urgent task of vested power – in whose ranks stood Katherine Graham and her fellow proprietors – to contain and deflect that urge. Graham called for a return to basics. Journalists, she said, should stop trying to be sleuths. Her demand that they behave with more deference towards the powerful was widely noted. It helped set the tone for the post-Watergate period." Ibid.

[6] Block, *Sins of the Fathers*, Avon, New York, 1991, p. 2.

[7] Behm, "The Eye of the Beholder", *Three Novels by Mark Behm*, Zomba, London, 1983, p. 9.

[8] Amongst Block's many works of fiction are two books that relate directly to the Vietnam era, a series of instructive softboilers featuring burglar and second-hand bookseller Bernie Rhodenbarr.

[9] Op cit., Block, p. 156.

[10] Block, *Eight Million Ways to Die*, Avon, New York, 1993, p. 179.

[11] Ibid., p. 56.

[12] Ibid., p. 182.

[13] Ibid., p. 164.

[14] Op. cit., Zinn, p. 545. One should note the propensity for such polls to repeat themselves, particularly when it comes to matters of faith. Ever since the Eisenhower administration, America has been in a spiritual crisis. In a recent poll (cited by *Newsnight*, BBC2, London, December, 1996), 71% of Americans believe the country is in a long-term spiritual decline.

[15] Op cit., Block, p. 8.

[16] Ibid., p. 184.

[17] Ibid., p. 191.

[18] Ibid., pp. 193–194.

[19] Ibid.

[20] Ibid., p. 217.

[21] Ibid., p. 228.

[22] Block, *A Ticket to the Boneyard*, Avon, 1990, New York, p. 79.

[23] Ibid., p. 130.

[24] Ibid., pp. 285–286.

[25] Ibid., p. 232.

[26] Dobyns, *Saratoga Trifecta*, Penguin, London, 1995, p. 343.

[27] Ibid., p. 494.

[28] Ibid., p. 186.

[29] Ibid., p. 218.

[30] Ibid., p. 84.

[31] Ibid., p. 52.

[32] Ibid., p. 75.

[33] Ibid., p. 18.

[34] Ibid., p. 90.

[35] Ibid., p. 122.

[36] Burke, *Neon Rain*, Pocket Books, New York, 1988, p. 12.

[37] Ibid., p. 36.

[38] Ibid., p. 255.

[39] Ibid., p. 46.

[40] Ibid., p. 146.

[41] Op. cit., Williams, pp. 58–59.

[42] Ibid., pp. 60–61.

[43] Op. cit., Burke, p. 129.

[44] Op. cit., Williams, p. 62.

[45] Ibid.

[46] Ibid., p. 62.

[47] Ibid., pp. 64–65.

[48] Op. cit., Burke, p. 263.

[49] Ibid., p. 263.

[50] Burke, *Cadillac Jukebox*, Orion, London, 1997, p. 28

[51] See Sabine Vanacker's "V. I. Warshawski, Kinsey Millhone and Kay Scarpetta: Creating a Feminist Detective Hero", *Criminal Proceedings*, ed., Messent, Pluto, London, 1997. Regarding the critique of the traditional detective-as-hero, Vanacker cites Barbara Wilson's *Murder in the Collective* and *Sisters of the Road* which "constitute probing interrogations of the crime genre and the dubious nature of the detective's search for knowledge and truth". Pam Nilsen, her detective, discovers that being a feminist and a detective are incompatible. Nilsen learns that to understand how the murder in her printing collective occurred she must show empathy with, and even trust in, others, when she would rather

question, analyse and investigate. Vanacker suggests that these might be the first and last examples of feminist crime fiction, since they invalidate the main thrust of the genre: "the investigative analysis of a crime by a ratiocinative male detective." Ibid., p. 63.

52 Paretsky, *Burn Marks*, Virago, London, 1991. Ibid., p. 29.
53 Paretsky, *Toxic Shock* (US title: *Blood Shot*), Penguin, London, 1988, p. 183.
54 Ibid., p. 191.
55 Paretsky, *Killing Orders*, Penguin, London, 1987, p. 46.
56 Paretsky, *Tunnel Vision*, Penguin, London, 1995, p. 373.
57 Ibid., p. 35.
58 Ibid., p. 47.
59 Op. cit., Paretsky, *Toxic Shock*, p. 280.
60 Op. cit., Paretsky, *Tunnel Vision*, p. 190.
61 Haywood, *Fear of the Dark*, Penguin, New York, 1988, p. 8.
62 Ibid.
63 Ibid., p. 141.
64 Ibid., p. 16.
65 Haywood, *Not Long for This World*, Macmillan, London, 1990, p. 129.
66 Op. cit., Haywood, *Fear of the Dark*, p. 16.
67 Ibid., p. 17.
68 Haywood, *You Can Die Trying*, Serpent's Tail, London, 1995, p. 208.
69 Ibid., p. 19.
70 Ibid., p. 211.
71 Ibid.
72 Davis, *City of Quartz*, Verso, London, 1990, p. 300.
73 Op. cit., Haywood, *Not Long for This World*, p. 30.
74 When Mosley first came to Britain to publicise *The Devil in a Blue Dress*, he maintained that Himes had not been a major influence on his work.
75 Mosley, *A Red Death*, Pan, London, 1993, p. 259.
76 Ibid., p. 71.
77 Ibid., pp. 229–230.
78 Mosley, *Black Betty*, Serpent's Tail, London, 1994, p. 145.
79 Ibid., p. 157.
80 *A Little Yellow Dog*, Serpent's Tail, London, 1996, p. 266.
81 Duncan, ed., *The Third Degree*, No Exit, Harpenden, 1997, p. 159.
82 "In the black", *Time Out*, London, September 4–11, 1996, p. 50. In Sallis's *Eye of the Cricket* – received too late to be given adequate attention in this study – Griffin's son finally reappears. Picaresquely viewing a range of disappearing souls, Lew conveys the sense of a decaying culture. Here Sallis again plays on the ambiguity existing in the relationship between author and protagonist. Having by now written a number of other novels, Lew is called to the local hospital to identify a young man, apparently homeless, whose only possession is a well-worn and notated copy of one of Griffin's out-of-print novels, one which bears an inscription from the author to his son. When he regains consciousness,

the young man claims to be Lew Griffin, and, in a notebook left to him by his *doppelgänger*, says he has already begun work on a new novel. Facing a long-term writer's block, Griffin endures another dark night of the soul, after which he can begin on a novel which may or may not be the one the young man has claimed as his own.

[83] Precedents for the use of a black protagonist by a white writer can be found in the work of such writers as Jim Thompson, Ed Lacey (*Black and Whitey*) and Shane Stevens (*Go Down Dead*).

[84] Op. cit., "In the black."

[85] Sallis, *Moth*, Avon, New York, 1993, p. 1.

[86] Op cit., Duncan.

[87] Op. cit., Sallis, *Moth*, p.180.

[88] "The real present of the Oulipo, that state which is ever so transitory, almost imperceptible between the past and the future, is . . . distinguished by this question: where is the Oulipo's end? . . . Its end is in its beginnings. 'One cannot wash one's feet twice in the same water,' wrote Queneau, paraphrasing the amazed Heraclitus confronted with the phenomenon of a flowing river that prevented him from washing himself twice in the same water. Sophism (before the fact), no doubt, but even if one accepted it as philosophical truth, one could still quench one's thirst from the same water without putting one's feet in the same river: one has merely to walk along the riverbank, on solid ground." *Oulipo, A Primer of Potential Literature*, ed., Warren F. Motte Jr., University of Nebraska Press, Lincoln, 1986, p. ix.

[89] Op. cit., Duncan.

[90] Sallis, *Black Hornet*, Avon, New York, 1996, p. 109.

[91] Ibid., pp. 278–279.

[92] See Sallis, *Difficult Lives*, Gryphon Press, Brooklyn, 1993.

[93] Op. cit., Duncan.

[94] "Roaches Ate My Face", *Your Flesh*, Seattle, 1996, p. 58.

[95] Pelecanos, *Nick's Trip*, St Martin's Press, New York, 1993, p. 141.

[96] Ibid., p. 265.

[97] Ibid., p. 257.

[98] Pelecanos, *Down by the River Where the Dead Men Go*, Serpent's Tail, London, 1995, p. 1.

[99] Ibid., p. 9.

[100] Pelecanos, *Nick's Trip*, St Martin's Press, New York, 1993, p. 13.

[101] Ibid., p. 234.

[102] According to an interview, Pelecanos's obsession with violence and particularly facial wounds originated in an incident that occurred when Pelecanos, as a seventeen-year-old, shot off half the face of his sixteen-year-old friend. Op. cit., "Roaches Ate My Face", p. 58.

[103] Op. cit., Pelecanos, *Nick's Trip*, pp. 235–236.

[104] Pelecanos, *Shoedog*, St Martin's Press, New York, 1994, p. 80.

[105] Karras's son is the protagonist in Pelecanos's *Mr Suckerman*, Little Brown, New York, 1997. Set during the bicentennial celebrations in

Washington DC, the young Karras gives the even younger Nick Stefanos some advice before the latter leaves on the trip which forms part of the narrative in *Nick's Trip*.

[106] Pelecanos, *The Big Blowdown*, St Martin's Press, New York, 1996, p. 238.

[107] Op. cit., Anderson, *Zone of Engagement*, p. 281.

[108] Ibid., pp. 279–280.

[109] Ibid., p. 283.

5. Extremists in Pursuit of Vice

[1] Constantine, *Cranks and Shadows*, Mysterious Press, New York, 1995, p. 1.

[2] Ibid., p. 11.

[3] Op. cit., Davis, *Prisoners of the American Dream*, p. 136.

[4] Cited by Vietor, *Contrived Competition: Regulation and Deregulation in America*, Belknap, Cambridge, USA, 1994, p. 1.

[5] It is left to the late Marxist crime writer Gordon DeMarco to give Carter his do. In his wicked and witty *Elvis in Aspic* (West Coast Crime, Portland, 1994), he explains why the CIA would want to assassinate Carter. The reasons are almost convincing. DeMarco points out that Carter infuriated the CIA by trying to replace Bush as head of the Company with liberal Ted Sorenson. Though Carter failed, alarm bells sounded, and the old guard, including Angleton, Shackley and Clines, resigned. The latter two agents resurface in the Iran-Contra scandal. Other reasons include Carter's refusal to back the CIA war in Angola; his appointment of former Martin Luther King associate Andrew Young as UN representative; negotiating a deal with the Marxist Torrijo to hand back the Panama Canal; reprimanding the chief of US military forces in Korea, James Singlaub – who also crops up in the Iran-Contra scandal – for criticising the President's decision to remove ground troops from Korea; angering Miami Cubans by exchanging diplomats and negotiating fishing rights with Castro. DeMarco's plot turns fanciful when the protagonist insists that Elvis was killed by the CIA because he knew – through James Earl Ray – about their plot to kill Carter.

[6] Op. cit., Constantine, p. 82.

[7] Ibid., p. 86.

[8] Deregulation allowed Savings and Loan companies to raise the rates on their deposits, resulting in severe operating losses and the failure of numerous companies. Further deregulation allowed S&Ls to purchase junk bonds and indulge in construction loans and brokered deposits. In effect, government insured policies were funding a variety of risky investments. Since the government had neither the manpower nor the money to enforce the closure of S&Ls, shadier players entered the market, while the Reagan administration, not wanting to divert money from pet projects like the CIA, the Stealth bomber, the Salvadorean army,

and Star Wars, turned a blind eye.

[9] "Deregulation poses a major threat to overall economic stability. Financial markets, under the impetus of the profit-motive and competition, and in environments of prosperity and euphoria, have always tended to take on more and more risk, until the bubble bursts." Herman, *Triumph of the Market*, South End Press, Boston, 1995, p. 16.

[10] Amongst those agencies affected were the Environmental Protection Agency, Occupational Safety and Health, Food and Drug Administration, Securities and Exchange Commission, and the Federal Home Loan Bank Board.

[11] Op. cit., Constantine, p. 297. "In the late 1960s or early 1970s . . . employment in private security firms . . . began to exceed that in public law enforcement agencies. From the mid-1970s, when municipal budgets began to tighten, public agencies have grown to a much smaller extent than private firms . . . From the viewpoint of political economy, the withdrawal from public to private security employees is part of a general shift to privatization." Zukin, *The Cultures of Cities*, Blackwell, Oxford, 1995, p. 40.

[12] Ibid., p. 221.

[13] "The mid-1980s were years of unprecedented growth, experimentation, and innovation among multiple murderers, years in which all previous 'records' were broken and sacrosanct social barriers were pierced." Leyton, *Hunting Humans*, Penguin, London, 1989, pp. 12–13.

[14] This would be mirrored in the political world, where deregulated policies in one area would lead to regulation in other areas, such as the Reagan–Bush era's deregulation of the airlines and social services. While the former would lead to the regulation of the price of air travel and a person's ability to travel, the latter would lead to the regulation of policies regarding the family and reproductive rights.

[15] The dangers of such criticism can be seen in George C. Chesbro's story "Imagine This", in which the same crime story has been found on twenty murder victims. The author is interviewed by the FBI. Though he believes he is being questioned because of his anti-Reagan–Bush views, it's simply a case of the FBI investigating the circumstances of death, while trying to comprehend why anyone would write a story in which the narrator expresses a desire to kill someone. Says the narrator, "I think fiction has largely exhausted itself in the past twenty years. How can you out-fantasise the headlines in the daily newspapers? *Ideas* can still be explosive, but the most explosive ideas can't – maybe shouldn't – be written about . . . This country has been destroyed by a succession of leaders who've corrupted language and substituted symbols for thought, as witness George Bush clowning around a flag factory." Chesbro, "Imagine This", *The Crime Lover's Casebook*, ed., Charyn, Signet, New York, 1996, pp. 43–44.

[16] Haut, "Demonic Cops", *Rolling Stock*, No. 19/20, Boulder, ed., Dorn, 1991, pp. 26–27.

[17] See Wollen, "Compulsion", *Sight & Sound*, April, 1997, p. 14.
[18] Ibid.
[19] From 1951 to 1970, Leonard authored a number of westerns, including *Hombre* and *Valdez is Coming* (Estelman, Lonsdale and Woodrell have also written westerns). If Leonard's westerns can be thought of as crime novels on horseback, then his early crime novels can be thought of as urban westerns without horses. In homage to his former genre, and to note the similarities between the genres, Leonard subtitled *City Primeval, High Noon in Detroit*.
[20] Leonard, *Glitz*, Penguin, London, p. 45.
[21] Shelley, "The Detroit Spinner", *Guardian Weekend*, London, March 9, 1996, p. 31.
[22] Ibid.
[23] Leonard, *City Primeval*, Star Books, London, 1983, p. 3.
[24] Ibid.
[25] Ibid., pp. 26–27.
[26] The best analysis of Leonard's work, and the origin of some of the ideas in this section, can be found in Barry Taylor's " Criminal Suits: Style and Surveillance, Strategy and Tactics in Elmore Leonard", *Criminal Proceedings*, Pluto Press, London, 1997, pp. 22–41.
[27] Leonard, *City Primeval*, Star, London, 1982, p. 272.
[28] Leonard, *Maximum Bob*, Penguin, 1992, p. 171.
[29] Leonard, *Split Images*, Star, London, 1984, p. 61.
[30] Leonard, *Gold Coast*, Star, London, 1983, p. 59.
[31] Leonard, *Freaky Deaky*, Warner, 1988, p. 13.
[32] Leonard, *Get Shorty*, Penguin, 1991, p. 33.
[33] Ibid., p. 132.
[34] Ibid., p. 160.
[35] Ibid., p. 332.
[36] Ibid., p. 33.
[37] Op. cit., Shelley, p. 34.
[38] Op. cit., Leonard, *Get Shorty*, pp. 358–359.
[39] According to Leonard, "He made it look so easy." Op. cit., Shelley.
[40] Op. cit., Haut, "Demonic Cops".
[41] Ellroy, *White Jazz*, Arrow, London, 1993. p. 274.
[42] Ellroy, *The Black Dahlia*, Arrow, London, 1987, p. 87.
[43] Ellroy, "My Mother's Killer", *Bouchercon Souvenir Programme*, Ringmaster, Manchester, 1995, p. 12. Originally written for *GQ*. Also published in *Granta* (UK). The subject would later be investigated at greater length in Ellroy's *My Dark Places*, an autobiographical account of his mother's death, the years leading up to the beginning of his writing career, and the reinvestigation of his mother's murder.
[44] Ibid., p. 13.
[45] Ellroy, *The Black Dahlia*, Arrow, London, 1987, p. 3.
[46] Ellroy, *The Big Nowhere*, Mysterious Press, New York, 1988, p. 39.
[47] Ellroy, *LA Confidential*, Arrow, London, 1990, p. 21.

[48] Op. Cit., Ellroy, *White Jazz*, p. 1.

[49] Ellroy describes his early right-wing views and activities, including wearing a Nazi arm band at the predominantly Jewish Fairfax High School: "My exhibitionist flair was purely self-destructive. I couldn't tone down my act. I was programmed to grandstand and alienate. My efforts to adapt triggered an internal backlash." Ellroy, *My Dark Places*, Arrow, London, 1996, p. 112.

[50] Op. cit., Haut, "Demonic Cops".

[51] Davis, *City of Quartz*, Verso, London, 1990, p. 45.

[52] Coburn, *Voices in the Dark*, Onyx, New York, 1995, p. 109.

[53] Coburn, *Love Nest*, Secker, London, 1987, p. 22.

[54] Ibid., p. 26.

[55] Coburn, *Sweetheart*, Secker & Warburg, London, 1985, p. 65.

[56] Coburn, *Off Duty*, Sphere, London, 1982, p. 11.

[57] Coburn, *Widow's Walk*, Sphere, London, 1987, pp. 222–223.

[58] Ibid.

[59] Vachss, *Batman: The Ultimate Evil*, Warner, New York, 1996.

[60] Vachss, *Flood*, Pan, London, 1986, p. 7.

[61] Ibid., p. 7.

[62] Ibid., p. 13.

[63] Ibid., p. 9.

[64] Ibid., p. 14.

[65] Ibid., p. 18.

[66] Ibid., p. 217.

[67] Ibid., p. 217.

[68] Ibid., p. 107.

[69] Ibid., p. 120.

[70] Ibid., p. 197.

[71] Ibid., p. 123.

[72] Vachss, *Hard Candy*, Signet, New York, 1990, p. 11.

[73] Op. cit., Williams, p. 229.

[74] "The fact that something like 'daily life' can exist in the ruins turns American values upside down. If you can still have something like a life with so little, then who needs so much? If art and language and music flourish as they do here [the South Bronx], so that the whole country is imitating them, what does that mean?" Ventura, "A Dance Among the Ruins", *Letters at 3 AM*, Spring Publications, Dallas, 1995, p. 56.

[75] Published by Black Lizard in the 1980s, Nisbet, like Mark Behm, remains more available in France than in the US or Britain. Meanwhile, when Black Lizard, once the best small publisher of crime fiction, was bought in the late 1980s, its catalogue (including the work of Nisbet, Heath, Willeford, Goodis) was reputedly destroyed.

[76] Nisbet, *The Damned Don't Die*, Black Lizard, Berkeley, 1986, p. 1.

[77] Ibid., p. 4.

[78] Nisbet, *Lethal Injection*, Black Lizard, Berkeley, 1987, p. 13.

[79] Ibid., p. 68.

80 Ibid., p. 75.
81 Ibid., p. 90.
82 Ibid., pp. 120–121.
83 Nisbet, *Death Puppet*, Black Lizard, Berkeley, 1989, p. 97.
84 Ibid., p. 97.
85 Novelist Steve Erickson, driving through America with the novels of Charles Willeford, reports hearing a similar story – this one set in a Las Vegas hotel: "[One] of those stories that confounded assessments of credibility: too horrifying to be true, or too horrifying not to be true. A story that lurched beyond the bounds of apocrypha." Erickson, *American Nomad*, Henry Holt, New York, 1997, p. 177.
86 Nisbet, *Prelude to a Scream*, Carroll & Graf, New York, 1997, p. 307.
87 Ibid., p. 203.
88 Ibid., p. 143.
89 Ibid., p. 250.
90 Woodrell, *The Ones You Do*, No Exit, Harpenden, 1992, pp. 16–17.
91 Woodrell, *Woe to Live On*, No Exit, Harpenden, 1990, p. 39.
92 Ibid., p. 54.
93 "The guerrilla fighting in Missouri produced a form of terrorism that exceeded anything else in the war. Jayhawking Kansans and bush-whacking Missourians took no prisoners, killed in cold blood, plundered and pillaged and burned . . . William Clarke Quantrill . . . initiated the slaughter of unarmed soldiers as well as civilians, whites as well as blacks, long before Confederate troops began murdering captured black soldiers elsewhere. Guerrilla bands in Missouri provided a training ground for outlaw gangs that emerged after the war . . . The war of raid and ambush in Missouri seemed often to have little relation to the larger conflict of which it was a part." McPherson, *Battle Cry of Freedom*, Penguin, London, 1990, p. 784.
94 Woodrell, *Under the Bright Lights*, No Exit Press, Harpenden, 1997, p. 1.
95 Hendricks, *Miami Purity*, Pantheon, New York, 1995, p. 113.
96 Woodrell, *Give Us a Kiss*, No Exit, Harpenden, 1996, p. 134.
97 Op. cit., Hendricks, p. 3.
98 Ibid., p. 5.
99 Ibid., p. 193.
100 Kellerman, "Bonding", *Hard-boiled Fiction*, eds, Adrian and Pronzini, Oxford, p. 477.
101 Hendricks's second novel *Iguana Love* (Serpent's Tail, London, 1999) is thematically similar to *Miami Purity*, and every bit as humorous, blunt and subversive. Set in the predominantly male subculture of Miami body builders and divers, the novel is narrated by Ramona, a woman who would like to gain control of her life. But, like Sherri Parlay, she is driven by her desires, only to become involved in the seedy affairs of those who control the dream she pursues. Interestingly, Hendricks's original US publisher thought the novel unfit for publication. Given that she is one of the more interesting and original of contemporary noir writers, one

wonders if their rejection was based on Hendricks's attitude and narrative voice, as much as her depiction of Ramona's sexuality – including an intimate relationship with a dead iguana – the revenge she exacts, or the portrayal of steroid abuse.

[102] From 1973 to 1993, the number of those held by the police went up 258%. Misdemeanours reported to the police increased by 42%, while violent attack, theft, armed robbery, and rape went up by 82%. Therefore the number of those held by police increased faster than the actual rate of crime, whose level is, nevertheless, the highest in the industrial world. While 47% of murders are committed by members of the same family or persons known to the victim, in 70% of murders a firearm has been used. 92.7% of African-American murder victims have been killed by fellow African-Americans, while 84.7% of Caucasian murder victims have been killed by fellow Caucasians. *The State of the USA Atlas*, ed., Doug Henwood, Penguin.

[103] Op. cit., Constantine, p. 76.

6. From Mean Streets to Dream Streets

[1] An early version of this chapter was delivered at the University of North London, November, 1996.

[2] Chandler, "Introduction", *The Smell of Fear*, Hamish Hamilton, London, 1973, p. 9.

[3] Walter Benjamin was the first to use the term in the context of the modern city. According to Benjamin, the flâneur observes and classifies the city. Like Raymond Chandler, the flâneur reads people's characters not only from the physiognomy of their faces but from objects and the social physiognomy of the streets.

[4] Chandler, *Farewell, My Lovely*, Penguin, London, 1994, p. 250.

[5] Hammett, *Red Harvest, The Novels of Dashiell Hammett*, Knopf, New York, 1965, p. 132.

[6] Op. cit., Zukin, *The Culture of Cities*, pp. 39–40.

[7] Leonard, *La Brava*, Penguin, London, 1985, p. 132.

[8] "The private detective who stakes out street corners is about to be brushed aside by a new brand of private eye that will orbit the Earth and accept all major credit cards." From Spring, 1997, those wanting to monitor another person or business can contact Earth Watch who are about to launch a private satellite using the CIA and Pentagon's most advanced technology. The commercial use of spy technology was sanctioned by President Clinton in 1994. It is largely a spin-off from defence cuts, including Star Wars and NASA. Another company, Space Imaging, a subsidiary of Lockheed, is also launching a satellite at the end of 1997. It is run by Jeffrey Harris, former director of the National Reconnaissance Office, the secretive body that oversees the government's spy satellites. Vulliamy, "US firm set to launch PI in the sky", *Guardian*, UK, February 12, 1997.

[9] Illustrative of the genre's popularity and influence is the fact that while TV cop programmes – from *Dragnet* to *Hill Street Blues* – once influenced noir fiction, these days noir fiction influences such cop programmes as *NYPD Blue* and *Homicide: Life on the Streets*.

[10] Op. cit., Pelecanos, *Shoedog*, pp. 49–50.

[11] Op. cit., Block, *The Devil Knows You're Dead*, p. 43.

[12] Op. cit., Mosley, *Black Betty*, p. 216.

[13] Estelman, *Sweet Women Lie*, Fawcett, New York, 1992, pp. 134, 97–98.

[14] Op. cit., Constantine, *Always a Body to Trade*, p. 79.

[15] Op. cit., Himes, *Blind Man With a Pistol*, p. 187.

[16] Tosches, *Trinities*, Bantam, London, 1996, p. 21.

[17] In 1975 there were only five new high-rises above the old height restriction of thirteen storeys, while, in the early 1990s, there were nearly fifty. Downtown banks and oil companies, with their cashflow problems, began to sell equity. By 1979 a quarter of Downtown's major properties were foreign-owned. Six years later 75% to 90% would be foreign-owned. Op. cit., Davis, *City of Quartz*, p. 135.

[18] Bunker, *Dog Eat Dog*, No Exit, Harpenden, 1996, p. 95.

[19] The railroad and massive doses of capital changed the traditional notion enunciated in the 'Law of the Indies': "The square ceased to be the center; it no longer was a reference point in generating new urban space. Town squares became random dots amidst the block after block of building plots, as in a plan for Santa Monica as part of the 'new' Los Angeles in 1875, and then entirely disappeared, as when the 'new' Los Angeles on paper became a fact a generation later." Sennett, *The Conscience of the Eye*, Faber, London, 1993, pp. 49–50.

[20] Though too complicated a subject to be discussed fully in this context, the relocation illustrated how, through the careful manipulation of local politicians and the public, an ideology can be established and the electorate can be pushed into a particular political position. See Sullivan's *Dodgers Go West*, Oxford University Press, New York, 1987.

[21] Lyons, *Other People's Money*, No Exit, Harpenden, 1996, p. 2.

[22] Ibid., p. 46.

[23] Ibid., p. 213.

[24] "My biggest influence and I'd make a case for him being the best there is, Joseph Wambaugh." Op. cit., Haut, *Demon Cops*.

[25] Wambaugh, *The New Centurions*, Sphere, London, 1987, pp. 41–42.

[26] Ibid., p. 64.

[27] Ibid., p. 79.

[28] Otis, *Upside Your Head*, Wesleyan, Hanover, 1993, pp. 2–3.

[29] Mosley, *White Butterfly*, Serpent's Tail, London, 1993, p. 63.

[30] Ibid., p. 100.

[31] Op. cit., Mosley, *A Little Yellow Dog*, p. 20.

[32] Phillips, *Violent Spring*, Berkeley (Prime Crime), New York, 1996, p. 15.

[33] Ibid., pp. 152–153.

[34] Leonard, *La Brava*, Penguin, London, 1985, p. 31. Over 55% of the

current population of Florida in 1990 lived in a different state in 1985, and the percentage of those born in a foreign country stood at 12.9%. Henwood, *State of the USA Atlas*, Penguin, London, 1994, p. 21.

[35] Didion, *Miami*, Flamingo, London, 1994, Ibid., pp. 31–32.

[36] Leonard, *La Brava*, p. 39.

[37] Miami as a city comprised of those working in the service sector was first publicly displayed in *Miami Vice*, a TV programme in which only cops were gainfully employed.

[38] Op. cit., Leonard, *La Brava*, p. 116.

[39] In 1995, the cities with the most murders per 100,000 were Gary, Indiana – 118, New Orleans – 73, Washington DC – 62, Detroit – 46, Atlanta – 45, Chicago – 29, Dallas – 26, New York – 16. *Guardian*, "Dead End Streets," August 27, 1996. However, 1996 saw the number of murders fall in a number of US cities. In Los Angeles and New York, the murder rate declined by 17%, Detroit by 15%, Chicago and Philadelphia by 4%. Miami is not mentioned. "New York, new safety", *Guardian*, January 2, 1997.

[40] Op. cit., Leonard, *La Brava*, p. 226.

[41] Ibid., p. 69.

[42] Hiassen, *Skin Tight*, Pan, London, 1991, p. 9.

[43] Ibid., p. 10.

[44] "Figures released by the New York Police Department showed that, while general crime had fallen, race crimes in the city had increased by 27 per cent. Although it is only the 119th most dangerous city in America, New York tops the league in race crimes, and most of those, said the police chief, were 'anti-Semitic' – invariably 'Black on Jew,' as people say." Ed Vulliamy, "New York Race War Hits New Heights", *Observer*, February 9, 1997.

[45] From an unpublished interview with Charyn, March, 1994.

[46] Ibid.

[47] Charyn, *Metropolis*, p. 59.

[48] Op. cit., interview, 1994.

[49] Ibid.

[50] Charyn, *The Issac Quartet*, Zomba, London, 1984, p. 400.

[51] Op cit., interview, 1994.

[52] Charyn, *Maria's Girls*, Serpent's Tail, London, 1993, p. 51. This is more wholesome than selling drugs for arms. According to *Guardian*, August 22, 1996: "CIA-run contras in Nicaragua benefited from the profits of a drug ring in the San Francisco Bay area during the 1980s, the San Jose Mercury has claimed. Attempts to prosecute the ring's kingpin were thwarted by the CIA, possibly to cover up ties between the traffickers and contra leaders . . . It also claims that the drug network sold tons of cocaine to Los Angeles gangs and is partially responsible for the city's crack problem." These reports have led to a court case in Los Angeles and investigations within Congress and the CIA. See "Dirty Hands and Fingers of Guilt", by Christopher Reed, *Guardian*, November 19, 1996.

53 Interview.
54 Op. cit., Charyn, *Maria's Girls*, p. 155.
55 Ibid., p. 250.
56 Op. cit., interview, 1994.
57 Due to a crackdown in extortion and racketeering, the Mafia, according to New Jersey police, has moved into white-collar crime, arranging medical, dental and optical care for more than one million patients in group plans throughout the country. It is also involved in the theft and reselling of phone cards, which grosses $1 billion per year. Another lucrative enterprise has been the Mob's infiltration of public offerings of stock by over-the-counter brokerage firms. Offering loans to brokers needing capital, the Mob forces them to sell the low-priced shares in companies before the stocks become available. With the brokers' help, mobsters inflate the value of the shares by trading among themselves in paper or fake transactions. The brokers are made to inflate the prices of the new shares by recommending them to unsuspecting investors. Selwyn Raab, "Mafia moves into white-collar crime", *Guardian*, February 11, 1997.
58 Tosches, *Trinities*, Bantam, London, 1996, p. 15.
59 Tosches, *Cut Numbers*, Mandarin, London, 1989, p. 181.
60 Ibid., p. 123.
61 See "Making Prisons Pay", by Christian Parenti, *The Nation*, January 29, 1996. According to the Rand Corporation, prison building will eventually break state banks. The solution put forward by state officials has been to harness the vast pool of idle prison labour in the hope that prisons will pay for themselves. Since 1990, thirty states have legalised the contracting out of prison labour to private companies. In cases where the companies pay the minimum wage for menial work, prisoners see 20% of their pay. The rest goes to state governments or prison managers. It's their lack of rights that makes prisoners a profitable labour force, undercutting an already deteriorating labour market. Presumably, the long term unemployed, to get back on the labour market only need to commit a crime. Meanwhile, according to Mike Davis's "A Prison-Industrial Complex: Hell Factories in the Field", *The Nation*, February 20, 1995, as colleges and universities were shedding 8,000 jobs between 1984 and 1994, the Department of Corrections hired 26,000 employees to guard 112,000 new inmates (a ratio of one guard for every 4.3 prisoners). To house the projected 1999 inmate population at the already intolerable 185 per cent occupancy level, the state will have to build twenty-three new prisons (as well as the twelve authorised at the time). Within ten years the penal population of California will increase 262 per cent, to 341,420, compared with 22,500 in 1980.
62 Op. cit., Pelecanos, *Nick's Trip*, p. 232.
63 O'Connell, *Box Nine*, Pan, London, 1993, p. 14.
64 Ibid., p. 42.
65 In 1992, according to a study by the US Department of Education, 49

per cent of US citizens were classified as having a low literacy level. Op. cit., *The State of the USA Atlas*, p. 57.

[66] Op. cit., Zukin, *The Culture of Cities*, p. 41.

[67] Attempts to enhance the visual appeal and value of public spaces, which began in the late 1960s and 1970s, were "a watershed in the institutionalisation of urban fear". At the time, voters could have chosen to approve government policies to eliminate poverty, manage ethnic competition, and integrate everyone into common public institutions. Instead, they chose to buy protection, fuelling the growth of the private security industry while severely affecting the evolution of street culture, a reaction that was "closely related to a perceived decline in public morality, an elimination of almost all stabilizing authority". Op. cit., Zukin, *The Culture of Cities*, p. 37.

[68] O'Connell, *Skin Palace*, Pan, London, 1997, p. 221.

[69] Op. cit., Pelecanos, *Shoedog*, p. 94.

7. Turning Out the Lights

[1] At the 1996 *Bouchercon* in Nottingham, journalist Duncan Campbell, delivering a talk, 'The Glamour of Crime: The Changing Face of Professional Crime in the UK', was asked if he thought the public's fascination with crime relates to the possibility that there exists an aesthetics of crime. Unwilling to consider the implications of the question, Campbell said, "No, I don't." Had he said anything different he might have had to entertain the possibility that there is more to his subject than mere reportage.

[2] Op. cit., Leyton, *Hunting Humans: The Rise of the Modern Multiple Murderer*, p. 26.

[3] DeQuincey, *The Confessions of an English Opium Eater and other essays*, Signet, New York, p. 278.

[4] Ibid., p. 279.

[5] Op. cit., Mandel, *Delightful Murder*, p. 47.

[6] Ibid., p. 41.

[7] "This fundamentally rebellious . . . nature of their protest is undoubtedly why so few government and police resources are allocated to the capture of these killers . . . for they pose no threat to the established order – neither in ideology nor in their acts." Op. cit., Leyton, p. 26.

[8] Ibid., pp. 103–104.

[9] Mailer, "The White Negro", *Advertisements for Myself*, Panther, London, 1970, p. 268.

[10] Ibid., p. 364. According to Leyton, the war in Vietnam was a factor in the sudden increase of multiple murderers.

[11] Op. cit., Mandel, p. 101.

[12] Poet Fiona Templeton believes that, in an unjust society, one is sometimes obligated to be a criminal: "When Reagan was elected I resolved to commit a crime a day until he was gone. There are easy

crimes and difficult crimes . . . No one should be harmed, and only those penalized who could afford it. So what would be the point? To what should attention be brought? . . . Who or what deserved the offence? Who was I to judge? . . . Was it just government I wanted to wound . . . ? Who and what is that? The thorn of the decision was in my side, a daily reminder that all is not right, but that all is not lost, but that fighting is hard . . . There are deeds more subversive than crimes." Templeton, "Talk About About", *The Gertrude Stein Awards in Innovative American Poetry*, ed., Messerli, Sun and Moon Press, Los Angeles, 1995, pp. 34–35.

[13] Straley, *The Curious Eat Themselves*, Gollancz, London, 1996, pp. 193–194.

[14] Kelly, *Payback*, Orion, London, 1997, p. 93.

[15] Masters, "Why are so many serial killers gay," *Observer*, July 20, 1997.

[16] Op. cit., Tosches, *Trinities*, p. 168.

[17] Op. cit., Bunker, *Dog Eat Dog*, p. 79.

[18] Wajnarowicz, *Close to the Knives*, Serpent's Tail, London, 1992, p. 236.

[19] Op. cit., Tosches, *Trinities*, p. 39.

[20] Ibid., pp. 39–40.

[21] Goines, *Black Gangster*, Holloway, Los Angeles, 1977, p. 208.

[22] Cruz, *Straight Outta Compton*, Fiction Collective, Boulder, 1992, p. 29.

[23] Cooper, *The Scene*, Payback, Edinburgh, 1996, p. 3.

[24] Ibid., p. 25.

[25] Himes, *The Harlem Cycle, Vol. 2*, "The Dilemma of the Black Writer in America", Payback, Edinburgh, 1996, p. xiv.

[26] There was one serial killer during the 1950s, six during the 1960s, 17 during the 1970s, and some 24 within the first four years of the 1980s. Op. cit., Leyton, pp. 356–367.

[27] Interview with Elliott Leyton, *The Third Degree*, ed., Duncan, No Exit Press, Harpenden, 1996, pp. 220–227. Past FBI forensics are now considered so flawed that the Justice Department has recently said that 50 cases may have ended in improper prosecutions due to questionable forensic procedure at the FBI laboratory. This constitutes "a challenge to the veracity of US justice. A leading source . . . said 'every major bombing case handled by the FBI needs reviewing.' That could total thousands of cases." Cases affected include bombings at the World Trade Centre and Atlanta Olympics, the Lockerbie and Long Island TWA 800 air disasters, and the assassination of Martin Luther King. "FBI in tainted evidence scandal", by Ed Vulliamy and Peter Marshall, *Observer*, February 16, 1997. From 1992 to 1996, out of 226,186 FBI referrals, only 57,871 resulted in convictions, 67,719 were ruled legally insufficient, 25,599 were rejected because of insufficient evidence, 28,680 were rejected because there was no evidence that an offence had been committed, 10,243 were thrown out because there was "minimal federal interest", 3,188 were rejected because there was "no known suspect". Burnham, "The FBI", *The Nation*, August 11, 1997.

[28] Op. cit., Douglas, *Mindhunter*, p. 173.

[29] Ibid.

[30] Harris, *Red Dragon*, Corgi, London, 1991, p. 349.

[31] The notion of the fallible professional female is subverted in Wozencraft's *Rush* when the federal drug agent ends up addicted to drugs, as much of a criminal as those she pursues.

[32] Sallis, "Troubled Souls: Tales of Murder, Mystery and Obsession", *The Washington Post*, May 2, 1993.

[33] Denton, *Blackburn*, Picador, New York, p. 101.

[34] Ellis, *American Psycho*, Picador, London, 1991, pp. 376–377.

[35] "It was [Joe Hunt's] belief that every relationship in the world was producible to paradox. Yet this underlying truth went utterly unaccounted in Judaeo-Christian doctrine. The moral and ethical code of that system propounded absolutes: do's and don'ts, shoulds and shouldn'ts. Life's lesson, though, was that reality is situational. Even morality was contingent upon circumstances: On the one hand, 'THOU SHALT NOT KILL,' while on the other hand even homicide could be justified by self-defense or national interest. The only integrity available to a human being was arrived at by the elimination of 'internal impediments', Joe asserted." Sullivan, *The Price of Experience: Money, Power, Image and Murder in Los Angeles*, Grove Press, New York, 1995, p. 65.

[36] "[There] is a growing body of people these days beginning at last to understand the increasing perils of the technosphere we have created. For, as the *New Yorker* recently put it, there's a little of the unabomber in all of us." Kirkpatrick Sale in *The Nation*, September 25, 1995, p. 311.

[37] Op. cit., Denton, p. 211.

[38] Ibid., p. 211.

[39] Ibid., p. 212.

[40] Ibid., p. 213.

[41] Ibid., p. 239.

[42] Ibid., p. 240.

[43] O'Connell, *The Skin Palace*, Mysterious Press, New York, 1995, p. 394.

[44] Jameson, *Post-Modernism, Or the Cultural Logic of Late Capitalism*, Verso, London, 1991, p. 17.

[45] Morse, *The Big Enchilada*, Blue Murder, London, 1991, p. 7.

[46] Ibid., p. 36.

[47] Lethem, *Gun, with Occasional Music*, New English Library, London, 1993, p. 39.

[48] By the 1970s, public corporations like Sheraton, Hilton, and MGM, Wall Street investment bankers, and Michael Milken's Drexel Burnham Lambert, became interested in Las Vegas. " From 1970 to 1980, Las Vegas would double the number of its visitors, to 11,041,524, and the amount of cash left behind by those visitors would increase 273.6 per cent, to $4.7 billion. The heart of all this growth was, of course, the casino business – and by 1993 visitors had dropped $15.1 billion in town." Pileggi, *Casino*, Corgi, London, 1996, p. 14.

BIBLIOGRAPHY

Primary Neon Noir Texts

Behm, Marc: *The Eye of the Beholder* (1980), *Three Novels by Marc Behm* Zomba, London, 1983.

Bergman, Andrew: *The Big Kiss-Off of 1944* (1974), Arrow, London, 1975.

Blauner, Peter: *Casino Moon* (1994), Simon & Schuster, New York, 1994; Penguin, London, 1995.

Block, Lawrence: *A Dance at the Slaughterhouse*, Avon, New York, 1992; Phoenix, London, 1997. *The Devil Knows You're Dead* (1993), Avon, New York, 1994; Orion, London, 1996. *Eight Million Ways to Die* (1982), Avon, New York, 1993; Phoenix, London, 1998. *The Sins of the Fathers* (1976), Avon, New York, 1994; Orion, London, 1997. *Such Men are Dangerous* (1969), Carroll & Graf, New York, 1993. *A Ticket to the Boneyard* (1990), Avon, New York, 1991; Orion, London, 1997.

Bunker, Edward: *Dog Eat Dog* (1996), St Martin's Press, New York, 1997; No Exit, Harpenden, 1997. *Straight Time* (*No Beast So Fierce*, 1973), Corgi, London, 1978; No Exit, Harpenden, 1997.

Burke, James Lee: *Cadillac Jukebox* (1996), Hyperion, New York, 1997; Orion, London, 1997. *Cimarron Rose*, Hyperion, 1997; Orion, London, 1997. *Heaven's Prisoners* (1988), Pocket Books, New York, 1996; Vintage, London, 1997. *Neon Rain* (1987), Pocket Books, New York, 1992; Vintage, London, 1996. *A Stained White Radiance* (1992), Avon, New York, 1993; Arrow, London, 1996.

Charyn, Jerome: *Blue Eyes*, Warner, New York, 1993. *The Crime Lover's Casebook* (ed.), Signet, New York, 1996. *The Issac Quartet: Marilyn the Wild* (1976), *Blue Eyes* (1974), *The Education of Patrick Silver* (1976), *Secret Issac* (1978), Zomba, London, 1984. *Maria's Girls* (1992), Warner, New York, 1993; Serpent's Tail, London, 1997. *Metropolis* (1986), Avon, New York, 1987; Abacus, London, 1988.

Coburn, Andrew: *Goldilocks* (1989), Secker & Warburg, London, 1990. *Love Nest*, Secker & Warburg, London, 1987. *Off Duty* (1980), Sphere, London, 1982. *Sweetheart*, Secker & Warburg, London, 1985. *Voices in the Dark* (1994), Onyx, New York, 1995. *Widow's Walk*, Sphere, London, 1984.

Constantine, K. C.: *Always a Body to Trade*, Godine, New York, 1983; Hodder

& Stoughton, London, 1983. *Cranks and Shadows* (1995), Mysterious Press, New York, 1997.

Cooper, Clarence Jr.: *The Farm* (1967), Old School Books, Norton, New York, 1998; Payback, Edinburgh, 1996. *The Scene* (1960), Old School Books, Norton, 1996; Payback, Edinburgh, 1996.

Crumley, James: *Bordersnakes*, Warner, New York, 1997; Flamingo, London, 1998. *James Crumley – The Collection: The Wrong Case* (1975), *The Last Good Kiss* (1978), *Dancing Bear* (1983), Picador, London, 1997. *The Wrong Case*, Random House, New York, 1986. *The Last Good Kiss*, Random House, New York, 1988. *Dancing Bear*, Random House, New York, 1984. *The Mexican Tree Duck*, Warner, New York, 1994; Picador, London, 1995. *One to Count Cadence* (1969), Vintage, New York, 1996; Picador, London, 1996. *Whores*, Dennis McMillan, Missoula, 1989.

Cruz, Richard Cortez: *Straight Outta Compton*, Fiction Collective, Boulder, 1992.

DeMarco, Gordon: *Elvis in Aspic*, West Coast Crime, Portland, 1995.

Denton, Bradley: *Blackburn* (1993) Picador, New York, 1995; Macdonald, London, 1995.

Dobyns, Stephen: *Saratoga Trifecta: Saratoga Longshot* (1976), *Saratoga Swimmer* (1981), *Saratoga Headhunter* (1985), Viking Penguin, New York, 1995; Penguin, London, 1995.

Ellis, Brett Easton: *American Psycho* (1991), Simon & Schuster, New York, 1991; Picador, London, 1997.

Ellroy, James: *American Tabloid* (1995), Fawcett, New York, 1997; Arrow, London, 1998. *The Big Nowhere*, Warner, New York, 1998; Arrow, London, 1998. *The Black Dahlia* (1987), Warner, New York, 1998; Arrow, London, 1997. *Blood on the Moon* (1984), Avon, New York, 1985; Arrow, London, 1997. *Brown's Requiem* (1981), Avon, New York, 1981; Century, London, 1998. *LA Confidential* (1990), Warner, New York, 1997; Arrow, London, 1997. *My Dark Places* (1996), Random House, New York, 1997; Arrow, London, 1998. *Silent Terror* (1986), Avon, New York, 1986; Arrow, London, 1997. *White Jazz* (1992), Fawcett, New York, 1993; Arrow, London, 1998.

Estelman, Loren: *Sweet Women Lie* (1990), Fawcett, New York, 1992; Macmillan, London, 1990.

Goines, Donald: *Black Gangster*, Holloway, Los Angeles, 1997.

Gores, Joe: *Hammett* (1975), Raven, London, 1977.

Hammett, Dashiell: *Red Harvest* (1929), *The Novels of Dashiell Hammett*, Random House, New York, 1989; Picador, London, 1997.

Hansen, Joseph: *Fade Out* (1970), No Exit, Harpenden, 1996.

Harris, Thomas B.: *Red Dragon* (1981), Doubleday, New York, 1998; Arrow, London, 1996. *Silence of the Lambs* (1988), St Martin's Press, New York, 1991; Mandarin, London, 1996.

Hasford, Gustav: *A Gypsy Good Time*, Washington Square, New York, 1992.

Haywood, Gar Anthony: *Fear of the Dark*, Penguin, New York, 1988. *Not Long for This World* (1990), Macmillan, London, 1991. *You Can Die Trying* (1993), Serpent's Tail, London, 1997.

Hendricks, Vicki: *Miami Purity*, Random House, New York, 1996; Minerva, London, 1997. *Iguana Love*, Serpent's Tail, London, 1999.

Hiassen, Carl: *Skintight* (1989), Fawcett, New York, 1992; Pan, London, 1997. *Tourist Season* (1986), Warner, New York, 1987; Pan, London, 1997.

Higgins, George V.: *A City on a Hill* (1975), Critic's Choice, New York, 1985. *A Choice of Enemies* (1983), Robinson, London, 1985. *The Friends of Eddie Coyle* (1970), Henry Holt, New York, 1995. *George V. Higgins – Three Complete Novels*, Robinson, London, 1995.

Highsmith, Patricia: *The Talented Mr Ripley* (1956), Random House, New York, 1992; Penguin, London, 1997.

Himes, Chester: *Blind Man With a Pistol* (1969), Vintage, New York, 1989. "The Dilemma of the Black Writer in America" (1948), *The Harlem Cycle* Vol. 2, Payback, Edinburgh, 1996. *Plan B*, University of Mississippi, Jackson, 1994.

Hunter, Stephen: *Black Light*, Doubleday, New York, 1996; Arrow, London, 1997.

Jeter, K. W.: *In the Land of the Dead*, Onyx, New York, 1989.

Kellerman, Faye: "Bonding", *Hard-Boiled: An Anthology of American Crime Stories*, ed., Adrian, Prozini, Oxford University Press, Oxford, 1995.

Kelly, Thomas: *Payback*, Orion, London, 1997.

Leonard, Elmore: *City Primeval* (1980), Avon, New York, 1982; Penguin, London, 1997. *Freaky Deaky* (1988), Morrow, New York, 1998; Penguin, London, 1997. *Get Shorty* (1990), Delacorte, New York, 1995; Penguin, London, 1998. *La Brava* (1983), Morrow, New York, 1998; Penguin, London, 1997. *Maximum Bob* (1991), Dell, New York, 1998; Penguin, London, 1997. *Riding the Rap* (1995), Dell, New York, 1998; Penguin, London, 1997.

Lethem, Jonathan: *Gun, With Occasional Music* (1994), Tor Books, New York, 1995; New English Library, London, 1997.

Lopez, Steve: *Third and Indiana*, Penguin, New York, 1994; Penguin, London, 1995.

Lyons, Arthur: *Other People's Money* (1989), Mysterious Press, New York, 1989; No Exit, Harpenden, 1996.

MacDonald, John D.: *Dress Her in Indigo* (1969), Fawcett, New York, 1996; Pan, London, 1972.

Macdonald, Ross: *The Underground Man* (1971), Random House, New York, 1996; Allison & Busby, London, 1997.

Morse, L. A.: *The Big Enchilada* (1982), Blue Murder, London, 1991.

Mosley, Walter: *A Little Yellow Dog*, Pocket Books, New York, 1997; Serpent's Tail, London, 1997. *A Red Death* (1991), Pocket Books, New York, 1997; Serpent's Tail, London, 1997. *Black Betty* (1994), Pocket Books, New York, 1995; Serpent's Tail, London, 1997. *Devil in a Blue Dress* (1990), Pocket Books, New York, 1995; Serpent's Tail, London, 1997. *White Butterfly* (1992), Pocket Books, New York, 1993; Serpent's Tail, London, 1997.

Nisbet, Jim: *Death Puppet*, Black Lizard, Berkeley, 1989. *Lethal Injection*, Black Lizard, Berkeley, 1987. *Prelude to a Scream*, Carroll & Graf, New York, 1997. *The Damned Don't Die* (1981), Black Lizard, Berkeley, 1986.

O'Connell, Jack: *Box Nine* (1992), Warner, New York, 1993; Pan, London, 1996. *Skin Palace* (1995), Mysterious Press, New York, 1996; Pan, London, 1997.

Paretsky, Sara: *Burn Marks* (1990), Dell, New York, 1991; Virago, London, 1997. *Killing Orders* (1985), Dell, New York, 1993; Penguin, London, 1997. *Toxic Shock*, US title: *Blood Shot* (1988), Dell, New York, 1989; Penguin, London, 1997. *Tunnel Vision* (1994), Doubleday, New York, 1994; Penguin, London, 1997.

Pelecanos, George P.: *A Firing Offense* (1992), St Martin's Press, New York,

1992; Serpent's Tail, London, 1997. *Nick's Trip*, St Martin's Press, New York, 1993, Sepent's Tail, London, 1998; *Down by the River Where the Dead Men Go* (1995), St Martin's Press, New York, 1995; Serpent's Tail, London, 1997. *Shoedog*, St Martin's Press, New York, 1994. *The Big Blowdown*, St Martin's Press, 1996. *King Suckerman* (1997), Little Brown, Boston, 1997; Serpent's Tail, London, 1998.

Phillips, Gary: *Violent Spring* (1994), Berkley, New York, 1997; No Exit, Harpenden, 1997.

Pileggi, Nicholas: *Casino* (1995), Paperback, New York, 1996; Corgi, London, 1996.

Sallis, James: *Black Hornet*, Avon, New York, 1996; No Exit, Harpenden, 1997. *Eye of the Cricket*, Walker & Co., New York, 1997; No Exit, Harpenden, 1998. *The Long-Legged Fly* (1992), Avon, New York, 1994; No Exit, Harpenden, 1997. *Moth* (1993), Avon, New York, 1995; No Exit, Harpenden, 1996.

Simon, Robert L.: *The Big Fix* (1973), Pocket, New York, 1974.

Stark, Richard: *Point Blank* (aka *The Hunter*, 1962), Warren, New York, 1998; Allison & Busby, London, 1997.

Stone, Robert: *Dog Soldiers* (1973), Houghton Mifflin, Boston, 1997; Picador, London, 1988.

Straley, John: *The Curious Eat Themselves* (1993), Bantam, New York, 1995; Gollancz, London, 1996.

Thompson, Jim: *Child of Rage* (1972), Blood & Guts, Los Angeles, 1991. *Nothing But a Man*, Popular Library, New York, 1970. *King Blood* (1973), Corgi, London, 1989.

Thornberg, Newton: *A Man's Game*, Forge, New York, 1996. *Cutter and Bone* (1976), Little Brown, Boston, 1976; Blue Murder, London, 1988.

Tosches, Nick: *Cut Numbers* (1988), St Martin's Press, New York, 1996; Mandarin, London, 1989. *Trinities* (1994), Doubleday, New York, 1996; Bantam, London, 1996.

Vachss, Andrew: *Flood* (1985), Random House, New York, 1998; Pan, London, 1997. *Hard Candy* (1990), Random House, New York, 1997; Pan, London, 1996.

Valin, Jonathan: *The Lime Pit* (1980), Avon, New York, 1983; Keyhole, London, 1982.

Wambaugh, Joseph: *The New Centurions* (1970), Dell, New York, 1972; Futura, London, 1991.

Willeford, Charles: *Cockfighter* (1972), Black Lizard, Berkeley, 1987; No Exit, Harpenden, 1997. *Miami Blues* (1984), Dell, New York, 1995; No Exit, Harpenden, 1997. *New Hope for the Dead* (1985), Dell, New York, 1996; No Exit, Harpenden, 1997. *The Way We Die Now* (1988), Dell, New York, 1996; No Exit, Harpenden, 1997.

Williams, Charles: *Don't Just Stand There* (1966), Panther, London, 1969.

Woodrell, Daniel: *Give Us a Kiss*, Pocket Books, New York, 1997; No Exit, Harpenden, 1997. *Muscle for the Wing* (1988), No Exit, Harpenden, 1997. *The Ones You Do* (1992), Onyx, New York, 1993, No Exit, Harpenden, 1997. *Under the Bright Lights*, Avon, New York, 1988; No Exit, Harpenden, 1997. *Woe to Live On* (1987), TDR, New York, 1987; No Exit, Harpenden, 1997.

Woods, Paula L., ed. *Spooks, Spies & Private Eyes: An Anthology of Black Mystery, Crime, and Suspense Fiction of the 20th Century* (1995), Payback, Edinburgh, 1996.

Supplementary sources

Anderson, Perry: *Zone of Engagement*, Norton, New York, 1992; Verso, London, 1997.

Caputo, Philip: *A Rumor of War* (1977), Henry Holt, New York, 1996.

Davis, Mike: *City of Quartz*, Random House, New York, 1992; Vintage, London, 1997. *Prisoners of the American Dream*, Norton, New York, 1986; Verso, London, 1986.

Docherty, Brian: *American Crime Fiction*, Macmillan, London, 1997.

Douglas, J., Olshaker, M.: *Mindhunter: Inside the FBI Elite Serial Crime Unit* (1995), Scribner, New York, 1995; Heinemann, London, 1996.

Duncan, Paul: *The Third Degree: Crime Writers in Conversation*, No Exit, Harpenden, 1997.

Hasford, Gustav: *The Short-Timers* (1979), Bantam, New York, 1987.

Haut, Woody: *Pulp Culture: Hardboiled Fiction and the Cold War*, Serpent's Tail, London, 1995.

Henwood, Doug: *The State of the USA Atlas*, Simon & Schuster, New York, 1994; Penguin, London, 1997.

Herman, Edward S.: *Triumph of the Market*, South End Press, Boston, 1995.

Herr, Michael: *Dispatches* (1977), Random House, New York, 1991; Picador, London, 1997.

Jameson, Frederic: *Post-Modernism, Or the Cultural Logic of Late Capitalism*, Verso, London, 1997.

Leyton, Elliott: *Hunting Humans: The Rise of the Modern Multiple Murderer* (1986), Pocket Books, New York, 1990; Penguin, London, 1989.

McCauley, Michael J.: *Jim Thompson: Sleep With the Devil*, Mysterious Press, New York, 1991.

Mandel, Ernest: *Delightful Murder*, Pluto, London, 1984.

Messent, Peter, ed.: *Criminal Proceedings: The Contemporary American Crime Novel*, Pluto, London, 1997.

Naylor, R. T.: *Hot Money and the Politics of Debt*, Unwin Hyman, London, 1987.

O'Brien, Tim: *Going After Cacciato* (1978), Dell, New York, 1992; Flamingo, London, 1997. *If I Die in a Combat Zone* (1973), Dell, New York, 1992; Grafton, London, 1997.

Polito, Robert: *Savage Art: a Biography of Jim Thompson*, Random House, New York, 1996; Serpent's Tail, London, 1997.

Reisner, Robert: *Cadillac Desert: The American West and Its Disappearing Water*, Penguin, New York, 1993.

Sallis, James: *Difficult Lives: Jim Thompson, David Goodis, Chester Himes*, Gryphon, Brooklyn, 1993.

Spanos, William V.: *The Errant Art of Moby Dick: The Cannon, the Cold War, and the Struggle for American Studies*, Duke, Durham, 1995.

Sullivan, Randall: *The Price of Experience: Money, Power, Image and Murder in Los Angeles*, Grove, New York, 1996.

Wajnarowicz, David: *Close to the Knives*, Serpent's Tail, London, 1992.

Warpole, Ken: *Reading by Numbers*, Comedia, London, 1984.

Willett, Ralph: *The Naked City: Urban Crime Fiction in the USA*, Manchester University, Manchester, 1996.

Williams, John: *Into the Badlands: A Journey Through the American Dream*, Paladin, London, 1991.

Zinn, Howard: *A People's History of the United States*, Harper & Row, New York, 1998; Longman, Harlow, 1997.

Zukin, Sharon: *The Cultures of Cities*, Blackwell, Oxford, 1995.

SCREENING NEON

A personal selection of modern film noir adapted from, or influenced by, neon noir fiction:

Point Blank (1967): Adapted from the novel by Richard Stark. Directed by John Boorman; screenplay by Alexander Jacobs, David Newhouse, Rafe Newhouse; starring Lee Marvin and Angie Dickinson. Arguably the first modern film noir, *Point Blank* reflects the explosiveness of the 1960s and the era's interest in the politics of crime. Though the scriptwriters have restylised the narrative, Boorman retains the flavour and politics of the novel. Lee Marvin plays the violent and paranoid Walker, the anti-hero who threatens the world of corporate crime. His visage is a picture of alienation and the focal point around which the narrative – told from the viewpoint of a walking dead man – unfolds. Playing with time and space, Boorman's film wears its influences proudly: Kubrick, Alain Resnais, a touch of Fritz Lang and a large helping of *nouvelle vague*. Viewed thirty years later, the film remains hard-edged and subversive.

Friends of Eddie Coyle (1970): Adapted from the novel by George V. Higgins. Directed by Peter Yates; screenplay by Paul Monash; starring Robert Mitchum and Peter Boyle. An often overlooked example of early nouveau noir. With the benefit of an excellent script, Yates gives *Friends* . . . the feel of a 1940s film noir. There is very little of Boorman's *nouvelle vague* cutting or excessive existential violence here. Like Higgins's novel, Yates' unusually static film concentrates on dialogue and characterisation rather than montage. Mitchum, recalling his earlier outings, such as *Out of the Past* and *Angel Face*, gives a moving performance as the aging low-life Coyle. With its overwhelming mood of corruption and crime, *Friends* . . . typifies the end of the 1960s when optimism appeared to have run its course and, with Vietnam still dominating the news, the state was momentarily called to account.

Chinatown (1974): Directed by Roman Polanski; original screenplay by Robert Towne; starring Jack Nicholson and Faye Dunaway. Perhaps the finest example of modern film noir. Towne's screenplay is of such a standard as to qualify him as a fully-fledged noir writer. "Talking about the past bothers everyone because you can't always tell what's going on," says Gittes, a private eye with middle-class pretensions, played to perfection by Jack Nicholson. In *Chinatown* the past is the present in embryonic form. Recalling the opening chapters of Robert Reisner's *Cadillac Desert*, Townes's script portrays California's narrative as the story of the politics of water. Though one does not see Chinatown until the end of the film, it is ever-present as a state of mind, a place within a place called Los Angeles. As in work of James Ellroy, progress becomes an excuse for corruption. Cinematographer John Alonzo, while filming interiors with claustrophobic panache, portrays LA as a supremely parched culture. A film that revives the genre, revises Raymond Chandler, and promotes Los Angeles as a post-modern dystopia.

Cockfighter (1974): Adapted from the novel by Charles Willeford. Directed by Monte Hellman; screenplay by Willeford; starring Warren Oates. A quintessential film noir. Willeford's script is a near-perfect recreation of the novel. Warren Oates at his best as the mute protagonist who refuses to speak until he wins the cockfighting championship. Oates becomes a blank slate on which the culture and its crimes are written. With Willeford's assistance, Hellman takes the viewer on a tour of small Southern towns. This is a bleak saga of macho America. Though the Vietnam war goes unmentioned, its presence and effect are ever-present. Here cockfighting becomes a substitute for sex, war and everything else under the hot Southern sun. As of this writing, the only Willeford novel to be adequately rendered onto film. Also, if you can find it, Willeford's book on the making of the film is well worth reading.

The American Friend (1977): Adapted from the novel *Ripley's Game* by Patricia Highsmith. Directed by Wim Wenders; screenplay by Wenders and Fritz Muller-Scherz; starring Dennis Hopper and Bruno Ganz. A mixture of influences, Wenders' film, with its many moments of brilliance, is a homage to Hitchcock (*Strangers on a Train*) and a tribute to film noir (Nick Ray and Sam Fuller both appear in the film). But this poses a problem for Wenders, who seems undecided whether this should be a film noir or a psychological thriller. Consequently, its diversity, intelligence and dispersed narrative prevent the film from fulfilling its potential. However, this and Wenders' next project, *Hammett*, contributed to the renewal of interest in noir film and fiction. Though lacking the depth of Highsmith's anti-hero, much less past noir protagonists, Hopper's Ripley retraces the narrative path of other Wenders principal characters, and reminds the viewer that this neo-thriller, which, thanks to cinematographer Robby Muller, never fails to look good, is, in the end, a glossy version of Wenders' early work.

Straight Time (1977): Adapted from the novel *No Beast So Fierce* by Edward Bunker. Directed by Ulu Grosbard; screenplay by Bunker, Alvin Sargent, Jeffrey Boam; starring Dustin Hoffman, Teresa Russell, Harry Dean Stanton. A moving portrayal – nicely underplayed by Hoffman – of recently released and likeable criminal spiv who finds himself in a culture that pushes him back into a life of crime. Filmed and edited in a workmanlike fashion, Grosbard, thanks to Bunker's input and expertise, impartially addresses the problems facing ex-cons, and the bankrupt values of middle-class American life. Reminding one of social problem films from the 1930s and 1940s, *Straight Time* gives no quarter to romantic notions about the criminal class, nor to the notion that crime might pay. Here the ex-con cannot do anything other than wage a war of attrition against those who have placed him behind bars. *Straight Time* is undervalued, important and memorable.

Dog Soldiers (1978): Aka *Who'll Stop the Rain*. Adapted from the novel *Dog Soldiers* by Robert Stone. Directed by Karl Reisz; screenplay by Judith Roscoe; starring Nick Nolte, Tuesday Weld, Michael Murphy. "In a world where elephants are pursued by flying men, everyone's gonna want to get high." Accordingly, Reisz's *McGuffin* is a bag of heroin. Murphy is the plodding war correspondent, Nolte the existential outsider who mules Murphy's drugs, while Weld plays Murphy's drug-addicted wife who runs off with Nolte and the dope. Without being cinematically excessive, Reisz captures the mood of the book and the era, as the war – in the form of drugs – is brought home, affecting everyone it touches. Moving from Vietnam to California to Mexico, *Dog Soldiers* moves fast, and might be mistaken for a road movie. Yet, as the sixties are uneasily laid to rest, this is, in effect, a character study and a portrayal of an era whose anti-moral moral remains relevant.

Cutter and Bone (1981): Adapted from the novel by Newton Thornberg. Directed by Ivan Passer, screenplay by Jeffrey Alan Fiskin; starring Jeff Bridges, John Heard and Lisa Eichhorn. A hard-edged embittered film noir, *Cutter and Bone* depicts the post-war years. From the exposition – a parade that seems more like a hallucination than a celebration – highlighted by some tight editing and Jordan Cronenweth's insightful camerawork, this could be mistaken for a 1980s take on German Expressionism, and reminds one of Passer's European credentials. But Passer quickly shifts gears and cultural emphasis, moving seamlessly into pulp-noir territory. Likewise, the narrative moves from a sordid, but all-American, nightmare to a sleazy and paranoid confrontation with reality. This is not *California Dreaming*, but the last embers of a burnt-out counter culture. Moving performances by the three main accomplices. *Cutter and Bone*, in its own way, is a classic depiction of the era.

Hammett (1982): Adapted from the novel by Joe Gores. Directed by Wim Wenders; screenplay by Ross Thomas and Dennis O'Flaherty; starring Frederic Forrest, Peter Boyle, Marilu Henner. A mess that could have been a classic. Substantially different from Thomas's conventional but ground-breaking novel, *Hammett* still manages to be interesting. Contributing to a new noir aesthetic, this is not so much a film biography, as, moving from fact to fiction, an attempt to tackle the subject of writing and the relationship between myth and reality. However, as film noir it is curiously lightweight. Originally filmed on the streets of San Francisco, Wenders chose to reshoot in an LA studio. Rejecting realism, and opting for artifice and artificiality, *Hammett*, despite some sharp angles, noir lighting, and eye-catching textures, illustrates what can happen when an independent director is co-opted by the likes of Coppola, or perhaps it's just that one writer too many can spoil a promising project.

Prizzi's Honor (1985): Adapted from the novel by Richard Condon. Directed by John Huston; screenplay by Richard Condon and Janet Roach; starring Jack Nicholson, Kathleen Turner, Angelica Huston. About love, death, air travel and organised crime, Huston's cinematic swan song is a homage to his various past noir excursions. With close-ups reminiscent of *The Asphalt Jungle*, this film, beyond its obvious signs of modernity, feels as though it could have been made at any time over the last fifty years. Condon's work (*Manchurian Candidate*) has always contained a noirish element – here its sharp script, brilliant observations, grand gesture and humour, remind one of Jerome Charyn. Huston, always a master at handling plot, mood and tone, provides a sophisticated take on the genre. Not quite for purists, but a wonderfully acted, over-the-top black comedy that moves beyond parody to create a style of its own.

Manhunter (1986): Adapted from the novel *The Red Dragon* by Thomas B. Harris. Directed by Michael Mann; screenplay by Mann; starring William Peterson and Brian Cox. Mann's noirist tendencies, which rely on visual impact and minimalist dialogue, can be traced from early *Miami Vice* episodes to his made-for-TV version of *Heat*. In *Manhunter*, a pared-down script, flashy camerawork and emotionally-draining editing, create a menacing atmosphere, one which gives everyone their due. It's hard to say who is more frightening: Peterson, who, with cold precision, plays obsessed FBI agent Graham; or Cox, who, as Lecter, is more menacing than Hopkins's stylised interpretation of the killer in Demme's less interesting *Silence of the Lambs*. With the hunter and hunted interchangeable, society is here divided between victims and psychotics; while the state, with its sophisticated technology, and an agent who puts his life and sanity on the line, will always get its man. Though the ending – different from the novel – is overly artificial, Mann avoids Harris's political reductionism, while capturing the novel's voyeurism, paranoia, and fin-de-siècle sense of doom.

Cop (1987): Adapted from the novel *Blood on the Moon* by James Ellroy. Directed by James B. Harris; screenplay by Harris; starring James Woods. Former Kubrick associate Harris strips Ellroy's novel down to its essentials, but, in doing so, ignores much of what is interesting in the novel. Without Ellroy's manic prose, Harris's narrative becomes facile, if not prurient. Nevertheless, the director does manage to capture the bleakness of Ellroy's world, while offering an interesting take on male paranoia regarding middle-class feminism. Woods is excellent as Lloyd Hopkins, the psychopathic cop who traipses through LA's mean streets like a demented speed-freak. Worth seeing if only for the scene in which Woods tucks his daughter into bed with grisly cop stories about the scumbags he's encountered – she is clearly headed for an adult life filled with psychoanalysis and truckloads of Valium.

Ironically, *Cop* conveys a seediness that the more accomplished *LA Confidential* lacks. Yet the problem remains: how to capture Ellroy's fractious narrative style and ambiguous politics without succumbing to cinematic excessiveness.

Cat Chaser (1988): Adapted from the novel by Elmore Leonard. Directed by Abel Ferrara; screenplay by Leonard and James Borelli; starring Peter Weller, Kelly McGillis, Frederic Forrest. Kings of sleaze, Ferrara and Leonard make an intriguing team. After all, *Cat Chaser* represents Leonard in his transitional period, when he was still writing hardcore noir fiction rather than crime comedies. For Ferrara, it represents a period when he still believed he could become a mainstream Hollywood director. Yet the project doesn't live up to expectations. The script, though interesting, gets lost in its narrative glare and detail, while the voice-overs quickly become intrusive. On the other hand, the film's transition from black and white to sun-soaked colour is both effective and evocative. Ferrara's non-judgemental perspective, and portrayal of hustlers, sleazy motels, and casual violence, have led some to describe *Cat Chaser* as a cross between *Blood Simple* and *The Killers*. While it's less gripping than either of those films, it still might be as down-beat a screen version of Leonard as one is going to get.

Miami Blues (1990): Adapted from the novel by Charles Willeford. Directed by George Armitage; screenplay by George Armitage; starring Fred Ward, Alec Baldwin, Jennifer Jason Leigh. This and Hellman's *Cockfighter* are presently the only film adaptations of Willeford's extremely cinematic but complex fiction. Armitage appreciates Willeford's humour and Miami's economic and cultural discrepancies, but, despite his workmanlike script, the film lacks conviction. This might be because Armitage isn't sure whether he wants *Miami Blues* to be a film noir or a comedy. Of course, Willeford evades categorisation and his take on the world might well be too subtle to make him accessible to mainstream studios and directors. But thanks to some hilarious scenes – including that in which a Hare Krishna airport collector dies of a broken finger – and a superb cast – particularly Ward who makes a convincing Hoke Mosely – this remains one of the better Miami-set crime films. Armitage revels in his portrayal of *lumpen* life, but Willeford deserves a sharper interpretation, and a more capable interpreter.

The Grifters (1990): Adapted from the novel by Jim Thompson. Directed by Stephen Frears; screenplay by Donald Westlake; starring John Cusack, Angelica Huston, Annette Benning. Because Thompson's career just barely edges into the neon noir era, *The Grifters* is listed here mainly for Westlake's – aka Richard Stark – excellent screenplay, one which captures the nuances of Thompson's novel. But perhaps his script is too subtle. At least for Frears, whose film, however worthy, is rather antiseptic and unable to convey the twisted extremism that underpins Thompson's work, or the way the latter colours his characters in various shades of black and white. Even the lighting and camerawork – particularly the interiors – create an ambience at odds with Thompson's oeuvre and emotional textures. Yet Frears is not one to shy away from the Oedipal aspect of Thompson's narrative. Though a competent production, one which introduced many viewers to Thompson's work, this is another example of a noir writer in need of a more hard-edged and obsessive director.

Dark Wind (1991): Adapted from the novel by Tony Hillerman. Directed by Errol Morris, screenplay by Neil Jiminez, Eric Bergren, Mark Horowitz; starring Lou Diamond Phillips, Gary Farmer, Fred Ward. Robert Redford's production company planned this as the first in a series based on Hillerman's reservation crime novels. However, this is the only one to have made it onto the screen. Here Hillerman's Navaho cop, Jim Chee, investigates a drugs related murder, and finds himself at odds with local FBI agents. Interesting in terms of setting, culture, and characterisation, *Dark Wind* remains a worthy but uninspired effort. One might have expected more from Morris, who directed the docu-thriller *The Thin Blue Line*. Nevertheless, worth seeing for the landscape, Stefan Czapsky's sympathetic cinematography, and performances by Phillips, Farmer and Ward. It makes one wonder if modern film noir might not have some way to go before catching up with neon noir fiction, or if some noir fiction loses its power and political impact when translated to the screen.

Casino (1995): Adapted from the novel by Nicholas Pileggi. Directed by Martin Scorsese; screenplay by Pileggi and Scorsese; starring Robert DeNiro, Sharon Stone, Joe Pesci, James Woods. About the changing face of Las Vegas and the nature of organised crime, *Casino* is an example of a film that enhances the book. While Pileggi's docu-novel is merely interesting, Scorsese, with help from the author, transforms it into a flawed masterpiece, and a successful follow-up to his near-flawless *GoodFellas*. What makes this sophisticated, if occasionally long-winded, script effective is its adherence to both cause and effect. Meanwhile, its portrayal of crime as having become indistinguishable from legitimate business concerns makes it particularly relevant to *Neon Noir*. With its excessive use of voice-overs, *Casino* resembles a glossy version of 1940s and 50s drama-documentaries like *Naked City*. Indulging his life-long fascination with film noir, Scorsese dazzles the viewer with narrative excursions, and cinematic technique, sometimes to brain-numbing effect.

Devil in a Blue Dress (1995): Adapted from the novel by Walter Mosley. Directed by Carl Franklin; screenplay by Franklin; starring Denzil Washington. Ultimately a better film than the hype surrounding it originally suggested. Faithful to Mosley's novel, Franklin's film investigates post-war Los Angeles and the politics of the era. Tak Fujimoto's camerawork and lighting contribute greatly to recreating a part of history that has long been mis-portrayed, if not absent from the screen. Washington makes an ideal

Easy Rawlins, while the script conveys the political ambiguity and subtlety of Mosley's fiction. Franklin, who can always be counted on to be true to his subject, makes no attempt to preach to the converted, yet manages to retain Mosley's evocative minimalism. With racism existing alongside disparities in wealth and power, Franklin's film, like the novel, sometimes seems like a subtext searching for its plot.

Get Shorty (1995): Adapted from Elmore Leonard's novel. Directed by Barry Sonnenfeld; screenplay by Scott Frank; starring John Travolta, Gene Hackman, Danny DeVito, Rene Russo. *Get Shorty* has always been a novel in pursuit of a screenplay. While one awaits the inevitable onslaught of Leonard-inspired films, Sonnenfeld's effort will stand with the best of them. Thanks to Frank's snappy script, the director lets Leonard's novel speak for itself. Like the novel, this is a contemporary comedy of manners, and subtly political. But, because it's a deconstruction of the film industry, *Get Shorty* tends to suffer from its own stylisation: the dialogue is often too off-hand, the acting too defined, the lighting too obvious, the editing unadventurous, and the likes of Chilli Palmer are only partly examined. By opting for a self-consciousness that has little to do with the novel, the impact of the narrative is curtailed. Despite its high points, this one might have been more interesting had it been left to the likes of Abel Ferrara.

Things to Do in Denver When You're Dead (1995): Directed by Gary Fleder; original screenplay by Scott Rosenberg; starring Andy Garcia, Treat Williams, Christopher Walken. Though not derived from noir fiction, its script – like that of *The Usual Suspects, Seven,* and *The Last Seduction* – is imaginative enough that it could have been. Turning the conventions of film noir upside-down – as they say in the film, "Give it a name." – Fleder populates his film with characters that could have come from the pen of Elmore Leonard. Rosenberg's script is noteworthy for its linguistic invention. With Jack Warden as a one-person Greek chorus, the plot remains subservient to the noir poetry of the script. With off-beat performances by Williams and Walken, this is a bleakly humorous view of the world – the notion that Garcia can make money from shooting videos for posterity seems all too real. About eternal values and predicaments, it's a shimmering portrait of the criminal world and contemporary society, and illustrates, if nothing else, that Denver is more than LA with cows.

LA Confidential (1997): Adapted from the novel by James Ellroy. Directed by Curtis Hanson; screenplay by Brian Helgeland and Hanson; starring Kim Bassinger, Russell Crowe, Guy Pearce, Kevin Spacey. Because Hanson sanitises Ellroy for mass consumption, *LA Confidential* becomes almost too easy to criticise. Lacking Ellroy's seedy reality and sense of evil, the film has gained such plaudits that what was once an overrated film might, by now, have become underrated. Cinematographer Dante Spinotti and Hanson work to recreate 1950s LA, but end up with a packagable artefact –

more Chandler than Ellroy – an exercise in nostalgia and another piece of LA revisionism – not really what Ellroy's fiction is about. Unlike *Devil in a Blue Dress*, whose LA is tinged with a mild expressionism, Hanson does not allow his reality-fixation to run its course. Though Dudley Smith is less plausible than in Ellroy's novel, the homoerotic relationship between Exley and White is quite pronounced. With the scriptwriters condensing Ellroy's wild prose and labyrinthine narrative, the person capable of retelling the plot invariably gets the promotion.

Jackie Brown (1998): Adapted from the novel *Rum Punch* by Elmore Leonard. Directed by Quentin Tarantino; screenplay by Tarantino; starring Pam Grier, Samuel Jackson, Robert DeNiro, Bridget Fonda. Having learned something about restraint and subtlety, Tarantino has put together a complex and mature film, one that moves from blaxploitation parody to a Cassevetes-like narrative in which brains defeat brawn. Leonard's anarchic narrative and stripped-down street-speak are perfect for Tarantino, whose script is razor-sharp, if occasionally excessive. What the film might lack is a mechanism that critiques various cultural and linguistic transgressions. About adjusting to middle-age, seduction, nouveau wealth, scam and counter-scam, Tarantino's film, whether the close-up of Grier walking through LAX, Jackson explaining to DeNiro – who manages to convey his ex-con status purely through visage and posture – about modern weaponry, or the final series of scams, is a visual and verbal delight. As usual in Leonard's later work, the women – Grier and Fonda – prove the most intelligent, while the state lags far behind.

INDEX

Hitchens, Dolores 98, n227
Holiday, Billie 191
Hughes, Dorothy B. 4, 98, n227
Hughes, Howard 147, 153
Hugo, Richard 63–4, n238
Hunt, Joe 220, n255
Hunter, Stephen 222, 258

Izzi, Eugene 1, 34, 55, 98, 127, 132
Izzo, Jean-Claude 14

Jacobs, Alexander 264
Jeter, J.W. 171, 225, 258
Jimenez, Neil 269
Johnson, Lyndon 13, 46, n235

Khan, Herman 33
Kellerman, Faye 177, n248, 258
Kelly, Thomas 209, 258
Kemper, Ed 217
Kennedy, John F. (JFK) 34, 62, 109, n233
King, Martin Luther 22, 62, 109, n233
King, Rodney 192, 213
Koenig, Joseph 217

Lacey, Ed n243
Laidlaw, Mark 171
Lansky, Meyer 33, 195, n227
Leonard, Elmore 3, 4, 11, 28, 34, 39, 47, 55, 66, 124, 128, 129, 130–44, 145, 153, 173, 182, 193–5, 197, 217, n246, n249, n251, 259, 268, 270, 271
Leone, Sergio 37
Lethem, Jonathan 224–5
Lewin, Michael 74
Lewis, Ted 15
Leyton, Elliott 206, 207, 216, n236, n245, n253, n254, 263
Lindsey, David 215
London, Jack 218
Lonsdale, Joe n246
Lopez, Steve 222, 258
Lovecraft, H. P. 169

Lynch, David 156
Lyons, Arthur 11, 74, 188–9, n250, 259

McBain, Edward 7, 139
McCarthy, Cormac 173
McCarthy, Joseph 7, 8, 40, 107, 109, 180
McCaulay, Michael n231, 262
MacDonald, John D. 13, 18–20, 40, n230–231, 259
Macdonald, Ross 8, 13, 15–18, 19, 40, 56, 62, 73, 81, 149, n227, n230, 259
McGinnis, Joe 128
McGovern, George 69
Mailer, Norman 128, 208
Malcolm X. 22
Manchette, Jean-Patrick 14
Mandel, Ernest 207, n227, n253, 262
Manning, Marable n231
Marlowe, Dan C. 78
Master, Brian 209
Medina, Enrique 15
Messent, Peter n238, n239, n241–2, 262
Metcalf, Paul n239
Monash, Paul 264
Monk, Thelonius 191
Montalban, Manuel Velazquez 15
Morris, Errol 269
Morse, L. A. 223–4, 259
Mosley, Walter 7, 11, 72, 105, 106–110, 116, 173, 183, 190–2, n242, n250, 259, 269–70
Motley, Williard 98
Muller-Scherz, Fritz 265
Muskie, Edward 69

Nader, Ralph 73, 184, n237
Naylor, R. T. n229, n233, n237
Neeley, Barbara 222
Newhouse, David 264
Newhouse, Rafe 264
Nisbet, Jim 124, 165–72, n247–8, 259

Vachss, Andrew 2, 124, 127, 159–
    65, 167, n247, 260
Valin, Jonathan 75, 260
Vanacker, Sabine n241-2
Ventura, Michael n247
Vietor, Robert n244
Vullaimy, Edward n249, n251, n254

Wajnarowicz, David 211, n254, 262
Wambaugh, Joseph 189–90, n250,
    261
Warpole, Ken n227, n228, 261
Welty, Eudora 16
Wenders, Wim 265, 266
West, Nathaniel 139, 221
Westlake, Donald 33, 268
White, Lionel 128, 136
Whittington, Harry 128
Willeford, Charles 7, 8, 11, 13, 20,
    28–33, 40, 92, 94, 131, 139,
    140, 174, n227, n228, n233,

n247, 261, 265, 268
Williams, Charles 7, 20, 92, 143,
    n227, n228, n231, 261
Williams, John n238, n239, n247,
    263
Woodrell, Daniel 55, 124, 172–5,
    n248, 261
Woods, Paula 261
Woodward, W. E. n232-3
Woodward-Bernstein 73–4
Woolrich, Cornell 16, 131
Wozencraft, Kim 215, n254

Yates, Peter 264

Zinn, Howard 72, n230, n231,
    n233, n235, n240, 263
Zukin, Sharon 203, n245, n249,
    n252, n253, 263

Also published by Serpent's Tail

Woody Haut

PULP CULTURE: Hardboiled Fiction and the Cold War

PULP CULTURE takes the reader on a walk down the Mean Streets of post-war America to investigate the classic texts of American hardboiled crime fiction and the era from which they came. With crooks hiding in every doorway and commies lurking under every bed, crime fiction – its gaudy paperback covers portraying men with guns and women with low necklines – was avidly read by a nation adjusting to the Cold War and the Atomic Era.

Beginning with Dashiell Hammett testifying before Senator Joseph McCarthy, *PULP CULTURE* pursues the lives and work of crime writers who approached the genre at street level: David Goodis, Chester Himes, Jim Thompson, Dorothy B Hughes, Dolores Hitchens, Leigh Brackett, Raymond Chandler, Mickey Spillane, Howard Browne, Gil Brewer, William B. McGivern, Lionel White, Ross MacDonald, Horace McCoy, Charles Willeford and Charles Williams.

PULP CULTURE gives post-war crime fiction a political and irreverent reading, examining the politics of paranoia, private detection and criminality; the origins of crime fiction; the role of women in a male-dominated genre; and why the early 1960s marked the final days of classic hardboiled fiction. It also considers the genre's influence on contemporary crime writers and film-makers. *PULP CULTURE* is essential reading for anyone interested in noir writing, films and the post-war era.

Praise for
PULP CULTURE

'Literature percolates society, and fiction, says Woody Haut, has been refracted by the class war and Cold War of this century. As the American yellowbrick road became an urban mean street, the likes of Dashiell Hammett and Raymond Chandler enunciated the paranoia and guilt of the American nightmare. Reds were under beds, UFOs were in the skies; a president was pulped, and culture turned decidedly noir. Fiction was full of trench coats and trilbies, square jaws and handguns. The Cold War may have thawed, but Haut recreates its chill, and brilliantly analyses the paperbacks that preempted the dystopian worlds of film directors David Lynch and Quentin Tarantino.' *Tobias Jones, Observer*

'A fascinating insight into the history of American hardboiled fiction and its origins in the Cold War. It will become a major work of reference in the field, encompassing as it does thorough analysis of the works of Jim Thompson, David Goodis, Chester Himes, Charles Willeford and many other vital writers who are only now getting the appreciation they failed to get when they were alive. Essential reading for all crime readers.' *Time Out*

'Haut examines the hardboiled novel in the context of postwar American politics – the anti-communism paranoia and the Cold War (Dashiell Hammett appeared before Senator McCarthy's committee) and also the liberal resistance to right-wing excesses. He charts, too, the economic and social development of the private eye in a rapidly changing America. *PULP CULTURE* has a serious intent, but it is easy and fun to read.' *The Times*

'A fascinating insight into the roots of modern American hard-boiled fiction and its development. There is little doubt in my mind that *PULP CULTURE* will become one of the major reference books in our field.' **Maxim Jakubowski**

Jonathan Romney

Short Orders

The nineties has been a turbulent and changing period for cinema. The film critic Jonathan Romney has spent the decade at the pictures making sense of things. *Short Orders* is a collection of his sharp, inquiring and entertaining writings on film, from art house to multiplex, and featuring his unique take on the likes of Tarantino, Jarman, Scorsese and Almodóvar. The collection also includes extended reflections on the end of cinema's first century and Hollywood's entry into the digital age and, with it, the end of the reign of the 'real' on-screen.

'I've long felt that Jonathan Romney was one of the sharpest film critics writing in English. Reading his collected pieces in *Short Orders* has confirmed and deepened this feeling. Moving with breathtaking confidence, from the American mainstream to the more obscure byways of World Cinema, *Short Orders* is bursting with dazzling and provocative observations. Written with verve, bold intelligence and dead pan wit, *Short Orders* is the most exhilarating collection of film criticism in a very long time.'

Howard Schuman

Lynne Tillman

The Broad Picture

Lynne Tillman's essays are irreverent, smart, funny – evidence of her playful, rebellious mind. They are collected here together for the first time. Her subjects range broadly and widely, from Matisse and 'reading women' to the issue of race in *The Bodyguard*, from Ray Charles' voice and lyrics to narrative theories, from cat therapy to sex, memory and death. An exceptional writer, Tillman takes the reader on an expansive tour of 20th century life and culture to unearth and enlighten its preoccupations, fears and obsessions.

'Adding to her daring feats in fiction, Lynne Tillman is now an essayist for our times. A private eye in the public sphere, she refuses no assignment and distils the finest wit, intelligence and hard evidence from some of the world's most transient artifacts and allegories. This is a truly memorable book.'

Andrew Ross,
author of 'The Chicago Gangster Theory of Life'

'Tillman's work is always intelligent, always subtle, and very often funny, and the scalpel she uses for slicing it into the American order of things has a decidedly wicked edge to it.'

Patrick McGrath